The Selected Writings of

JACK B. YEATS

edited by
Robin Skelton

André Deutsch

First published in 1991 by
André Deutsch Limited
105–106 Great Russell Street
London WC1B 3LJ

British Library Cataloguing in Publication Data
Yeats, Jack B. (Jack Butler) *1871–1957*
 The selected writings of Jack B. Yeats.
 I. Title
 828.91209

 ISBN 0 233 98646 4

Phototypeset by
Input Typesetting Ltd, London
Printed in Great Britain by
Billing & Sons Ltd, Worcester

EDITORIAL NOTE

In none of his novels and romances did Jack B. Yeats extend himself to create chapter headings or even chapters. Consequently I have been obliged to invent headings for the passages I have selected. In one instance, *Hartigan Talking* from the undateable play *The Silencer* which he left in manuscript at his death, I have collaged passages from the play. The texts I have used have been checked against the existing typescripts and proofs, and I am grateful to Senator Michael Yeats and Ann Yeats for permitting me to study these papers, and especially to Ann Yeats in whose home I laboured. The labour was not hard as regards the prose, for in all the published works I discovered only one instance where the publisher had overridden the wishes of the author. I have myself overridden the publisher. The texts of the plays have been taken from my own edition of *The Collected Plays of Jack B. Yeats* (Secker & Warburg, 1971). In putting this book together I have been assisted by Tammy Liddicoat to whom I am grateful. I must also thank W. L. Webb who thought of the book and insisted that I, and not he, should compile it.

Robin Skelton
Victoria, BC
1990

The Selected Writings of

JACK B. YEATS

CONTENTS

INTRODUCTION

THE VISION OF JACK B. YEATS*

"But all wild sights appealed to Synge, he did not care whether they were typical of anything else or had any symbolical meaning at all. If he had lived in the days of piracy he would have been the fiddler in a pirate-schooner, him they called 'the music—' 'The music' looked on at everything with dancing eyes but drew no sword, and when the schooner was taken and the pirates hung at Cape Corso Castle or the Island of Saint Christopher's, 'the music' was spared because he *was* 'the music'." This comment upon Synge by Jack B. Yeats reveals as much about its author as its subject and hints at attitudes which persisted throughout Yeats's paintings, writings, and life. Jack Yeats, like Synge, was—to use my own words—"an observer, a recorder, a satirist and in many ways a romantic." Like Synge, he was passionately interested in the life of the people and viewed planned societies with scepticism, even while objecting to capitalist materialism. Like Synge, he relished the wild and the odd, and he perceived and commented, both affectionately and sardonically, upon the contrary nature of humankind and upon the conflicts in human society. He was, like his brother, W. B. Yeats, concerned not merely to work in one medium but in several, and he was, like both W. B. Yeats and Synge, an innovator. Moreover, once one surveys all his work—the drawings, the paintings, the prose works, the plays—one discovers an overmastering unity, a bringing together, not only of "beggar and nobleman" but even of the media themselves. For the prose works frequently include minidramas and the plays, stories; and both are supported, and sometimes accompanied, by sketches and paintings. Students and lovers of twentieth-century art are already well aware of the importance of Jack B. Yeats as a painter, but readers interested primarily in

*Robin Skelton, *Celtic Contraries* (Syracuse: Syracuse University Press, 1990), by permission of the publisher.

literature may not be familiar with his life or his writings. It seems sensible therefore to begin with a few biographical facts.

Jack Butler Yeats was born on 29 August 1871 and was the youngest of John Butler Yeats's children, W. B. Yeats being the eldest. He spent the greater part of his childhood in Sligo, where early he showed his fascination with both drawing and the theatre, writing and illustrating childish plays and acting them out in a toy theatre. He studied art at Westminster School, and before the turn of the century, first in London then in Manchester and later at Dartmouth, he had established himself as a cartoonist and illustrator. His work of this early period is bold in line and dramatic in concept, the drama often approaching in mood the melodramatic directness of folktale or of those pirate stories he delighted in reading.

His childhood experiences and enthusiasms clearly coloured his imagination. He showed a love of the fantastic and of the savage innocence of Irish peasantry. His delight in dreams of far lands and strange countries was one he shared with the poet John Masefield, who contributed verses to his early plays for children and who clearly intensified his interest in things piratical. Indeed, in old age when told that there was a rumour that, as a youth, he had fallen out with his brother and gone to sea for seven years, after commenting, "I was never at sea in my life", he explained the influence of the sea upon his work with the single name "John Masefield".

It was in the first decade of the century that Jack Yeats began to show his paces most clearly. In 1902, with Pamela Colman Smith, he produced a series of broadsheets, each of which contained verse and two illustrations, one at least of which was hand-coloured. This clearly emanated from a feeling which he shared with his brother that art could be "taken to the people" in this way and reflected the strong influence of the thought of William Morris upon the Yeats family generally. These broadsides led W. B. Yeats and his sisters to issue a similar monthly series from the Cuala Press from 1908 to 1915, and a later series in 1935 and 1937.

In 1905, Jack Yeats first began to paint consistently in oils. His work in this medium between 1905 and 1924 still made use of the heavy outlines he had used as a book illustrator, and he took his subject matter frequently from his memories

of the peasants, beggars, and tinkers of western Ireland whom
he knew so well, and whom he also portrayed in his illus-
trations to Synge's *Aran Islands* and to the articles on the
Congested Districts which Synge wrote for the *Manchester
Guardian*. He also, however, made great use of the circus,
which he used to visit with Masefield. These circus and peas-
ant paintings have a solidity reminiscent of Millet; the paint
is applied with heavy insistence, and the colour is much more
drab than in his later work. His work of this period has been
associated with that of the London group, and, in its strange
combination of anecdotal realism and symbolic distortion has
been compared with that of Sickert. Even though realism
seems a part of his work at this time, he never painted from
actuality but always from memory; the distortions are less
the product of a fallible memory than of an intention to
transform, dignify, dramatise, and elucidate the actual and
to cast over it "a colouring of the imagination". Moreover,
in even the most serious or pathetic of these works there is a
quirkishness, a flicker of humour, a fascination with and a
delight in oddity. This is particularly evident in his picture
book, *Life in the West of Ireland*, which was published in 1912.

This delight shows itself even more openly in his writings
of this period. Jack Yeats was the author of a number of plays
for children with hand-coloured illustrations. Their titles are
indicative of their contents: *James Flaunty: or, The Terror of the
Western Seas; The Scourge of the Gulph; The Treasure of the Garden:
A Play in the Old Manner*. This last is advertised by Elkin
Matthews, who published a whole series of *Jack Yeats's Chap
Books* with the note: "Stages with Prosceniums designed by
the Author, Footlights, Slides, and Scenes, can be had, price
5s net each." Apart from these plays he wrote a story, *The
Bosun and the Bob-Tailed Comet*, and an account of the toy boats
made by himself and his friends as children, with the title *A
Little Fleet*.

Setting aside the exuberant drawings with their superbly
rhythmical use of line and their masterly compositions, the
plays themselves include, for all their manipulation of the
clichés of childhood adventure, a disturbing juxtaposition of
the ebullient and the macabre. The plot of *The Scourge of the
Gulph* is as follows:
Captain Carricknagat, a black-bearded pirate, aboard his

ship off the Isle of Plumes, learns that his wife has been captured and eaten by cannibals. The message is brought by Bosun Broad, who has lost an arm in the fight but has escaped with a letter from the unfortunate woman. This letter asks the Captain to find her body, remove her skull, place it in a black box with silver hinges, and bury it on the round hill on the Island of Plumes. The Bosun and the Captain find the skull, but the Bosun dies of "the black thirst" before the Captain is able to dig a grave with his sword to bury what he calls "This sad piece of ivory". At that point Joe Miles, a sailor who has earlier been marooned, comes upon the Captain and, believing the box contains treasure, kills the Captain. On opening the box he discovers the skull and brings the play to an end with the words: "An empty skull, a black box, a dead skipper! Have I done anything or nothing?"

This is, indeed that dying fall, that weary or appalled asking of the cosmic riddle with which much poetic tragedy ends. The note of soliloquy is necessarily frequent in these plays, for the nature of the cardboard theatre, with its figures held perpetually in the pose in which they have been painted, requires a somewhat static drama. Thus Jack Yeats's plays for children have the same restricted or formal pattern of movements as that provided by W. B. Yeats for his plays, though for a different reason. Ernest Marriott in his small monograph on the work of Jack Yeats makes the point:

> It seems to me that these diminutive dramas show something of the fanciful simplicity and directness of phrase which we find in the work of the better-known dramatists of the Irish movement . . .
>
> Bosun Hardbite addressing McGowan who is seated on a mooring post on the quay says, "Sit there on yer old iron mushyroom till the seaweed grows you." An Emigrant replies, "The poor captain is feeling sad in his heart. The poor man, like the rest of us, doesn't like leaving the dear silk of the kine." At the beginning of [*The Treasure of the Garden*] the captain ruminates, "What a roaring life it is too, chasing the rich ships—the big fat pigeons with crops full of gold. But it's the other thing that sickens—fighting two great ugly frigates in a little ditch of a creek . . . they fall across you and lie on you

like a dead horse." The impressive scene where he makes this speech is a battered deck with bullet-riddled pirates hanging from the shrouds in the last horror of bodily death.

If Jack Yeats took the role of "the Music" in his pirate drama, he also took it in many of his drawings and prints of this period. The series of hand-coloured prints by him which were issued by the Cuala Press almost all belong to his earlier manner. In them one can see certain themes emerging over and over again—the solitary watcher, caught up in reflective nostalgia; the sailor, with his eyes full of strange places, walking alone through the city street; the ballad singer, a vehicle for songs even odder and older than himself; the peasant inextricably a part of the rude barren landscape. These are often accompanied by images of physical exuberance and energy, even of a kind of brutality, as they are also accompanied in the work of his friend Synge and in much of the work of Masefield. In these prints, he makes use of the bright colours and bold forms of an art both emanating from and directed at popular tastes and notions.

Their "Gaelic" quality attracted AE who wrote in 1909, "We have had abundance of Irish folklore, but we knew nothing of folk art until the figures of Jack Yeats first romped into our imagination a few years ago. It was the folk feeling, lit up by genius and interpreted by love. It was not the patronage bestowed by the intellectual artist on the evidently picturesque forms of a life below his own. I suspect Jack Yeats thinks the life of a Sligo fisherman as good as any, and that he could share it for a long time without being in the least desirous of a return to the more comfortable life of convention." The folk art quality which AE detects not only emerges from the use of themes which excite the common "folk"—races, hurling matches, circuses, outlaws of the land or sea—but also from a curious wonderment and rhythmic stridency. His coloured prints and drawings frequently use large areas of bold colour and contrast them simply. His greens and blues are more intense than natural, just as his figures are also exaggerated in shape and gesture. In the black and white drawings, he uses a multitude of lines, covering earth, sky, and clothing with closely packed ripples, so that the whole

THE MUSIC

picture is often throbbing with rhythm. The heavy outlines are not, thus, imposed upon the figures but are developed from the pressure of life within them. This is, for all the apparent calm of many of the resting or idly talking figures, a tumultuous art.

It was not until 1924 that a similar turbulent quality emerged in his oil painting and in his writing. Perhaps his best prose work is *Sligo*, first published in 1930. This is a helter-skelter of freely associated memories, reflections, fantasies, and jokes. There is no shape to it; its form is that of the rhythms of the mind alone, and in this it occasionally reminds one of Joyce's *Ulysses* and *Finnegans Wake*. Yeats, however, is an original, not a disciple. His high jinks are like nobody else's, though his methods in this, and in his later *The Amaranthers*, do seem to anticipate many of those used by Flann O'Brien in *At Swim Two Birds* (so praised by Joyce) and by T. H. White (especially in *The Elephant and the Kangaroo*). His particular vein in *Sligo* emerges clearly from his account of the reason for the title. It is given after forty pages.

About a name for this book. I was making some notes one day while travelling in a train through a boggy country in Ireland when a melodeon player opposite me asked me if I wouldn't stop and "give out a tune" and he handed the melodeon towards me. "I have no ear," I said. "Ah, to hell with ears," he said "I play it with my body. Are you writing a book?" he said. "Well I am making notes for one," I said. "What are you going to call it?" he said. "I don't know yet," I said. "Call it Sligo. It's the name of a town," he said, "the only town in Ireland I never was in. I was near it once but I stopped on the brink and took the long car with a unicorn yoked to it for a town called Ballina. Call it Sligo, it ought to be a lucky name." So Sligo it is. When he asked me to play a tune he pronounced it Chune, a very good way too. If they give me music to my grave I will sooner they will call it a Chune than a Toon: there is a want of dignity about the word "Toon" and I would not look forward to it.

This, in its inconsequence and dry humour, is reminiscent of Sterne. In other passages, however, we find a satirical absurdity that is Swift without Swift's anger.

But why tow, why not let others tow as they like it. There
are more up-lifters in the world than subjects of uplift.
Let them uplift us, shoulder high. Then we will be able
to see over their heads to the several promised lands,
from which we have come, and to which we trust to go.
When the uplifters are wedged and milling together, and
we are tired of sitting, we can stroll about on their solid
heads, and view these lands.

An even more Swiftian quality emerges in the passages
about the Ropes family and its ancestors in which the evolu-
tion of a society is parodied. Jack Yeats, however, unlike
Swift, wrote from affection and believed in the basic goodness
of humanity. One need only compare Swift's accounts of
sectarian conflicts, political and religious, with Jack Yeats's
account of how the Ropes family explained the nature of the
tides: "They all sat in a ring on the warm sand and settled
about it. Not all at once. But after a good many days they
reduced the idea to two parties. Those who held that the sun
drew the water up and down and those who held that the
water was working the sun. The usual thing. And there was
very little hope of anything being settled, until a small wedge
party got up an idea that the whole place was pulsing any
way it liked if you were satisfied. So they all agreed on that."
The lighthearted, but in no way trivial satire of *Sligo* is
attached to a pseudo-autobiographical thread of narrative
and reflection, as it is also in later works, the most notable
of which is *And To You Also* (1944). This book is even more
exuberant than *Sligo*, and its prose is even more carefully
slapdash. Here Jack Yeats expresses yet again his strong
feeling of the limitations of language as a medium of
expression and attempts to expand its boundaries in a number
of ways. One of these is the use of the incantatory and absurd
list—as practised by Rabelais. His introduction to one mag-
nificent list is as follows:

Now—thinking of you also I would like to give you from
my store a really full-waved chapter heading, and we are
in luck for I have under my hand a list of suggestions
for the contents of a chapter which I will not write. But
I will not waste the list so here it comes, and as you have

been standing up to breast the gravelly storm as far as this without a breather, I'll call it

Chapter Two

and here goes:

J. Toole, and Cook, and James Sullivan, and his great poster. Swede turnips, Weight-lifting, man in his walking clothes grunting. Swan song, heard record and refused to die. Vale of Aylesbury and all the falls. Waterfalls everywhere—Jem Mac. Jem Smith. The Lord Mayor's coachman. Paintings outside booths at the Fairs. The private performance of the little play called Hand Knocks. Bob Habbijams. The M. C. Harris. Pictures on walls of Inns, and of the Lambeth School of Arms. Shapes the bus conductor. Rain. Glissade. House Boats. Walking by Seashores. Song Book Shops.

And so it continues for four pages, showing a dexterity in free association, a verbal music, a capacity for pattern making that are truly astonishing.

Jack Yeats's novels and stories are as original as his memoirs. His first full-length novel, *The Amaranthers*, divides itself into two parts. In the first one the members of the club are introduced to us and are shown to be (among other things) devoted to the making of toy boats behind the sober facade of the island's only (small) skyscraper. The remainder of the book chronicles the adventures of James Gilfoyle who finally reaches the island and befriends the Amaranthers, who had suffered the effects of an earthquake.

In *The Amaranthers*, as in *Sligo*, digression is frequent and amusing. We have a full description of the performance of a play which sounds, in some respects, like a drama concocted by a combination of Anouilh, Ionesco, and Jean Genet, with Robert Louis Stevenson supervising. We have the life stories of several bizarre characters. There is a sudden death, banditry, high finance—it is a gallimaufry of a book. Some parts of Gilfoyle's adventures are distinctly reminiscent of the adventures told by Masefield, especially in *Odtaa*, but they are odder and parody the adventure story rather than exploit it seriously. The book is also, however, filled with radiance, gaiety, and intense enjoyment of physical beauty, so that even while the reader is laughing, he is also being charmed.

In *On the Boiler*, W. B. Yeats wrote of his brother's *The Charmed Life* (1938), "He does not care that few will read it, still fewer recognise its genius; it is his book, his 'Faust,' his pursuit of all that through its unpredictable, unarrangeable reality least resembles knowledge. His style fits his purpose for every sentence has its own taste, tint and smell." This is true also of *The Amaranthers*. It is one of the most original of books, though it clearly relates to the Irish tradition, having Swiftian passages, as well as passages that remind us of the broad and magical comedy and adventure of Irish epic. Moreover, as in Irish epic the magical adventure often approaches farce but is countered and qualified by an underlying romantic seriousness, so that the grave and the gay remain in tension and give the book a fundamental ambiguity of outlook as they do so often in Joyce. It is perhaps this balance of the grave and gay, this combination of the tragic and comic, that is characteristic of much of the best Irish writing. It is notable in Synge, O'Casey, Joyce; it is present, though to a muted degree, in Goldsmith; it is characteristic of the best of Wilde and Congreve, and it appears in heroic proportions in Swift.

It is also present in Jack Yeats's last, energetic, prose work, *The Careless Flower* which was published in 1947, when he was seventy-six years old, and which contains, yet again, a wealth of shrewd observation, a perpetual dance of language, and the same romantic-sceptical view of human affairs that animates the earlier work.

The energy which is so remarkable a feature of Jack Yeats's writings of his old age is also characteristic of his paintings of the same period. In these the colour has become hectic, challenging, expressionist. The rhythmic vitality of line in his earlier drawings has now been transformed into thick oil colour, so that the landscapes and figures are all trembling with the same gay vitality, even though the total symbolism of the pictures may be tragic or pathetic.

Jack Yeats was not only an innovator as both painter and novelist, however. He was also a formidable playwright, and the plays he created in the period from 1933 to 1949 are as different from his early drama for the toy theatre as are his last oils from his drawings for the sporting magazine *Paddock Life* in the 1890s.

It is not easy to sum up the character of these plays without lapsing into dangerous generalisations, but it seems clear that Jack Yeats used them even more than he used his novels to present his philosophy of life, which was as riddling, as lively, as romantic, and as satirical as one might expect. There are a number of recurrent themes. In every play there is talk of death and in seven of them a death, or a presumed death, is central to the pattern the play makes. In half of them a central character is a much travelled stranger whose arrival on the scene sets off a chain of events that appears to have its own interior logic rather than to be caused wittingly by any of the characters. In most of them we are given the strong impression that the characters are caught up in a pattern of destiny which they recognise only dimly, if at all. Human intentions are pointless: we are prisoners of a will greater than our own: we can only, if we are wise, accept what life brings us and live as much by chance as by choice.

This last contention is particularly obvious in *The Deathly Terrace*, which seems to be the first play of this series. Andy, a film producer, and Sheila, an actress, land by boat at a terrace on which they intend to film a scene of "the dead man by the sea". They find the corpse of Nardock who appears to have killed himself and they make the film. However, when the film is given its premiere, Nardock appears in the theatre alive. In the next act Andy catches up with Nardock, and they exchange stories of their experiences. When Sheila appears in a boat they both fake suicide and leave her to think they died of love for her and so to regard herself as a goddess who can "dance in and out of the hearts of men". The play is ill proportioned, the greater part of it being taken up by the conversation between Andy and Nardock, but, in fact, this conversation is the heart of the play's vision. Nardock tells Andy: "Time has no meaning to me, I am embedded in time and floating in eternity. I have seen the Peruvians in pigtails and the Chinese in kilts. I have gone down into the heart of the volcano, and placed my hand where the pulse should be and called on it to shake. And I have stepped from the fragment of one star to the nucleary fragment of another, and I have looked at myself so doing . . . I am an Egoist steeped in generosity and seethed in affection."* He describes his travels and tells how he invented the circle, fire, and the "sinking of the stone in the pond". He invented "continuosity" and everywhere he went he left a blessing behind him and everywhere he showed himself to be a joker, a leg-puller:

> A poet has shown us the sadness of the last man, the hangman with no one in the world left to pull his legs. But I can see another picture of the last man looking with desolated eyes searching for the last leg but two, just to pull it, and his mind will be brimming with splendid schemes for leg-pulling—too late, and he could not stoop to pull his own leg . . . Too late, that is a sad word, never say it, say too soon, perhaps. But never say too anything, there is no such thing as redundancy to those who are embedded, as you and I are, in continuosity, because if there is too much of anything at any moment, we only hold it over in the heel of the fist and later link it up with the coming event, and so linked together we get continuosity, impetuosity and exuberance.

If Nardock is the prophet of a new, or a very old, creed, Andy is his fitting disciple. Andy tells Nardock the following story about his father: "[he] decided that I must be dedicated to luck, that chance should rule my life, not premeditation. So when at the age of five years, my education having got beyond my mother's powers, I chanced to spell out the word 'school' without having any idea what it stood for, I was taken to board school but on the way I lost my little shoe in the mud opposite a small house which had a notice in the window DOWTON COLLEGE, I went there. It had style, that College. There were eleven pupils. I made up the dozen and we wore mortar boards. The school caught fire and was burnt out, when I was ten years of age. So my father came to the conclusion that my school days were over."

Andy's life story continues, fantastic in invention, witty in implication, and exuberant in feeling. The inventiveness and exuberance of his tale may remind us of the tales of Baron

*All quotations from Robin Skelton, ed. *The Collected Plays of Jack B. Yeats* (London: Secker & Warburg, 1971).

Münchhausen. Jack Yeats certainly read Münchhausen, for his wife Cottie gave him a paper-covered edition. Nardock and Andy, however, are not derived creatures; their combined philosophy is central to Jack Yeats's own vision. In his prose works he utilises that very continuosity Nardock claims to have discovered and with an appropriate "impetuosity and exuberance." The "egotist steeped in generosity and seethed in affection" appears over and over again in the prose romances, and if one looks at the painting *The Two Travellers* of 1942, one might well feel, from the loquacious stance of the figures and their relationship to the moving and changing landscape, that the travellers represented portraits of Nardock and Andy contemplating another venture into the magnificently absurd.

The word *absurd* had to crop up sooner or later; and, perhaps, it is as well that it should do so here, for the theatre of the absurd as practised in some of the works of Beckett, Genet, and Ionesco is not infrequently Nardockian, and the spirit of continuosity, of flux, and the theme of man ridiculously embedded in time yet floating in eternity, is present in Beckett's novels as well as in those of Flann O'Brien. I am not, at this point, attempting to make out a case that Jack Yeats was the teacher, directly or indirectly of these later writers (none, in any case, could have read *The Deathly Terrace*), but I am concerned to show that the Nardockian viewpoint is much more than a whimsical piece of ingenuity; it is one statement of an attitude which pervades an enormous amount of European literature of the last forty years. One can understand why *The Deathly Terrace* was never performed or published. It is structurally ill balanced, and it demands an audience that was not available at the time it was written. To move from that play to the first three plays that were published is to be initially a little disappointed. *Apparitions* is no more than a folk anecdote of a practical joke, and its main interest is the fact that Yeats used the practical joker once again as a central character and did so in such a way as to portray the folly of self-importance and vanity. On the other hand, *The Old Sea Road*, the second play published under the general heading *Apparitions*, is a different matter.

The Old Sea Road, like the *Camino Real* of Tennessee Williams, is a highly metaphysical entity and the play is a parable.

It opens with two labourers, Nolan and Dolan, spreading stones on the road. They are dully clad, and throughout the play, we are told, "The sky, sea and land are brighter than the people." Nolan tells Dolan—and the chiming names suggest, deliberately, a cross-talk act: "it's time I retired, but the times we live in won't let me. Fancy me, let alone yourself, spending the whole blessed day laying stones on the Old Sea Road. We spread them here, and in the fullness of time they roll down the hill until they reach the charming village of Cahirmahone, where they lie night and day to trip up the feet of the ancient warriors of the place." Along this road walk many people, the schoolteacher and her favourite pupil, the student of mathematics, the policeman, the ballad singer, the postman, the publican, and an old peasant man and woman. Along the road too comes Michael of the Song, a wanderer, and he meets Ambrose Oldbury, a practical joker of whom there has already been much talk. Michael, despite his poverty and hunger, is excited by life. He tells the mathematics student, "the whole world's exciting. If it was the least tint more exciting the unfortunate inhabitants would be exploding into fragments making star sparks of themselves." He is very much his own man, saying, "To Hell with the departmental store all under one roof. I'm under my own roof, and I don't want yours. Every man under his own thatch and the ladies under their own, if you like." When he meets Ambrose he asks him why he is a practical joker. Ambrose tells him:

> If I could bring off a solid joke with four dimensions I'd be satisfied. But I never saw one that had more than two, here and there. All I ask is reasonable fun and that's denied me by a benighted people.

MICHAEL: That's because you are not able to consume your own amusement as it comes, and carbonise it for further use, if you did . . .

AMBROSE: Pardon me. If I did I wouldn't be sitting out on an old bank talking to you at this time of evening. I'd be sitting in lonely study regaling myself on my own regalia and chuckling to myself.

MICHAEL: You've had your last chuckle long ago. You've lost the instinct, you common omadhaun.

AMBROSE: I've lost nothing, everything is sticking to me. I'm smothered with it. I tell you I'm the fella with the grand piano legs that carries the world on his back. I'm the fella that's full to the brim. I'm the brim myself in fact, I'm the end of everything.

MICHAEL: You flatter yourself, you've just come on the wrong pitch and now you're all het up about it. What you want is a good sleep, and a think it over.

AMBROSE: I'll think nothing over again. I'm done with thinking things over either before or after the event. I'll open my mouth and swallow the wave.

Ambrose's last practical joke is to burn all his money, tell Michael, "from now on I'm a living joker starting in on the ground floor" and to offer him a drink from his flask. The drink kills them both.

Ambrose's surname, "Oldbury", is an obvious indication of his character as a death bringer, but he is not really the medieval figure of Death walking the roads. He is one who challenges, by means of his jokes, the validity of life itself. He tells Michael: 'I'll show you something you've never seen before, I'll warrant you. I'll show you Man upright defying the slings and arrows and getting away with it. I'll show you how the rich can dissolve in their own essence in the twinkling of an eye." The essence of the practical joke is the way it makes its victim feel insecure and unable to trust his own eyes or own ears. It peoples his world with delusions; it takes his realities and proves them illusion. Thus it might be said that Death is the greatest practical joker of all. In the midst of life we are in death; in the midst of reality we are insubstantial. We are, to quote Nardock, "embedded in time and floating in eternity."

The deaths of Ambrose and Michael do not have the same miraculous effect as those of Nardock and Andy; they alter no one's lives. Ambrose's practical jokes, unlike Nardock's, leave no blessings in their wake. Nevertheless both Nardock and Ambrose, like Jimmy in *Apparitions*, take pleasure in challenging the supposed stability of the day-to-day world.

Rattle, the last of three plays published in 1933, is equally concerned to present a disruption of the norm. The firm of Gardeyne and Golback is on the point of collapsing. Those involved in it are trying to decide what to do with the wharf and warehouses, and it is thought that the site might be sold for a cinema. While these discussions are going on Ted Golback receives a letter telling him that he has inherited "property in mines, lands, forests and lakes" in the South American country of Pakawana. In due course the Pakawanian representatives arrive, and a presentation of the deeds is made. The final movement of the play shows us Ted in Pakawana, where he is told about the country and its ways by the philosopher Dr. Canty. Unfortunately there is an apparently rather token rebellion in progress, and Ted is shot and killed before ever reaching the capital.

This is an unfair summary of the play, for it leaves out the exuberant speculations and dreams of many of the characters; it omits all the wit of the conversations and the humour of the Pakawanian speeches and the fantastic description of Pakawanian society by Dr. Canty. Nevertheless, this bald account does indicate that the play deals both with hope and with death, and that its structure is rather that of an adventure narrative than of the usual drama of tension and confrontation. It appears to flow along as if the characters were borne upon a tide they could not control or even clearly recognise. The image of the wave is, in fact, central to the drama. When the plan for building the cinema falls through, Alec Gardeyne tells his brother William: "My disappointment about the Picture House has depleted me for the time being. But no doubt, if I had a long rest somewhere, I could lay out a plan of some sort. But of course I see that something must be done almost at once." William replies:

> That's it. It's this "almost at once" business that bothers me. There's something in this "almost at once" which grits against . . . No, grits is not the word. But there's something that stems the flow and ebb. Can you be said to stem an ebb? There is something which is the exact opposite of the steady ebb and flow, flow and ebb, of the tide up and down this river, just at our doorstep, as we might say. Why yesterday (*He gets up and walks to river door and looks out*). Ah, and there it is still! Why, yesterday there was a piece of broken wood, off a packing case with some letters on it, P.E.A.C., I think—and then it was

broken off. It may have been for peach or peaches, per-
haps tinned peaches. But there's the bit of wood again.
Yesterday I watched it go up with the tide, and again
come down with the tide. And then I saw it get caught
in an eddy just beside our wharf where there were some
other things floating. There it stayed caught up. It
seemed to me as if it was symbolical of something. It
was specially odd that I should see it because, if I hadn't
got the day for our meeting wrong, I wouldn't have been
here at all yesterday, and so I would not have seen the
peach on the deep (*He laughs*) going up and down. But
there is some symbol there. Perhaps this vagrant wood
is to show that the rhythm that cannot be mastered can
be enjoyed until it laps you gently into a state of static
bliss with a number of other pieces of drift.

It is certainly no coincidence that when the Pakawanian depu-
tation arrives Dr. Canty tells Ted: "we do now with the hand
of General Golmozo, assisted by the hand of Dr. Canty, we
make you Edward Golback, a brother of the Golden Wave,
and do wrap you in the cloak of waves." When Ted is dying
in Pakawana, he asks to have the decoration, the Wave,
placed around his neck.

"The rhythm that cannot be mastered can be enjoyed,"
said William Gardeyne and his words remind us of Nardock's
notion of continuosity and Andy's adherence to chance. It is,
however, necessary to forgive the rhythm its mastery. Dr.
Canty, when asked where the General is, tells Ted: "Oh, in
Vino Veritas at first, later, Golden Slithers on a new moon
with appropriate music. In Vino Veritas the wondering ques-
tioning alcoves of the brain get filled with activity and the
victim wants to know, O Jehovah, why? To know all is to
forgive all. To forgive all is not to want to know all." The
theme is repeated when Ted is dying.

TED: To know all is to forgive all, and doesn't that cut both
ways?
CANTY: Yes, yes. To forgive all is to know all.

It is with solicitude for the dying man rather than with any
sense of personal guilt that the leader of the rebels, Gossgo-

cock, bends over Ted and asks Canty, "Can he give forgive-
ness?" Canty tells him, "His forgiveness flows from him in a
straight line to you."

Life acceptance must finally include death acceptance. It
must also include a capacity to be carried along by the rhy-
thms of apparently chance events and to enjoy the hope or
dream as much as the substance, the joys of speculation as
much as those of realisation. Thus Ted dies contented with
his experience of the dream of Pakawana and does not resent
the loss of the reality; thus the Gardeyne brothers enjoy their
plans for the wharf's destiny as much as they would the
success of those plans, and perhaps more. The commonplace
and the dull only exist if we allow them to do so; we can
always defeat them by an exercise of the imagination and by
the contriving of happy speculations.

It must have been with some such thoughts as these in
mind that Jack Yeats wrote *Harlequin's Positions*. As in *Rattle*,
we are presented with a disruption of ordinary events by the
arrival of someone from overseas. In this instance it is a
relative from abroad who visits a small group of people in a
little Irish town. He tells his new friends:

> I discovered that those positions the harlequin takes with
> the wand in his hands all have names. I don't know if
> his were peculiar to himself. He turned always from one
> to the other to complete the series, five in number:—

> Admiration
> Pas de Basque
> Thought
> Defiance
> Determination

> I committed them to memory—Harlequin positions—
> and have made them my order of—order of existence, if
> I may put it that way.

This speech gives us a clue to the intentions of the playwright,
a clue which is badly needed, for *Harlequin's Positions* flows
easily along from conversation to conversation and very little
happens that could be called obviously dramatic. Annie, the
orphan friend of the family, sells a piece of land and decides
to take everyone on a voyage round the world on the proceeds;

the voyage never takes place, however, for there are rumours of war and it is decided not to venture. As the talk of war grows more widespread the police suspect Alfred Clonboise, the visitor, of being some kind of spy. The war rumours prove false, and he is not arrested. There is, one might well say, nothing very much to it all.

And yet there is something in it. As Clonboise says, "There is something in everything." He goes on to say:

> There was a group of young men in Buenos Aires when I was there who tried to found a religion on that— something in everything. One of them, the Secretary of the Society, picked up a horseshoe nail, walking with me one day near the Market and he began, on that nail, expounding, expounding. At first I was dizzied, but after a little I was completely bored, and so was he. If I could have constructed the ambling pad, the horse, Aunt Claire, from the horseshoe nail, I would have mounted it and ridden away from the Secretary, leaving him nothing but my dust. I would have taken a taxi, and pushed him away as I pushed in, but at the moment, I was embarrassed to the point of not having a taxi fare. It was just before my fortunes took a sudden upward turn. You know, "the darkest hour" and that kind of thing.

It was Walt Whitman who once said, "All truths lie waiting in all things." Alfred Clonboise tells the young man, Johnnie, as they talk on the hill overlooking the little harbour: "Everything's symbolical if you look at in the right way."

It is not easy to look at *Harlequin's Positions* in the "right way" for the talk of which it is largely constructed is inconsequential, highly anecdotal, and seems rather aimless. Nevertheless, what does emerge finally is a picture of the different stances the characters adopt towards passing events and an affectionate, ironic attitude towards those stances. Whether or not all that is said and done can be labelled as one or more of the Harlequin's positions is hard to determine; what is clear though is that Jack Yeats was engaged in presenting us with a picture of a group of characters caught up in life's rhythm, each of them important to themselves and each of them uncertain of their proper roles. To the perceptive eye, everything is symbolical, for every moment links up with other moments and implies beliefs, values, and a history. One has only to watch the world around one to see drama and poetry. It is this demand which *Harlequin's Positions* makes on its audience, as also does the later drama of Samuel Beckett where a single simple event, two people upon a bench exchanging half-a-dozen words perhaps, is given symbolic intensity by forcing us to label it as "theatre" and to scrutinise it narrowly.

This is of course a partial truth. There are moments of melodrama, as when the Guard discovers Alfred Clonboise's revolver and when we are told of the way Johnnie's father and Mr. Bosanquet died. There are also passages of grotesquerie such as that in which the second Pilot describes the draper's assistant who broke his neck and who cannot be seen behind the counter "with his head on his shoulders": "It's a sin to laugh at him, but it's a fact he don't mind. He's a bit of a curiosity for everyone. It was the drink did it, and it didn't stop him drinking either. It costs him nothing. All the travellers that come to the town like to take him out and buy the stuff for him, anything he fancies. They like to see him pour it as if he was going to pour it in his ear." Nevertheless, *Harlequin's Positions* on the whole represents the farthest Jack Yeats went towards antidrama and the nearest he got to anticipating the methods of such later playwrights as Pinter and Mortimer. We are more entertained by the play than we may be by observing life itself, but we are equally unable to sum up the total implications of what we have seen, and the play does not end with any grandiose curtain to help us pretend a conviction. It is part of that continuity, that continuum which is life, and its rhythms are natural rather than theatrical. I am reminded of that picture by René Magritte in which a painting on an easel records that exact part of the landscape which the canvas hides from view; the painting is no more than a segment of the actual given significance by its utilisation of an artistic medium.

What I have said about *Harlequin's Positions* applies also in part to *La La Noo* and *In Sand*, where we are also presented with elements of antitheatre. It does not apply to *The Silencer*, which is similar to *The Deathly Terrace* in its use of melodrama and in its verbal exuberance. *The Silencer* opens in a pub where a group of businessmen are engaged in chatting idly about the weather and discussing life in general. Marshall enters with Hartigan whom he introduces to the company. Hartigan immediately reveals himself as a compulsive talker, a teller of tall tales and a spellbinder. One of the businessmen is so attracted by his zestful and curious view of life that he gives him a job but Hartigan's love of talk causes an appointment to be missed and business to be lost. Employed by another man, he pauses en route to the bank to give a stranger exact and lengthy instructions and is robbed of the money he is carrying. Thieves planning to rob a jeweller's then set Hartigan to distract the attention of the policeman with his stories and chatter while they carry out the operation. The scheme does not work, however, and all the would-be-thieves but Sam and Hill are captured. Hill revenges himself on Hartigan, shooting him down while he is talking to a man on the street and killing him instantly.

Hartigan's last speech before his death clarifies his role for us:

All deaths are game deaths, death sees to that. It's the penultimate moment that shakes the brave. Chinamen in all parts of the world where I have seen them, appear to me to be neither waiting, nor watching, nor regretting. And you are doing the whole three this moment I know; I know it in my bones. And you can't deny it; and you don't want to deny it . . . You are afraid and ashamed of what you cannot help. You are saying to yourself that I'm one of these dud inspirational philosophers given away with a penny paper and you think I am holding you against your will, and you have no will. You are listening to me because you have nothing to say yourself. You are not going away because you have nowhere to go. You have forgotten you have a home. You have forgotten you have a tongue. The bell has forgotten it has a clapper. Anyway, you have no one to pull the bell rope for you and the bell can't get outside itself and pull its own bell rope, now can it? Speak me fair! You cannot speak me fair or unfair! You're held with a basilisktic stare. A basilisk of your own creation. You love the sound of me and you hate the sense. You love time and hate the clock. You wade in stars and hate the ocean seas that lap over you like a sinking tent . . . Look at your boots; they're all smeared with stars.

And you don't know it, and could not say what street, what city you are in. You left a desk and you could not say where you left it. You are speechless because I talk for you. You think you speak yourself. You think I echo your thoughts. You have no thoughts; you never had thoughts. Those things that straggled across your brain were not thoughts, they were wheel tracks in the dust, it will make no difference to you. You have never existed in your own right. You exist now in mine. As the waves of the wind ripple the flag flying from its flag-pole, so you move and exist. As one ripple disappears on the flag's flying tail, another is beginning at the rope making its journey from the hoist to the fly. By my lips you live; by their stillness you pass away or back again into your solidity of a poised dust mote. You could wish yourself alive but you will never do it.

> The song says:
> "Even the dear little fish,
> Though they can't think they can wish."

Here again is the "Egotist", though he seems in his speech to be less "steeped in generosity and seethed in affection" than was Nardock. Like Nardock, however, he rejoices in life and perhaps even embodies all life's vitality. Hill, while visiting a séance later in the play, in order to ask forgiveness of Hartigan's ghost, is told by that ghost:

Stars pass in the sky, forgetting the sky they plough, and forgotten seed stars are sown in forgotten furrows, and a harrow comes a-harrowing, a harrow that is nothing but the breath of the memory of the breaths of all the birds; like the oranges, all thoughts here are fruit and flowers on the same stem. As the basket is woven on the uprights, which are the good thoughts, and the weaving osiers the bitter thoughts, so I know that one day by forgetting here and there we will arrive at but one thought—one thought to satisfy all needs, if needs there will be for the thinker. But not yet is that one thought

set for me. I cannot in the twinkling of a star be forgetting
the grey beards of the seas. In comfort of body I recall
dreadful days of old, fighting odds too heavy, far too
heavy. But then I was held in a body which has neither
fear nor ache, unless the misty vapour of the lake can
ache. Do the clouds ache in their hearts because the lake
distorts their reflections? Not they! They say if there were
no clouds there'd be no lakes. And what are lakes but
puddles grown up? And what are little puddles but little
drops of water, and little grains of sand too; they make
the mighty ocean and the pleasant land too. A song of
innocence; little drops of water and little grains of sand
are innocent because they are little. But why not big lakes
and roomy mountains innocent too? Is a little innocence
better than a big innocence? No, a thousand times, no!
Ten thousand times ten thousand innocences are just
that and nothing more, and what a lot that is. Oh, dear
Heart, be glad; dear Heart that had to be constantly
screamed at. Screamed at your ear to keep you up to
your best, if it did keep you so up, which I forget. But
now, dear Heart, be glad! Is a taking-notice-of a heart
necessary to make it glad! But is there a point where the
glad heart is so glad it doesn't know it's glad? But glad
eyes, I think, always knew when they were glad. But
that's a-going back; no, not a-going back exactly but a-
going out sideways into the realms of the days that are
no more. Not so much, no more, as forgotten . . . or
forgotten from their order. So that where we leave down
one gangway, we come aboard skipping up the next.
Ever ashore, ever a-floating; before the wind and in the
wind's eyes, in the trough and on the crest, forgetting
where the foaming stars come down and the twinkling
waters rush up.

This speech so irritates Hill that he puts a bullet into the
dictaphone from which the voice comes but the spectre of
Hartigan is not damaged; it continues to dance in mockery
and delight. Policemen enter and arrest Hill for creating a
disturbance, but it turns out that they are not real policemen,
only partygoers in fancy dress. Truth and justice, which Hill,
paradoxically, saw as his principles when he killed Hartigan,

and which are for him stable notions, are shown to be as illusory as everything else.

The Silencer is perhaps Jack Yeats's most complex play and the one which presents his philosophy most explicitly. In the two climactic speeches, the first coming just before Hartigan's death and the second just before his spectral voice is silenced by a bullet from Hill's gun (or 'silencer'), we are given the essence of his beliefs. We are told not to blind ourselves to the experience of life by waiting, watching, and regretting. We are accused of failing to notice the nature of the life we live, of ignoring the eternity upon which we are afloat. We are advised to see the unity of life, to perceive how the good thoughts and the bitter ones, the happiness and the pain are woven together into unity and are necessary complements to each other. We are warned against self-regard and self-pity; we must see ourselves as part of a total pattern and learn to forget the unimportant details of living and even, finally, our own identities, our own self-consciousness in order that we may become part of that "one thought" which, Blake tells us, "fills immensity." Hartigan's ghost, however, is not yet ready to become one with the spirit of the universe. His spirit is still chained to earth by memories; it is even possible that it may return to earth; having left down "one gangway", it may return by another one. Clearly, for Jack Yeats death is not a conclusion but a continuance and a change of perspective and brings an understanding and recognition of the overall rhythm of the universe.

Possibly it is necessary to see this philosophy as a background to the two other plays I must discuss, *La La Noo* and *In Sand*. It is also necessary to realise that the same philosophy imbues the paintings and the prose works. If we look at one of his last paintings, *Glory* (1953), we see, in T. G. Rosenthal's words, "youth, maturity and old age all talking and rejoicing in the glory of life." They are standing in a landscape so organised as to remind us of the rhythms of the sea, of the flow and ebb, of the rise and fall of waves; and we see that the turbulence of the figures is at one with the turbulence of their setting. We see their individual glory as part of universal glory. So it is also with the other paintings of the forties and fifties, and so it is with the prose memoirs and novels. There is an intense and zestful presentation of the way in which

sensation follows sensation as man is borne along in conti-
nuosity; there are marvellous wishes and fantasies, but there
is always also a mingling of the pathetic with the exuberant,
and a unifying theme of delight in evanescence. We must
delight in the transient because it is transient, because it leads
on always to the new, to something else. The hero is always
the wanderer, the man who does not attempt to impose fixity
upon a restlessly unfixed universe, who does not fear the
clock, but embraces the passing of time and accepts death
with a sigh for what has gone and with a trusting gladness
at what is to come. Jack Yeats's portrayal of people in his
books is enormously sympathetic but his sympathy extends
beyond the individual to the life process itself. He loves the
living human creature, but he is in love with life itself and
with the rhythm of the universe that contains and compre-
hends both life and death.

This may seem too weighty a series of considerations to be
applied to *La La Noo*, and yet, if it is kept in mind while
reading the play, it sharpens the edge of the irony. *La La Noo*
is set in a lonely Irish pub. The Publican and a Stranger are
talking together when they are interrupted by seven women
who have been to a nearby fair and who now wish shelter
from the rain until it is time to catch the bus on the road
some little distance away. The Stranger is much travelled,
somewhat loquacious and filled with interest in life. The
women are a mixed bunch; they all talk together and their
talk is of love and death as the talk of country people so often
is. The First Woman says:

> I would hate to see any man die. I didn't see my father
> die. He was away from me when he died. I have no
> brother or sister and my mother died when I don't
> remember her. And I thought I was going to see the
> Jockey boy die there on the Strand today. I was sick at
> it. I didn't want to see it. I am glad now, not only for
> him, but for myself. But surely I cannot expect to live
> all my life and see no man die. 'Tis too much to expect.

FOURTH WOMAN: I never seen them die. I seen them wither
and when my back was turned they died on me.
Wouldn't they put the life across you? They like to with

their tricky ways. They're in hands with death the whole
time, the dirty twisters.

FIFTH WOMAN: I don't care what you say, I'll see a man die
and then I'll die myself and it won't be long either.

Shortly after this exchange the women decide to leave the
pub and walk to the road to wait for the bus. They are
drenched by a sudden shower and return. The Stranger puts
them in another room, and they take off their wet things and
hand them to him round the edge of the door so that they
can be dried at the Smith's forge nearby. When the clothes
are dry and they are dressed again, they realise that it is
nearly time to catch the bus. The Fourth Woman runs for it.
The rest wait for the Stranger to drive them in the Smith's
lorry. The Stranger has never driven a lorry before, and he
runs it into a tree and is killed. It is only then that the Seventh
Woman reveals that she is able to drive a truck and so
the women leave the Landlord alone with the body of the
Stranger.

Although the play builds up steadily towards the catas-
trophe of the Stranger's death and the Fourth Woman's
prophesy is fulfilled in that she turns her back on the company
and runs off before the disaster occurs, *La La Noo* is more
than a macabre anecdote. The talk circles around themes of
universal significance. The Sixth Woman asks rhetorically,
"Are there not enough wounds on the creation of the earth?"
The Stranger tells the Publican he ought to thank God for
living in a quiet place and adds: "What do you want with
heavy death and destruction, doing no good to anyone only
cataracts of harm to man made in the image of God." There
is trivia in the talk too, talk of superstitions, of clothes, of the
weather, and almost all the talk is speculative. The Publican
frequently refers to myths of the heroes that had fought in
the near countryside, and he tells the Stranger: "The world
away from us this day is full of terrible cruel things. There
was vampires and dragons in the old days, long ago, if you
could believe the old tales, and I could believe them, for there
are raging vampires eating at the hearts of the people all over
the world this evening, while you and me here in the quiet,
are just talking a little encouragement to ourselves." *La La
Noo* was first performed in 1942, and this speech is an obvious

allusion to the Second World War. The Publican is a fearful man and afraid to wander. The Stranger is a travelled man full of talk of wonders. The women are all questioning and speculative. Indeed, the drama of *La La Noo*, though it seems at first sight to be a presentation of the theme that death lies in wait for us all and is always both awaited and unexpected, is something more. It is a portrait of a questioning, fearful, speculative mankind. Its dramatic technique is almost that of antidrama. The talk is unforced, natural, wayward. It is, one might say, a slice of life—and a slice of death. In its casual, fluid manner it anticipates once again the conversational mode of later theatre.

Nevertheless, behind it there lies something else. The women's nakedness, their stripping off their clothes, is clearly symbolic. But of what? We are reminded of Lear's "unaccommodated man". We are forced to recognise that all our trappings and our dignities are transient. We may even recall, thinking of the Publican's reference to the war, that in the chapter of Revelation which announces the coming of Armageddon we have seven angels, and we have the words: "Behold I come as a thief. Blessed is he that watcheth and keepeth his garments lest he walk naked and they see his shame." That Jack Yeats might have had this verse of Revelation in his mind and have wished to set his small country play against the backcloth of that terrific prophecy may seem improbable. And yet, when he painted a tinkers' encampment in 1941 (the year before *La La Noo* was produced), he called it *The Blood of Abel* and thus referred the spectator directly to a specific chapter of Genesis.

Jack Yeats was not an allegorical but a symbolist writer. He dealt not in precise references but in allusions and echoes. The meaning of his work is the meaning we find in it, and he gives us many meanings to choose from. This is one of the points made very clear by *The Green Wave*, a conversation piece which he intended as a prologue to *In Sand*. This consists only of a conversation between two elderly men about a painting. The heart of the question is displayed in one exchange:

2ND ELDERLY: What is it?
1ST ELDERLY: It is a wave.

2ND ELDERLY: I know that, but what sort of a wave?

1ST ELDERLY: A green wave—well—a rather green wave.

2ND ELDERLY: What does it mean?

1ST ELDERLY: I think it means just to be a wave.

2ND ELDERLY: I like things to mean something, and I like to know what they mean, and I like to know it at once. After all, time is important, the most important thing we know of, and why waste it in trying to find out what something means, when if it stated its meaning clearly itself we would know at once.

1ST ELDERLY: If that wave could speak it might say: "I'm an Irish wave and the Irish are generally supposed to answer questions by asking questions," and the wave might ask you what was the meaning of yourself!

At the close of the conversation the 1st Elderly Man tells his friend teasingly, "I see it's beginning to worry you again, so next time, before you come, I'll get some artistic friend of mine to paint some buttercups and daisies on the side of my green wave and turn it into a green hillside, and then it won't worry you any more." This is a very double-edged remark. Why should a hill be less disturbing than a wave? Is it the instability, the fluidity, the unfixedness of the wave that disturbs us? Or is it that we see in the wave what we are too blind to see in the land, the restless rhythm of life and its mystery? We know of course from Ambrose Oldbury's boast that he will swallow the wave, from the "Order of the Wave" in *Rattle*, from the talk of tides and gangways in *The Silencer*, and from the speeches of Nardock in *The Deathly Terrace* that the wave is for Jack Yeats an image of great significance and suggests the flux and rhythm not only of this mortal life but of the eternity upon which we are afloat. The picture of *The Green Wave* itself appears in number 4 of the Cuala Press Broadsides (new series) in 1937,* and it may be that it was the making or the publication of this print that gave rise to the writing of the play. The wave as presented in the broadside is not, however, simply green. It has red in it also and thus contrives to suggest the current of life itself, the tide of the

---

*I am indebted to Professor Norman Mackenzie for drawing my attention to the existence of this picture.

blood. Naturally, the sea is a central character in Jack Yeats's drama as in his novels: it certainly figures importantly in *In Sand*.

The theme of *In Sand* is, I suspect, taken from a poem by Walter Savage Landor which was once very well known and which was published in many anthologies including Palgrave's *Golden Treasury*. The poem goes:

> Well I remember how you smiled
>   To see me write your name upon
> The soft sea-sand . . . O! *what a child!*
>   *You think you're writing upon stone!*
> I have since written what no tide
>   Shall ever wash away, what men
> Unborn shall read o'er ocean wide
>   And find Ianthe's name again.

The story which the play tells is simple enough. Anthony Larcson, who regards himself as a "joker" and an "egotist", is dying, and he tells his lawyer to arrange that after his death a young girl should write upon the sand at low tide the words, "Tony, we have the good thought for you still." This is done and the girl, who was chosen by lot, also receives a bequest which enables her, when she comes of age, to go on a holiday and thus to meet the man she marries. The couple travel all over the world and on every beach she visits, the girl Alice writes the words, "Tony, we have the good thought for you still", though she has no recollection of Larcson himself at all. While visiting a tropical island her husband, Maurice, receives a cable which tells him he is ruined, and he dies within the same day. Alice remains on the island, living on the charity of the proprietor of the hotel. After her death a new Governor thinks to make the island a republic and he and a Visitor discuss plans to develop the island and even begin to put some of them into practice, though they are delayed by the early beginning of the tourist season. The play ends with two young people writing upon the sand the words, "Tony, we have the good thought for you still", not understanding them, but knowing that they bring good fortune.

The play is in three acts, each one presenting a different aspect of the main themes. In the first we are given Larcson's last words and the writing of the name on the sand by the young girl. His friend and confidant, Oldgrove, tells Larcson: "You always, in the past, had grand ideas. Indeed, you often told me ideas and plans that would have shaken up all the Bank Managers of this place, retired, and in active service. But you never put any of your plans into operation—you had too kind a heart to want to upset anyone." Nevertheless, the last plan of Larcson does upset people somewhat. The Mayor, after reading a part of his formal speech on the seashore, stops reading and reflects on the society of the town:

> It is only the hard who have survived in the last gener-
> ation in our town. Whatever may have gone on in other
> places, you know, as I know, here it has been tooth and
> nail. Get a good hold and never shift it till you get a
> better. It has been down, or be downed ... Maybe it
> would have been better if this man, whose wishes we are
> following out today, had never decided to leave these
> wishes which are in a sense a criticism of our bad old
> ways, and a criticism I say of even the best of our
> ways ... The ways of men, and especially men on their
> deathbeds, are strange ways, and can not be understood
> by those who stand in their full health, not thinking of
> their last hours, but of the hours which keep coming
> towards them like waves of the sea, some with crests of
> glistening foam on them and some dark as blood, no two
> waves alike.

In the second act we find Alice and Maurice "not thinking of their last hours" though Alice has written Larcson's message with its reminder of human transcience everywhere she has been. Maurice, however, just before he receives the fatal telegram, says: "We're fancy free, nothing to stop us except misfortune—other people's misfortune—or our own. We can keep moving like the finger on the wall but we don't write anything on the wall—only the sand of the sea-shore." All these images and thoughts come together in the last act of the play when we are told by the Old Sailor of the island's past, and the Visitor and the new Governor make their plans to create an autonomous republic.

It is in this act that Jack Yeats makes use of that theme of utopia which appears so frequently in his novels and which is also touched on in the last act of *Rattle*. The Old Sailor

tells the Visitor of the island's days of innocence. He was cast
away there as a young man, and says: "The people on the
Island thought a lot of me. For three years I never did a
stroke of work. The people brought me anything I wanted,
they thought I could work miracles . . . When they were tired
of feeding me for nothing, they gave me a little canoe and I
went fishing and by and by I got a little patch, and I found
I was able to grow a few sweet potatoes and, one thing and
another I made out." He describes the development of the
island society, and how there were some "Suppression Gover-
nors" eager to cut down trees and to ban pleasure, and some
"Earthly Paradise Governors" who attempted to build roads
which were washed away by the rains and to make improve-
ments which never lasted. It seems that the island insists on
retaining its own dreamy gentle identity and that no governor
can alter it.

This account prepares us for the new Governor who wishes
to modernise the island. The Visitor tells him that the island
needs a motor-road (there are no motors), a picture gallery,
a race course, and a swimming pool (everyone swims in the
sea). He suggests the formation of an army and the creation
of a prison. All these necessary attributes of modern society
can only be created symbolically. The motor-road must be
simply a track marked out on the sands and the swimming
pool a sea pool labelled in blue paint. What matters is not,
it seems, the thing itself but the idea of the thing. Whether
or not the army is needed it must exist for dignity's sake;
whether or not a flag is required it must be created for the
sake of show. It is curiously like a child's game. The Governor
is particularly insistent that the islanders must be prohibited
from writing the wrong kind of slogans on the seashore, and
he draws up a list of permitted slogans. When at the close of
the play the tourist season begins and occupies the attention
of the hotel people so that they have no time to spare for
creating a revolution, a brown boy and his girl friend write
upon the sand, "Tony, we have the good thought for you
still." The Governor, told that the slogan brings luck, then
writes the words himself and realises that he has broken his
own law.

What have I done, I who was given these Three Stars
(*he touches them with his fingers*) each for seven years obedi-
ence and for causing others to obey, I have disobeyed
my own ukase.
>   But I have obeyed alone.
>   I have disobeyed alone.
>   I will die alone.
(*He pulls revolver from holster and raises muzzle to his chin*)

The brown girl and boy and the Visitor prevent the Governor
from committing suicide and then the brown girl says: "Don't
be fretting yourself, Governor, look . . . look at the sea's edge!
The tide is coming in now fast, look, look, the waters are
covering up and washing away everything that we have
written."

Anthony Larcson's joke has worked. He has managed by
means of his words to prevent the island losing its innocence
and turning into the ruthless modern society he disliked and
accused. He has also reminded us that all mortal dignities
and hopes are ephemeral and that having "the good thought"
is more important than having the materially successful life.
The island that his words preserve from progress is like the
sea in the ebb and flow of its governors, its changes from
suppression to amelioration. Alice and the Old Sailor have
submitted themselves without resentment to the tide and
achieve not merely resignation to coming death but also con-
tentment. *In Sand* lacks the fiery exuberance of *The Silencer*,
and the bareness and directness of *La La Noo*, but it has its
own quality of lyric melancholy and easy philosophy. It is,
perhaps, an old man's play, but it is not a play of defeat—
for at the end one puts the book down with a feeling for
human warmth, affection, simplicity, and a faith in the mys-
terious good life can give if it is trusted.

Jack Yeats's drama was inimitable. There are no other
plays quite like his. He anticipated in his plays many later
fashions and the work of other playwrights. In *The Deathly
Terrace* there is a use of what we now call "high camp"
that anticipates much later theatre, including some scenes
by Beckett and Ionesco. In his antidramatic talk-plays he
anticipated Pinter and Beckett. His work fits more easily, it
might be said, into modern European literature of our time

than does that of his brother. It may be some time before his work is properly appreciated and evaluated. His prose works are still unavailable to all but wealthy and assiduous collectors. But I believe that, once the whole of his writing does become available, he will be recognised as being one of the most original and important of twentieth-century writers and as towering a figure in literature as he is in painting. Moreover, once the complete writings are set alongside the drawings and paintings, it will become apparent that there is, in all Jack Yeats's work, an extraordinary unity. Not only do paintings illustrate and extend themes of the writings, but the writings explore and investigate symbols and scenes presented in the painting. Jack Yeats, like his friend Synge, tackled "the whole of life".

from
THE
MANCHESTER
GUARDIAN

RACING DONKEYS

My friend Dan Vincent, the wise little sporting sweep who knows so much of London, met me by appointment one Bank Holiday morning by the omnibus yard where they change horses. We climbed up on top of a waiting 'bus, and were in time to see the work of changing. I watched carefully, as I had often done before, the whole ritual of the business, from the appearance of the fresh pair at the gate with the yardman, all of one dusty brown colour, with an old horse-girth around his waist, hanging on to the reins. I saw how he slapped the horses into the pole, and how every little thing was done in its proper order, till at last the driver dexterously caught the thrown-up reins on his whip, gathered his clean-groomed, sturdy pair together, threw some dark saying to the yardman, and we were away. Dan immediately began to converse with the driver. He told him how he was taking me a long way east to see some donkey-racing. He told him of some of the great donkeys of the past—of Dick Bird's Little Bird, and of Flying Scud, whose winnings ran well into three figures. But the driver was not interested. I do not think 'busmen are very catholic in their tastes. I knew one who liked to discuss religious questions and one who collected engravings, but they were exceptions. This driver did not laugh at Dan's taste for donkeys; he was not interested—that was all. A man with less poise than a 'bus-driver would have sniggered at least. Why is it that a donkey makes so many men laugh, I wonder? I know men whose very existence seems to me the grossest absurdity who will guffaw loudly at the mere sight of a small donkey. I wonder when the guffaw first originated—who first passed the word to laugh. Our driver was one of the dandy kind. He wore a deep crimson carnation in his button-hole, and his hat was very shiny. He drew our attention to a dark spot in the middle of the back of his light dustcoat. "One of them ole ladies done that," he said. "'Stop driver,' she says,

and she poked her dirty umbrella in my back. I talked to her;
I lost my temper; I lost my job. I was off the box a week."
He mourned his ruined overcoat as far as Knightsbridge.
Then he accepted a cigar with a band on it from Dan. He
did not light it, but rolled it across his mouth from corner to
corner, and told us yarns of his uncle who drove a 'bus along
the Edgware Road, and how we might know him when we
saw him, for he "allus wears a John Bull 'at." He also told
us how he was going to get married if he had any luck.

We left him at the Bank, and penetrated further east by
other omnibuses and a tram car. At Bow Church we got
down, and walked through strange, dull streets of little old,
ugly houses—everyone like its neighbour, except that some
had wax fruit in the front window and some had not. One
had a model of a ship, and in one there was a model of a
lighthouse. I wondered if the man of the house was a retired
light-keeper. If he was, how he must have longed of a morning
in that dark street for the salt breezes that blew around his
other home!

We turned a corner, and were immediately all among the
donkeys; here they were, in their light barrows, with the
donkey-owners all talking at once. We were outside the Irish-
man's running grounds, where the races were to be held.

Very soon the gates opened, and we paid our sixpences
and went in. We found ourselves in a fair-sized enclosure
with a high board fence around it, on which were notices of
future events written with white chalk in a large round hand.
Almost all the ground, as well as the track, was covered with
cinders. The track was an oval one, going a great many laps
to the mile. The place was soon full of people; the eel jelly
man was there—

> Jelly, jelly, jelly,
> All jelly,
> So nice,—

and a man with a jar of beer, which he doled out in a pint
milk can, had a great many friends. Many of the people had
whippets with them. If you own one of those speedy little
dogs you should wrap it up in its greatcoat and put the leg
of one of your old socks around its delicate throat, for their
health takes as much looking after as a prima donna's. There

was a small boy there dressed in the fashion of those parts—
in a sailor suit with lace collar and a velvet jockey cap. There
was the brother-in-law of a celebrated pugilist—he and his
bride; it was their wedding-day. She was a fine lass! She wore
an electric blue Newmarket down to her heels, and a white
hat and feathers. He won the barrow race, which came off
before the donkey racing commenced. He and others drew
costers' barrows around the track, each barrow having a
weight in it, in the exact placing of which much nicety is
required. Then the first heat of the donkey race started, and
Dan pointed out to me which was Seek Tommy, a donkey of
which I had heard, and he told me how his owner was nearly
the biggest owner of donkeys in the country; and he showed
me a very solemn donkey of a kind of piebald colour, and he
told me how every year her owner drove her down to Ascot
Races. The racing was very exciting, the light barrows spin-
ning round the bends on one wheel, with the drivers leaning
at fearful angles. Seek Tommy, running like a little steam
engine, with never a touch of the whip, won the first heat.
Some of the finishes of the various heats were very close. One
donkey when leading and within a few yards of the winning-
post made a determined rush against the fence, with the
intention, no doubt, of freeing himself from the barrow. The
harness broke, and the next donkey won.

After many of the heats the air was heavy with arguments.
I am afraid some donkey owners go a-racing on the old system
of win, tie, or wrangle. A rule that there was to be no passing
at the bends caused trouble. Hobson's Orme was disqualified
for this. Now, behind Hobson's Orme there was a party of
parties, as you might say, all in new black-and-white check
caps. After the decision was given against Orme they looked
very ugly. They rushed at the Irishman who owned the track.
They blacked his eye; they rent his coat from tail to collar;
while a horrible little man, perched high on the fencing, sang
out, loud and clear, "Tear 'im up! Tear 'im up! Tear 'im
up!" The trackowner gave way before the gang till he felt the
fence at his back. Then he sent their leader reeling through
them, with both hands to his broken face. Dan looked at me,
and said, "My word, they don't want no more; that satisfied
them."

The proprietor walked away to start the next heat. We

waited on till we saw Seek Tommy win the final—the day's racing was over. An owner, looking affectionately at his donkey, said, "He's done well today; he shall 'ave a bit of extra for 'is tea." Little groups of people still lingered on the track, but most mounted their barrows or got a lift in a friend's. One who drove a pair—one Ned in the shafts and one outside—gave a lift to three, who clung with their arms around each other's ample waists and smoked black cigars.

And so we all diverged away to our homes, at the different points of the compass, and our "little bits of extra" for our teas.

SHOVE HALFPENNY

I had seen a certain amount of shove halfpenny played, but never a really important match, so when my little friend Dan Vincent, the sporting sweep, on meeting me for what our grandpas used to call "a ramble," suggested we should see a match on the Surrey side of London, I was delighted. We took a blue 'bus, I think, "across the water." But before going to the small alehouse, called the Orphan Boy, where the match—for five pounds a side, by the way—was to come off, we had our evening meal in a cosy little eating-house—sizzling bacon and eggs and buttered toast! And there is no place where buttered toast is properly served except in the smaller kind of eating-house, especially in those where the proprietor and his missus do the work themselves. The buttered toast was real buttered toast, whole rounds of it, with the crust left on, and plenty of salt butter. The toast was so endearing that we stayed over it longer than we meant, and had to take a hansom to the Orphan Boy. So we arrived by its low door with a kind of mild glory about us, caused by the cab, which made the loungers outside cheer. Believe me, they took one of us for the shove-halfpenny challenger, for he too came from "across the water." We went inside, and presently the challenger drove up, and with his backer was taken into the landlord's private parlour.

By this time the bar was packed with the knowing and the curious ones of those parts. While we waited for the principals

to take the ring, as it were, a bearded old sportsman in the crowd played an exhibition game, doing, it seemed, anything he liked with the halfpennies. At last the landlord came into the bar carrying a new table, followed by the two principals and the backer of the challenger; the landlord himself was backing Val Dance, the local man. Bill Boland, the challenger, was a stranger to all in the bar, and no one spoke with him but his backer; he had a long face, with a weary, serious look. But Val Dance was the "life of the party," as the corpse's husband said in the story. He wore, I remember, a crimson silk kerchief about his neck, and exchanged remarks of a gay and witty kind with all about him. At last the polished table was in position. The referee, appointed by one of the big sporting daily papers, had lit a long presentation cigar. The two backers had taken their seats on each side of the table, with large lumps of chalk in their hands with which to score.

When Val, who had undressed himself to his shirt and trousers, so desperate was his mood, folded his arms across his chest and cried, "W'os 'appennies are we going to play with?" friends crowded round him and appealed to the generosity of his nature. After some time he yielded. "All right," he said, as if he was giving away half a stone at least, "I'll play with the gemman's 'appennies"; and he began to play. I remember he did some wonderful things with those polished halfpennies. Four halfpennies would by lying anywhere on the board when, with a little pat from his hand, he would shoot up the fifth; it slid from coin to coin, and lo! all five were in their places. He won the first game. Bill Boland seemed to play a good and a steady game—that was all. Val was full of glee; he called for a new clay, and during the next game he tried to smoke it, but there was a hole in the stem and it wouldn't draw. The man who got him the pipe called out advice as to the smoking of it from the back of the crowd. The second game was very close indeed. I remember while the excitement was holding us silent—indeed there were very few words spoken at any time among the audience while the play was on—the landlord's little boy upset a pot of beer over the official referee, who shouted loudly for a swab.

Boland won the second game. Honours were now easy, one game apiece. Three games the rubber. Immediately the backer of Boland arose and called out, loud and clear, to the landlord's wife, "Twelve pots in the bar, mam"—he was standing twelve pots of four-ale to us, the audience. Dan Vincent looked at me; he said "Bill's got 'im set," and then the twelve pots began their slow circle from lip to lip around the bar-room; as soon as one pot was fairly on its way another was started, and so for ten minutes the spectators were busy taking large or small gulps from the slowly moving pewters. Where I stood, on a settle, during the two games, I could see over into the next bar, and I saw there an old man of those parts, and he was trying to awaken some excitement in the bosom of the cabman who drove Bill Boland. At intervals the old man would say—"Five pounds a side! Whew! You never 'eared of such a game!" But the cabman showed no interest; he slowly lifted his tankard, and when it was empty he looked into it in a kind of melancholy way.

The third game began, and then I realised that Dan was right. Bill had Val Dance "set." Though his face never lost its subdued sadness, it was evident that Bill knew it. He did things to those halfpennies to learn which must have taken the practice of half a lifetime. It was all over. The local knowing ones looked at one another. "The man from across the water" had won. We spoke to the landlord; he seemed a little disappointed in Val Dance, but he asked us to take something "on the house." We wished him good night and better luck another time, and went back "across the water."

THE GLOVE CONTEST

I asked a man in the street for the hall where the boxing was to come off that night. He told me to follow the tramway tracks till I came to it. I found a large gloomy building with little knots of people standing about the door. As many of those who waited wore their hair very short indeed, I knew I wasn't far from the battle-field then. I paid my money, and, climbing the stairs, I found myself in a long assembly-room, packed with people all wearing about their eyes a keen look of anticipation. I passed by them to my seat, right in the front among the Corinthians, and very close to the raised platform on which were set up the stakes and ropes of that square which the old-timers loved to call "The Magic Circle."

The evening's work had not yet begun. I turned round and looked at my neighbours. Those near me were of that type who wear their hats a little sideways and are fond of a heavy Melton overcoat. On my right a splinter-bar pin gleamed in a voluminous cravat. Further away the benches were filled with those whose throats abhor the stiff foolishness of collars. Here were neckerchiefs of every colour, blue with a white bird's-eye, a winey red or a yellow fogle on a white ground. Here and there among the crowd one could see an old fighter, retired, the proud possessor of a pair of thick ears. But most of the people were of those who follow the art of "hit, stop, and get away" as spectators, not as professors of the art. But all the faces bore a look of eager intelligence, more like the faces of those attending a lecture, than, say, the audience of a musical comedy. Not that we didn't enjoy some comedy that night.

At last "The Announcer" stepped into the ring and told us of the exciting entertainment he had arranged for his customers next week. After that the first pair in the nine-stone competition for local lads climbed into the ring, and proceeded to punch each other with a kind of jovial wicked-ness that was cheering to see. Other pairs followed. Some were clever and some were only strong, but all gave punish-ment and took it with the best of good humour. Then we had the comedy I spoke of. An Italian, whose arm had grown strong perhaps scooping up parti-coloured ice-cream or in turning the handle of an organ with a picture of Garibaldi on the front, took the ring with a withered old boxer, a clever enough old man, but "a has been," as they say. The Italian took the attitudes of a fencer—the longe, the appel, the paradee,—and lightly patted the old man here and there, and turned and smiled to the audience as though he would say: "It is an old man; see, I strike him but lightly. I will not send him home to his grandchildren a shattered wreck." Sometimes, while his head was turned to smile at us, the old "has been" would hit him unexpectedly. Then the Italian would spring round the ring throwing fantastic postures as he went. All this we enjoyed very much, and we gave the pair of them plenty of applause. But the proudest man in that assembly was the Italian, and he put on his coat and swaggered up and down in front of the platform, obstructing the view of the ring until the crowd grew annoyed with him.

When the preliminary bouts were over the referee came to the front ropes of the ring, and, having told us once again what we were to see next week, he produced a belt with massive metal shields and clasps upon it bearing in relief the figures of men in fighting trim. He told us that the winner of next week's big contest should also win this belt. He then stuffed as much of it as he could into his trousers pocket, and by this time the two warriors in the important contest of the evening—a ten-round affair—had taken their seats. One was a Manchester lad, the other a lad of London. The referee introduced us to them and their seconds. Then he made us a straightforward little speech, the last sentence of which was: "Gentlemen, each of these lads, I know, has many friends in the house tonight, but I'm a friend of both lads." The contest began, as pretty and exciting a thing to see as heart could wish. They began quietly at first; then the London lad began to force the pace a little. The other acted on the defensive. The first followed him over the ring, and for round after round piled up the points, while the Manchester lad got weaker and weaker. Then those friends of which the referee had told us began to give tongue loud and deep, like a pack of hounds in a valley wood. Then a surprise came. The weakening man stiffened; he struck two heavy blows; they both told—he had his man in trouble; he followed London into his own corner. Then the time-keeper struck the triangle and the round was over. Immediately the seconds of London began to revive their drooping man. They blew water in his face; they sponged him; they fanned him with the towel punks; they had only the one minute rest in which to get their man himself again.

The triangle sounded, and the little boy above the crowd turned a fresh card with the number of the round upon it. The contest went on; the tables were now completely turned; Manchester began at once to attack, and London could only defend, holding himself ready always for an unguarded jaw and a lucky blow; while Manchester made up the points lost earlier in the contest, and now his friends began to give voice to their feelings. But he had a lot of leeway to make up, and

the other was fast shaking off the effects of those two stagger-
ing blows; so to the very end victory seemed hanging in the
balance. The triangle rang out for the last time. The referee
consulted the judges; he stepped to the front of the ring. "The
decision of the judges is—a draw," he said. "Now leave the
hall as quietly as you can."

THE CATTLE MARKET

I asked the conductor where I should best get off for the
Cattle Market. "See them men with sticks?" he said. "You
follow them." The Cattle Market is a very cheerful place for
everything—but the cattle; they look a little weary. I think it
is "them men with sticks"; everybody carries a stick, and I
think that wearies the cattle.

The constant movement and the fact of having got up when
the birds got up make the people in the market gay and
inclined for a joke. So when a buyer offers a preposterously
small price for some cattle he does not want, instead of a
surly answer, the owner will meet his mood and cry, "Oh,
go to—Heaven and be an angel."

Most men about the market are stout men, "beef to the
heels, like a Mullingar heifer," but there is a curious band of
lean and wizened men who all the time are flitting here and
there, some with dandy brushes bulging their pockets. Some
have hands dyed blue, and some have hands dyed red; they
are the drovers. Their hands are dyed with the colours with
which they put a new owner's mark upon the sheep.

If you do not feed in the market on pies or tripe, both of
which can be bought from perambulating merchants, you can
refresh yourself in a building with a steaming roof in the
centre of the market. But near the gate there is a big inn
where cattlemen and butchers dine at an ordinary; the long
corridors, the hurrying waiters, the profusion of food, the
jorums of hot toddy are the same exactly as you would meet
in some great old country town on a fair-day, where bull-
necked farmers eat like Jack the Giant-Killer. Here the con-
versation is all of cattle and cattlemen.

"How's that little fella that used to sell the little old
    cows?"
"You'll never see him no more."
"Not dead?"
"Yes; been dead all the winter."

After dinner you can wander back into the market, and
under an archway you will find a man who sells silk handker-
chiefs.

> Of every tint and hue,
> The green and red,
> The puce and black,
> The scarlet and the blue,

as the old racecourse ballad-singer sang. Buy the silvery one
with the big blue spots.

THE FLAT IRON

Everyone in Manchester knows the Flat Iron Market, and a
very large number do their fancy shopping there by night.
The market is the hunting-park of the bargain hunters who
want, or think they want, or imagine that they may some day
want—a trusty old cavalry sword, or a pair of skates, or a
bunch of curtain rings, or a pair of half-wellington boots, or
a toy engine, or a hank of cord, green or red, or a little round
looking-glass, or a pair of cork soles, or a bunch of old keys,
or an old rusty lock, or a pink ice-cream, or a handful of hot
chestnuts, or a small but cheerfully coloured copy of "The
Angelus," or a fuzzy toy animal, or a bottle of medicine that'll
cure anything that can be found in a medical dictionary, or
a "gigantic penny packet" of notepaper, or a roll of oil-cloth,
or a pair of stays—for a penny. The stay merchant said, "The
ribs is right," and a little man with a red nose bought a pair.
　You can buy thousands of different things. You can even
buy a policeman's helmet. Two heroes got one each, and after
buttoning their jackets up to the chin ran through the market
like a brace of Merry Andrews, startling timorous merchants

A JUNE FAIR

by suddenly popping their helmeted heads round the corners of the stall.

I think I should like to do all my marketing in the Flat Iron, for it is a real market, a place where you can swagger aloof if it suits your mind, or you can rub shoulders with the best of company, stopping occasionally to pass old-fashioned chaff. And when you stop to buy you plunge immediately into the old primeval realities of commerce. Here you do not stand sourly while a pale-faced, short-tempered shopman whirls your purchase into a dexterously twisted screw of pale brown paper and sends your money trundling in a globe along naked wires. No; here before you make a purchase you can slap and thump a thing, and abuse and sneer at it, and the man behind the stall will slap and thump it too, and praise it; and at last you'll get the price down to near to what he will take and you will give. Then perhaps some old split-the-differ of the market rolls up and makes it a bargain between you.

Oh, you can enjoy buying in the Flat Iron Market. And you can buy almost anything that heart could wish, but never a flat iron could I see. This surprised me, for you can get petticoats in Petticoat Lane. In my ignorance, I did not know, till I was told, that this market takes its name from its shape. The larger priced things, like clothes and oilcloth, are sold by Dutch auction, the auctioneer striding up and down the platform of his stall, by turns wheedling the people with a honeyed tongue, or with winks and sideway glances setting the women giggling and the men roaring, or browbeating them with his fiercer banter until he has them at his mercy. "Some of ye don't come to buy, s'elp me," he cries; "ye come to pinch."

If you go to the market for pleasure only, when tired of hearing others bargain and chaff among the flare lamps you can cross the road to where the merry-go-rounds are whirling. Also sometimes there is a boxing booth, and there are several kinds of throwing games, one where you hurl balls at strangely whiskered dolls, which fall over backwards like life itself if you hit them fair. Then there is "The Paralizer," in a tent with netted sides and top, and goal-posts at the far end, with a goalkeeper in a blue shirt. Here you pay an entrance fee, and if you are clever you kick a goal and receive a cash

THE BARREL MAN

The charge is a penny for three throws.   The barrel man defends himself with the
sticks in his hands, and if hard pressed drops down into the barrel.

reward, thereby, no doubt, imperilling your pure amateur status forever. But the goalkeeper is strong and nimble and stops more balls than he lets go by him.

A young man might easily stand in front of this goalkeeper and kick away all his spare change and borrow from his friends till he broke them, and when they left him he might, if allowed to kick on credit, stand there till he kicked away his inheritance, and until the copper-bag of the lady with the red motor-cap, who takes the money, became stuffed with his I O U's.

It is strange that show people, who are in their dress so conservative, should have taken so heavily to the red motor-cap. I think I saw the first to wear it. She drove twelve spotted horses yoked to the high band wagon of a road circus. She was perked up above the crowd like a pinnacle on a cathedral, and she had cotton wool in her ears. Her hands were light, but she had wrists of iron, and she tooled her long team down the hilly Market-street of Sligo town at a pace that made everything rattle, but she never made a mistake. I left "The Paralizer" and looked at the passengers on the merry-go-round, which had no dappled wooden horses, but cars in the shape of gondolas that not only went round and round but up and down with a sort of writhing motion. I did not mount the cars. I turned away from the Flat Iron and the revolving music and the smoking oil lamps.

'WHEN I WAS IN MANCHESTER'

Manchester is the only city in the world which has so pleased itself as to pay me a salary. And that was a long while ago. And the salary was not so enormous as for any part of it to remain with me yet. And of memories of Manchester when I lived there very few remain with me today. It was not that the city had an unkindly face to me, and I had good friends I went to see on Sundays. But I was the victim of a folly all the time, a folly of my own building. I overworked conscientiously. I thought then that I was investing in something which would pay me hereafter. But now I am afraid I may not find it so when I stand out on the whingey side of the gate, keeping the Recording Angel out with me while I try and convince him that he has forgotten some of my good deeds. I am afraid that when I say, "Well, I once followed overwork," he will say, "Tell us what's that!" I thought I was throwing my bread on the waters. Now I doubt it, and I believe I will, at that gate, have to rely on the quota of my nation. The song says,

God does love the Irish,

and well He might, for they never loved themselves.

The bread I threw on the water never came back to me, nor led me anywhere. It was not like that bread great Tom Sawyer knew about. That quicksilver-loaded bread, which sometimes thrilled the breast of Great Pappa of the Waters. But it is not fair to say the bread tossed never came back. It does come to me now. Two good crusts of memory.

Once, when I lived in Manchester in the very heart of the city, I came on an army pattering along on little round feet, some small soldiers were big enough to walk within themselves, but plenty were so small they had to hold each other's hands to give themselves a steadying comfort. And, looking away to right, down through the insurance offices and the heavy fortresses of heavy business, I could see the flailing, whirling drumsticks cutting capers in the air, and there I was watching the Catholic school children passing on their way.

BOWLERS

Another crust which comes to my feet now is when the city was entertaining two young cinnamon-coloured princes from the lands of the palms: and the fire brigade came out—horse engines in those gay days—and the water was fired into the air, and the sun was attracted to the spray and in return slapped a rainbow on it. I was not very near the princes, so I could not see if they were pleased, but I was. But fair play's a jewel, and, come to think of it, perhaps there was some quicksilver in the bread I tossed, for many years after I stopped living in Manchester I visited that old brown city again, with all overwork ideas by then thrown down the gully-hole of time. And in one crowded week I saw a play called "A Disgrace to Her Sex," and the comic man in it cut a loaf of bread into one long spiral; that would be a queer old bread

to throw on any water. And I saw Manchester "Concert Houses." I wonder do you have them still, where the juice of the hop, the barley, and the grape went down the long lane to song. A Derby hat on the side of the head signified a hunting song, with a view holloa and away we go, with a row tow tow tow towty. Another hard felt hat, a little one, like Charlie Chaplin's before Charlie Chaplin's day. This little one was placed suddenly by the chairman on his head, at one of the Forums of Manchester which I attended. This little hat over the great mound of thoughtful brow, which itself hung over a distinguished face, and a more distinguished long, white beard. The little hat was a sign that Parliament had adjourned, and the debater, who had been accused of throwing mud, had only just replied: "I didn't throw mud, I threw facts, facts, not mud!"

I went on a canal boat, and I saw other canal boats that had barrels with Corots on their ends, undoubted Corots. That was on the canal which links Manchester with inland towns. But I also journeyed on the canal which makes Manchester a seaport. And I am sure to-day there never is an hour in Market Street when there is not some man rolling with a deep-sea roll.

CLOGS

I saw a bold old knife-board 'bus taking 'old boys to a football match. I did not climb up on that omnibus, to let once again eat into my bones the thrill of the days of old.

Though after I left the Ship Canal I took an ancient vehicle. I was tired of looking at what we called the Foxfire rolling green and shining from her bows all down from Runcorn. And when I left the canal, where it meets the Mersey, I climbed inside a roomy great cab; it must have been a kind of between high and low tide cab, for the coachman cried "All clear aft!" and the boys astern cried "All clear," and they also cried "The Old Banjo"—that was the name of the cab, perhaps. The Old Banjo landed me on a tramcar, and I went under the Mersey, and I caught a train, forty miles, forty minutes, back to Manchester. There was a sweet in those old days called Ship Canal Block. I didn't eat it, but I think it was good.

I saw in that visit some good boxing, and jumping too,

hop, step, and a lep. And a Lightning Artist. Fresh they came from his fingers and his brain; you had to carry them home carefully. They were dripping, drip, drip.

I saw a nice little old man in the cattle market selling pork pies. Another nice little old man in the coal market selling umbrellas. And I heard again the rattle of the clogs. The first morning I woke in Manchester, long ago, I woke to their music.

Are there huge clogs as signs over clog-makers' shops still! Clogs with gold leaf nails in them. When I was a boy they used to talk of the "Whistle of a Racing Jacket," and it's like nothing else on earth. If I had the skeleton of an ear I could whistle it 'ayself, and, if so equipped, I could play "The Rattle of the Clogs" on a cornet, with a silk handkerchief just nestling in its spout.

I saw other plays as well as "A Disgrace to Her Sex." I saw "The Master Criminal"—the greatest scamp on earth. It must have been Crimes Week. Someone, not the scamp in the play sang "Everybody's loved by everybody." I missed "The Ugliest Woman on Earth," though I saw her, heavily veiled, impenetrably veiled, in a barouche, with a pair of flashing horses, a coachman and a footman, and she was accompanied by a man of the great world with a silk hat, and another in a peaked cap, with a large red feather like a ham-shank frill, and he was continually blowing a post-horn. And I missed the "Royal Divorce." I couldn't help it. It wasn't there till next week. But there were the posters with Napoleon sitting brooding on a stone seat in a lovely garden. I've always missed the "Royal Divorce." I've seen

OUR BOYS,

HARBOUR LIGHTS,

and

LONDON DAY BY DAY,

but not "The Lights of London," though I remember the posters of it. I mean the small poster with the small drawings on it, and the ballad: "A country lad and lass along a country road"—wasn't that the way!—"Oh, cruel lights of London," and I thought by Highgate they stood, where Whittington turned his head.

> Oh, cruel lights of London,
> If tears your lights would drown,
> Your victims they have wept them,
> O lights of London Town.

And I don't know whether it was so in the play or not, but I have always thought that those creatures, that country lad and lass, came from Lancashire.

from

SLIGO

UPLIFT

But why tow, why not let others tow as they like it. There
are more up-lifters in the world than subjects of uplift. Let
them uplift us, shoulder high. Then we will be able to see
over their heads to the several promised lands, from which
we have come, and to which we trust to go. When the uplifters
are wedged and milling together, and we are tired of sitting,
we can stroll about on their solid heads, and view these lands.
There will be very few of us and so, like weeks of Sundays,
the time will pass pleasantly, each in turn doing the honours
of each's own promised land. I suppose walking on heads will
be a little like walking on cobble stones. Of course all Uplift-
ing heads are exactly the same size and Uplifted come to
the same level, the skulls are thick and we will be wearing
pampooties, so they will not mind our strolling over the tops.
They will not know anything about it. How splendid! In fact
they will not know anything about anything. Better and
Better! We will speak kindly about them every now and then.
There will be enough of everything for everyone and there
will be no need to sell each other gold bricks. No one ever
offered me a gold brick, they tried me with a home-made ten
dollar bill. But to own a gold brick would be fine, or a
collection of them on your sideboard. With all the Cups won
on sawdust, cinders, grass, or water. They plug the brick with
a little pick of gold and have that little pick assayed which
convinces the buyer, of course, at once. How fine to have
your trepanned head trepanned with gold, instead of silver.
Have it assayed and sell yourself to some gaudy buyer of
human gold bricks. But those buyers are getting scarcer and
scarcer. The Big Talk Nations of the world must soon create
a gold brick buyer or hand in their checks. Imagining a gold
brick buyer is useless, also mugs don't stay mugs. That's
another danger, and drawing lots is hopeless. Better bury all
the gramophone records, smooth the earth over them with

our noses, and start again with the first man who can think of a wheelbarrow.

WHY SLIGO?

At the Fair of Barnet I was making a note in a notebook when a small figure with a sweeping moustache, which belonged to the days of old, said to me, "Ah, a correspondent I see!" "No," I said, "I was just amusing myself." So he talked with me a while standing there in the street, for he could not leave his post. He was holding a horse tackled to a horse jobber's high gig. He said "I am not illiterate, Sir. I have seen much of the world, Sir, and clothed my mind. I have heard the 'Chickaleary Cove' sung: and 'Champagne Charlie' was the song with which the dear old boys used to call me from my chambers, digs they say now, in the afternoon. I would immediately spring from my bed, run to the window in my dressing-gown, say 'one moment and I am with you,' and really in almost that space of time I would join them in the street below and we would be off on our rambles 'on the Shaugharaun' as your countrymen would say. Pardon me, Sir, your speech betrays you." He stroked his moustache and looked at me out of his small eyes, and something in the gesture told me I had seen him before, some years before, standing outside a Horse Auctioneer's yard in London: at the time he was talking to a man with a broken nose and to a man who had for sale a small white pup with a blue ribbon round its neck, and I remembered that my friend had not got any shirt on. "Ah, Sir, I have been in Ireland, I was sitting in a Hotel on the Dublin Quay, sitting by a window, blowing the soup out of my moustache and smoking a cigar, when a voice below cried, 'Here comes Tom Sayers,' so I sprang out of the Hotel window and there he was. I saw Jane Shore once." "Is it possible!" I said. "Yes," he said, "I saw Jane Shore and Robinson Crusoe." At that moment the owner of the gig came up and the man who had seen Jane Shore accepted some silver from the gig man with disdain and turned to me saying, "more of this anon." Then he led me by quiet back ways to a small, quiet, shaded public house where after some little playful argument he agreed to drink at my expense. "Jane Shore and Robinson Crusoe, I saw them walking side by side in the Lord Mayor's Show. They were looking well. I myself, Sir, have been something of an actor, minor parts nothing more: 'Harbour Lights,' 'The Broken Melody,' 'Fun on the Bristol,' 'Muldoon's Picnic,' 'The Waterman,' and I have not been a stranger to Rosherville and Ranelagh. A light voice I had but 'penetrating' they said, and I was also able to be of some slight assistance in Opera—

> 'Suddenly there comes a silence
> Ah Toreador
> Ah Toreador
> Beware.' "

The Landlord of the public-house came towards us, but the singer waved him away. "I was giving this gentleman here an illustration from other days: the days that are no more. I did not call you." So the Landlord faded away in his carpet slippers and, having first given his moustaches a sudden twirl, my friend hove ahead, "It was a pleasant life down through the bosky lanes of Surrey, sounding my post horn. I was quite an expert there. I trust I am not boring you, I do not believe there is any sight on the road to equal a four-in-hand, greys with red roses in the head stalls are my favourites. To them I give the palm. On a moonlight night with a coachman who can keep them all going like gentle waves on an ocean, no fuss, no flurry, but moving all the time under the broad pale moon. Sir, it was the month of June and besides the Coachman was sitting a lady tall and perfectly formed, a thing of beauty floating through the night. Can I offer you a fuzee?" he said, for I was about to light a cigar; he had insisted on buying one for each of us. "They are not regalias," he said, "but we must pass that over: one moment, a fuzee," and he opened his wirey old covert coat and I saw in that moment that he still had no shirt. His horny brisket was bare and as the Landlord was lighting his lamp the flash shone for an instant on his corrugated ribs. Dr. Freud, or somebody else, says character is formed once and for all at the age of five years. Had this man been without a shirt when he was five. Dr. Freud says, they tell me, that the Thumb Sucker of five becomes The Kisser, the Heavy Smoker and the Deep Drinker of maturity. Three Troubles. I knew an artist once, God rest his soul, who must have been an infant Thumb Sucker, known it, and feared those three troubles: For he ate raw onions for breakfast which made the first impossible, were a substitute for the second, and masked the third.

There is no padding in this book except the padding of the hoof. At the same time I write this Book because I want a couple of million (pounds) quickly, and as it may be the last Book written in the world it should have a very large sale. Though it may be the last Book it is quite likely that lectures will be arranged and Broadcast. They will be given entirely by the fair sex, interesting but monotonous.

About a name for this book. I was making some notes one day while travelling in a train through a boggy country in Ireland when a melodeon player opposite me asked me if I wouldn't stop writing and "give out a tune" and he handed the melodeon towards me. "I have no ear," I said. "Ah, to hell with ears," he said "I play it with my body. Are you writing a book?" he said. "Well I am making notes for one," I said. "What are you going to call it?" he said. "I don't know yet," I said. "Call it Sligo. It's the name of a town," he said, "the only town in Ireland I never was in. I was near it once but I stopped on the brink and took the long car with a unicorn yoked to it for a town called Ballina. Call it Sligo, it ought to be a lucky name." So Sligo it is. When he asked me to play a tune he pronounced it Chune, a very good way too. If they give me music to my grave I will sooner they will call it a Chune than a Toon: there is a want of dignity about the word 'Toon' and I would not look forward to it. Every town in Ireland has its cry. Of Sligo, they used to sing "Sligo where all the rogues come from": I am sure "the rogues" meant were the amusing kind those "wild pigs of the world" after which mothers used to call their children. There is "All on one side" like the town of Athlone, "Nothing for nothing at Borrisokane." But Carrick. Ah! "Carrick I dread you." That is Carrick-on-Suir. I was not in it yet, but I was often in Cork's own town among "God's own people." How grand it would be if individuals had mottoes and used them, I do not mean family mottoes, but individual Slogans. "Let me introduce you to my dear old friend Charles James——Pro aris et focis. Or you must meet each other, Mac let me introduce you to Mr.——— . Mr. Mac——— 'one of the good Boys.' Mr.——— 'Tout-a-fait.' " But the mottoes would have to be registered and the private property of the individual: not to be the happy, or unhappy, chancing of the moment on the lips of the Introducer.

THE ROPES FAMILY

Johnnie said to me one day, "Did I ever tell you about my people?" "Often, Johnnie," I said, "about your Aunt in Ballina with the long-tailed ten year olds, and your Uncle in Arndaree and the Spanish prisoner, and your brother-in-law with the secret for taming Lions with a mouth organ." "Oh, I don't mean those ones," Johnnie said. "I mean the Great People from whom I come."

They came, from Johnnie's account, down the biggest of the rivers (it would be the biggest or Johnnie's ancestors wouldn't be on it) on a kind of a raft as big as a parish, running with the stream, singing songs and dancing, and all talking at once; flowers they had and fruit and wine. Jars of it, and a flock of curlew for company. They had an easy time coming down the river. She was a heavy river, and when they got to the Heads at the mouth they were still bowling along good. And the pilot, they had a river pilot all right, had to leave them. He got over the side into his little dug out, they gave him a wreath of flowers, dead and the stalks stinking. But he put the wreath round his body like a bandoleer and dug for the beach with his old paddle; and he was crying. Well Johnnie's ancestors spent a pleasant evening swapping imaginary stories of the pilot and his ancestors back to the first rocking of time. When these lads and lasses on the raft hit the main ocean and lost the shore of the stream, they had an off shore wind, which suited them very well, for they hated to retrace a track. After a number of amusing experiments with the raft they discovered if they all crowded aft and cocked the raft's head out of the water, she'd keep going before the wind. A long time after that, drying their clothes in the sun up forrad on the branches of the bushes that were sticking up out of the raft, they discovered the Mystery of the Sail, and they made a lot of songs about it. Now do not let anyone think for a moment that the history of Johnnie Ropes's ancestors as told by him was in any way like Erewhon. Ropes had read it, he thought it a fearful bore. After a while a group of these ancestors of Johnnie's getting curious and experimental hit on the rudder. After that the raft's wake on those lovely seas was like a Jacob's ladder. Every one had to have a go at steering her, and all the time the curlew flying and perching and picking at their share of the grub and zigzagging about in the sky. The grub and the wine were holding out well. The wine was having a changeful life, cold for breakfast when the spray had been on the jars all night, and warm for supper after the day's sun, with the Bouquet drifting round everybody. Still nothing can last for ever, and it was just as well for Johnnie Ropes and me that an island hove in sight away on the sunset hand. A new group of curiosity manipulators trying to go one better than the group which hit on the rudder, discovered that by all sitting with their legs hanging over the edge of the raft they made a kind of leeboard and the raft would edge up a bit from dead before the wind, so they made for the Island on the sunset hand. But luckily before night came, and their legs got too numb, a vigilant soul spotted an Island dead ahead between sun rise up and sun go down. So they drew in their legs and massaged them and everybody had an extra go of the mulled, with nutmeg on the top, they'd discovered that too. No I think they knew about that before they started. Well, it was pretty dark when they grounded on the white beach on the Islands, and nutmeg and all, they slept sound. In the morning bright and early they turned out and stepped over the side onto the coral strand. The tide, such as it was, had gone down. That bothered them a bit. They thought it was the droughty weather. But when they saw the tide coming in again they were bothered more. So they all sat in a ring on the warm sand and settled about it. Not all at once. But after a good many days they reduced the idea to two parties. Those who held that the sun drew the water up and down and those who held that the water was working the sun. The usual thing. And there was very little hope of anything being settled, until a small wedge party got up an idea that the whole place was

pulsing any way it liked if you were satisfied. So they all
agreed on that. Ropes said his ancestors had superior minds
to a cat's. Because, a cat looking in a looking-glass, first spits,
then puts its paw round the back of the glass, feeling for the
other cat. Then gives it up. But Ropes's ancestors never gave
up anything until they were satisfied. When they had fixed
the tides they began to explore the island. It was the first,
sure enough, Island they had ever seen. There were islands
on the river but they didn't look like Islands: they lost their
coasts with the river coasts. But this island was the real thing,
with plenty of water all round it. You could walk round it in
a day. It had plenty of springs, a lake, a lagoon, and some
hills that looked like mountains, and it had woods with fruits
and flowers, in the glades, and the trees were so various that
everywhere you saw any kind of shelter you had a mind for.
The woods were the first place the Ropes explored, and as
soon as they saw the Green Houses on every hand, they let
slip out of their memories all the houses they had ever seen
before. That is what the stud groom said of Horses the day
he went down to the railway station to meet Ormond. Ropes's
people had a fine time, moving round and round the island,
and making camps and unmaking them, and living in valleys
and living on the tops of the hills, and rafting it on the lake
for a while. There was some business of re-acting annually
the scenes of their voyage from the river, on the lake with a
smaller raft and a procession representing the Sun, the Tides,
and the Perils of the Deep. But it upset the curlew who didn't
understand it all and everyone tired of it, so they let it lapse.

I asked Ropes how many of his ancestors came on the raft,
he said he couldn't say, but they had multiplied very much
before the raft lake pageant was started. It was intended as
an amusement, an improving amusement for the young fry.
I seldom asked Ropes questions. He hated being interrupted:
he said the young ones began to bother the old ones after a
while. They were getting difficult to keep amused in their
hours of leisure. Telling them stories was the main scheme.
However everyone brightened up when some bright girl dis-
covered the fun of drawing with a stick or a shell on the white
strand: she imparted the idea to a superior sort of sweetheart
she had at that time: and drawing plans, and pictures, and
caricatures of yourself, and other people, mostly, kept all

hands as jolly as could be for a long time. The great joy about the pastime was that if you were careful to draw between high and low water, all your drawings were washed out with the tide; and at low water you started everything afresh. This occupation appeared to have lasted for generations. I cannot understand from my friend why it should not have lasted till the crack of doom. Perhaps it would have if it hadn't been for the Conversation Trouble. The young ones were getting very tired indeed of the old stories of the raft history being told to them over and over again, and the old ones themselves hated telling them; for all the grown Ropes had a great dislike to ever repeating themselves. And it was getting, even among the Elder Ones, desperately hard to find anything new to say. For generations, with some shame, they took to their old raft trick of all talking at the same time. But that spoilt their voices and tattered their throats, so it was time for them to pull stakes, metaphorically, and push off from that shore. Rafting it again. On several rafts made fast to one another. They drifted and flapped along before the wind until they hit the Next Island, and so from Island to Island through the years. If the swimming was good, and different from the swimming in the last Island, that kept everyone interested for a good while; and there was always a completely new crop of adventures to work up so that they would hold an audience. They struck one bad Island where there were too many things that crawled and bit. However, tree top living is tiring, going on bridges up among the Toddy trees, but not too much Toddy; walking on single log bridges with a load of Toddy is too nervous work. All the tree roads ended in a good spring board sticking out far over the sea. So good diving was always to be had. But that Island was much better as a terror subject to frighten the young ones with, or as a contrast to make you enjoy better days, than it was to live in. Indeed it seems to have been a pretty bad Island. And then there was the first of the inhabited Islands they hit. That was a lucky strike of course. Their blood was thinning down and it Had to Be. They soon intermarried with the people on that Island and on the other inhabited Islands they drifted to, and of course they swallowed, more or less, a lot of new notions. And the raft idea gave them the canoe plan. I asked Ropes how many canoes. "Millions," he said. I should not have asked. As well as disliking questions Ropes objected to me taking any notes of what he told me while he was talking. So I always had to trust to my memory, and he would never allow me to read to him anything I had written afterwards of his yarn. He would have been better pleased perhaps if I had forgotten all he told me as soon as it was told. But still he had some little vanity about it. And if I could meet him now as in the days when he told me this tale and I should tell him I had put it in this book he would say "Good Enough." I asked him where his family got this name of Ropes, was it a word changed through the passage of the ages or was it a translation, or did it really at any time have anything to do with Ropes. He said, "Ropes right enough. They got the name because they invented the hay ropes: they never used anything else."

One of the Islands his people drifted upon had a rather stylish King and he was fond of having Plays acted and the Ropes showed an easy mark for this man's Theatrical activities. They acted an enormous number of plays for him, and became in fact as a people the most perfect Stock Company the world ever saw. The best the sun ever rose or set over. Well indeed there was a pure yarn about the sun refusing to set or staying hung up aloft, top side, right over the stage like a spot light in the sky while one of the Rope Companies finished the last Act of an extra long piece. They were a long time voyaging on their Stock Company reputation. More Islands. Appreciative audiences, And after a time paying audiences, paying, so they *had* to attend. But the whole thing came to change with a jolt. One of the Company was stabbing another with a trick dagger, which had a blade which slipped into the haft. But he got tired of the trick dagger. After stabbing with it several times, he threw it from him and pulled out a real dagger and introduced reality into the play. The audience were in two minds whether to hiss, or clap, so they booed. The Authorities after that shifted all the Ropes bag and baggage, canoes, face paint, and all, to a bunch of uninhabited Islands. So they drifted on doing their Show from Kingdom to Kingdom wherever there was a spare empty bunch of Islands for them to inhabit, and where the Good and True from the Kingdoms could come over and see them perform, always hoping to be there when they again introduced their reality stuff. But they refused to do it to order, and after a long time their desperate reputation died away and they got a mild one again. About that time they must have curled round in their tracks, for they hit an Island that was either Number One Island or a piece of it joined to some other Island; for they found a lot of fruit which were familiarly acceptable to their stomachs – also the Curlew made no mistake about showing by their cry, which took on some ancient note, that they knew the old spot. But after a while there was too much of the dim and misty past and piano memories for the Ropes; and they shoved off again. More Islands. Inhabited ones. Inhabitants a weariness to the Ropes: always these Inhabitants taken up with talking about the setting sun "going down in a slit in the Sea" or rolling straight away to where the whizz ends. So the Ropes got up an idea of their own that what they wanted to see was where the sun came up through the trap in the sea floor or whatever business it did. So at that time, there being a long spell of suitable gentle winds, they tied the canoes together and strung out towards the East and the upcoming sun. Any way they'd meet him when he came.

Somewhere about that time they must have bowed with a shore that was the shore of something a bit bigger than any of the Islands. A long stupid shaped Continent. Inhabited too: mostly cantankerous people. Some of them farmers too, grubbing away, growing corn and "making two blades of grass grow where one grew before" and a lot of other tedious copy book sort of stuff. The Ropes liked none of them. And all the time they were crossing that land they kept pretty close order. Especially at night. Viewed, in comparison with any other part of the charting of the Ropes, this time while they were driving across that Continent was short. Pushing back the spade, hoe, scythe, and reaping hookers. But among the Ropes there were plenty of bag and hatchet men, and when the enemy got up too close and began biting on the edges, where the stragglers were, then the bag and hatchet men began falling trees on them and that kept them back, and towards the last they gave the Ropes the road. And in a moderately small while they were all canoeing it again and plenty more Islands dead ahead in the Sun's eye. The curlew were glad, they didn't like the banging about crossing the

Continent and they stayed up aloft giving little cat cries all
night.

The Ropes continued turning towards the Sun with a fair
wind mostly. But sometimes they had to use their paddles a
good deal, and it was paddles and curiosity which took them
on a course with the sun shining on their right ears. After a
while of that, they beached on a long ridgey Island, with a
good flat beach at low tide; there was some talk of white
buildings there and some went to look at them. "Empty,"
they reported. All hands went and had a look at the buildings:
showey they were and stately. The Ropes camped there for
a long while. But there was a lot of easy tracks down to the
beach on the westerly side at the back of the white palaces.
There were miles of these white palaces splitting right across
the sun's track. It was rather a chilly Island. And down on
that beach was the first place that the Ropes began playing
a game with their paddles and a ball, which they whacked
from paddle to paddle, and high into the air. The curlew
liked it, they treated the ball as one of themselves when it
came up among them: they took it for a round curlew I
suppose. The game was started to keep the Ropes warm.
They played it on the beach because it was the only flat place
big enough: the rest of the Island was too ridgey and built
over with mouldy white palaces and white steps. It appears
to have been a good game and the Ropes always remembered
it with gratitude on account of it warming them up, and that
Island of white palaces. After a long time they whacked about,
here and there, from Island to Island still; but this part of
the world was running out of Islands for them, so when they
landed on an Island that suited them fairly well, for the time
being, they warmed themselves up with their paddle game,
for the Island was colder even than the White Palace one,
and thought they'd take a breather from travelling for a while.
But what bivouacked them for the time being was meeting a
whole lot of dun faced people looking out for the slit on the
Sea where the Sun went down. Ropes's people were disgusted.
It was so like the first old stories they used to hear that they
decided to rest on their paddles and bide their time.

And that's more or less Johnnie Ropes's story. He said that
he and I knew where they were standing to the paddles and

he seemed very set and certain about it: and he said the Curlew had got a special new cry that might mean anything.

GAMES AND RACES

Quoits is a pretty game to see played when there is importance in the game, and when the friend with the pieces of paper shows the thrower where to drop his quoit and allows the quoit to nip the paper from his fingers, and, if he calls out at the time, it adds to the excitement, "There's a nice bit of white, good, good lad you have it": an inch out and its fingers the quoit would find instead of paper. This calling to encourage the player has never been brought to that perfection which it might arrive at. Partly, I suppose, because in many games the player is too excited to be anything but deaf to the call of the encourager: and partly, perhaps, because encouragement would so easily lend itself to discouragement of the other player and where would that end. The ordinary combined and scattered shoutings of a crowd are not what is wanted, but something to cheer and encourage. To call to a Jockey through a Megaphone at the last of the flat races of the year, the name of his favourite dangerously fat-making dish might rise the hope in him and encourage him to encourage his horse. But of course as to some games I am pushing an open door: and the things pushed in a whisper into the open ear of a languid boxer in his corner by his second must be at times wonderfully well thought of from the way boxers will rise phoenix like and scatter the feathers of the other phoenix. That's what we all want, not advice, but helpful cheer. It was as advice that, coming from the country parts, I first heard the word Swank: it is a long time ago, and the word had a different meaning from the meaning it acquired later on in its useful existence. When I heard it, it was called as a warning to a boxer, to tell him to look out: his adversary was not as tired as he appeared to be, that he was in fact as the saying is "playing possum." This I suppose was much more in keeping with the dictionary meaning of the word. It was in the East End of London I heard it. But in no time it was in every mouth with the meaning it still has. It is always a pleasure to me to come on slang that will not travel or change so on the voyage that it becomes something else altogether. Slippers are personal as everybody knows who ever tried to find comfort among that extraordinary collection of old battered deceivers which the Boots at old-fashioned Hotels used to bring you, to choose from. Slang is like slippers, worn to fit the first users only.

A Goose Fair in the West of England was a fine sight; they didn't sell geese so much as eat them. It was in the good old days when money was a talisman as well as an ornament. That goose dinner. That Market Ordinary, what must a Market Extraordinary have been like, cost one shilling and sixpence. It consisted of hot goose and ham, cabbage, potatoes, salad, bread and cheese, beer and cider, a glass of gin, a long white clay pipe and a saucer of black tobacco, all for one and six! Before we started at it we shut all the windows, and steamed into it, heads down. Then we went out and stood about, sleepy, in the street in front of the Hotel and let the Fair, or what part of it was still alive and plunging, run over us. At Ballinasloe there was less eating; but there were horses everywhere, and when the Yorkshire buyer wants to attract the attention of a man riding by he does not say "Hi you in the blue coat and the purple muffler and the wideawake hat": no, he says, "Hi, grey mare." Men are called by their mounts in Ballinasloe. It's the horses that count. But every man is no doubt as clever as he can be. I was once at a little Race Meeting in Connaught, indeed it was an absolutely genuine Flapping Meeting, the cleverness displayed was, to my mild eye, extraordinarily far-seeing. Everything appeared to be arranged; there were many Bookmakers, about 7 per cent. of the people there that day were Bookmakers, and they had one chief leading Bookmaker, the Brains or the loins of the whole concern. He had his joint pitched so that he could see right into the little weighing enclosure. There were six races, and in every case all was settled in advance it appeared, and all went well, and only one horse on that land, that day, was a True Star of any magnitude. Five times by actual performance, or by deduction, had it been made perfectly clear to the simplest eye there that, Airyoh, we will say, was capable of beating any horse on the ground without exerting himself more than to

THE RACE DAY

keep himself from getting a chill as the autumn evening crept on: well Airyoh was to be a fiery hot favourite for the "getting home stakes." But the tentative prices of money on, even money, and two to one, had to be spat on and wiped away and he started at three to one. No fences. All plain sailing. As honest as a new pane of glass, or a bar of soap in the moonlight. And he won. The Jockey went into the little enclosure to weigh in and *he made the weight*. The Bookmaker's Chief saw it at once, he howled like a stricken factory chimney falling, and all the lesser Bookmakers joined him. It was of course "the double double" or the "double cross." That Jockey was not intended to make the weight. The Ring was absolutely under water, but they had to raise their hands to pay. They went home bag empty in their grimy old motors with the covers drawn as close together as they could be drawn, and inside flattened faces gazing at concave faces. They had given a whole day to the preliminaries of the skinning of one small town, and the town had won.

TIN CANS

I discovered the other day why bathing as a grown man is so different from bathing as a boy: I slipped and fell under water, with my mouth open, and as I spluttered I caught again the ardour of youthful bathing, so I suppose we always went under water with our mouths open: it had something to do with the event, just as tongue lolling was necessary for most penmanship. I have a new game, new to me, I discovered it for my own self, and now I give it to the World. Tin Can racing on a sandy shore. All you want is a gale of wind blowing parallel with the sea, and round tin cans: cocoa tins are good, but Golden Syrup tins if they have a rim on either end, are best, and keep a better course than all the others. Whack a hole through each end of the tin, pass a stick through so that it sticks out a foot at either end and thread square paper sails on the stuck out stick; then launch your tin before the wind. Tins will move without any sails in a good breeze, and if the gale is very strong even lids of tins will go good. The best joy comes from having tins of all shapes and sizes

matched against each other, a menagerie Race. I have seen tin cans on a strand within sight of Dublin throwing themselves through the brine-laden air in a way that would lift your heart up, and extend it as these Japanese ornamental flowers expand in tumblers of water, and you would purr to yourself "Isn't it a marvellous thing the way we do utilize the airs of Heaven for the purpose of making tin cans gallop like greyhounds."

from
SAILING
SAILING
SWIFTLY

JASPER AND O'MALLEY

The book and newspaper shop was on the same sunny side of the street, and had an awning out in front to protect the stationery and pens and ink. The ink might have fermented from the fierce rays of the sun, that were always shining in the summers in the late 'sixties or early 'seventies.

Both O'Malley and Jasper had to stoop going into the shop, which seemed just one pale brown shade, to set off a stately and demure young lady in black, with a neat cambric collar and cuffs, the collar turned down, and the cuffs turned back. She had an open leonine or lionessine face, large and luminous, and of that tinge, then, or just lately then, described as "alabaster." Her name was Miss Annette Dunaven, which generations ago, perhaps, had been Donnevan. She was at the moment giving change for what he called "a crown," to a gentleman with a ginger moustache and a very military appearance, a jacket-collar of Hessian shape, and buttoned so high as to almost hide his linen. Not that the Captain did not wear linen, or rather cotton; he wore cotton because of the variety of stripes and colours he could get in that material, and because he was on a holiday, and never sent his shirts to the wash; he just discarded them. This gave him a feeling of magnificence, and long after he visited any health resort, or holiday town, the poorer men of the district would, when taking off their coats, to do a turn of work, always be received with a murmur of applause, for the vividry of their shirt sleeves. His interest in Miss Dunaven was perfunctory. He was not a marrying man, and any other arrangement was repugnant to him, as it was impossible he well knew to Miss Dunaven. He was not a marrying man, for he well knew than no woman would put up with his shirt extravagance. He was called "the Captain," and the odd thing about him was that he really had held that rank in the army, and there was no doubt his small stature and sinewy arm would have carried

him where medals festoon the air. But he never saw war.
Once in the East he heard his regiment march away to battle,
but he heard them from the cold dungeons, for he was in
clink. Misappropriation of canteen funds, forgery, and all the
awful things that follow, and strangely enough he was not
guilty. He guessed who was the guilty man, but he doubted
he had proof. And when a low-sized, button-faced, grey-
skinned native woman of these parts, no longer young, and
a washerwoman, indeed she didn't take the basket off her hip
to do it, opened the prison door, he walked out into the jungle,
with a "Madame, I thank you."

At the mess table that night the guilty man drank to "good
riddance" and he drank with a full heart. It was a keen
squeak; he never sinned again, not once.

So "the Captain" was not a high-spirited man, and was
most trusted by the owner of a livery stable to send out as
shepherd with a parcel of young lambs, in black velvet, and
grey tweed, riding habits. He used to read a sporting paper,
standing at Miss Dunaven's corner. He liked to look on the
lashey eye of old Nunquam Dormio, which looked back at
him from the outside page. It meant the fear and love of God
to him.

The Captain was a brave man, but he knew he would die
slowly and would require help at that deliverance in reverse.
He earned his living at a seaside town, and owing to an

epidemic of mumps, of measles, or some other indignity, he had taken this little holiday, among the mineral springs, with his variegated shirts.

Miss Annette turned gravely towards Jasper, and was beginning to slowly say "Good morning, Mister New Biggings," but telescoped it into "Newbins," at the moment that she saw John Thadeus O'Malley. That was the first burst of the planet before the next came, like the tail of a kite all made of fireworks. "Miss Dunaven, allow me to have the pleasure of introducing Mr. Thady O'Malley."

"O'Malley" and "Thady," she almost swooned. "Be still heart." "Fate defend me." It was the attitude she saw her mother take, when her father lay cold and still, and the landlord, neither cold nor still, bounced into the little drab parlour demanding rent, rent, rent. It's true she knew the landlord did not know he was in the house of the dead, and when he knew withdrew himself for a few days, but came again back to the charge.

It was the attitude, the hand between the throat and heart, which her own landlady took, when, the second day at the lodgings, she asked if she could have another towel.

"O'Malley." Behind the counter on the shelf under the till was:

CHARLES O'MALLEY
THE IRISH DRAGOON
BY CHARLES LEVER

and a piece of cotton as a bookmarker in a place, about one quarter through the book. It was the only book Annette had ever attempted to read right through. She had been reading it all summer. Just before the water drinkers began to come she found it, and becoming so engrossed in it she withdrew it, partially, from the shelf of lending books, that is, she took it away and read it a little on Sunday afternoons, and at odd times when the heat, in those hot summer days, kept customers at home, and then, every now and again she would return it to the shelf of lending books. These books were not really lending books any more; they had been once, but the scheme had to be given up, for even the deposit of five shillings was no safeguard for the books. Sometimes the books just did not come back at all, and sometimes they came back with a page gone, used perhaps to wipe a soapy razor or twist up a soapy curl. And when a book was handed back over the counter it was impossible to hold a customer while the book was searched for the missing page. So the deposit system and lending of books to anyone was done away, and only a few very faithful invalids, or residents, were allowed to take a book when they felt like reading. The idea wasn't so bad. It introduced honour, and the borrowers had every now and then to bring custom, or at any rate, to recommend custom to the book and newspaper shop. And of course small things were for sale as well. Three different kinds of sweets, one kind, gelatine lozenges, had a worker's existence as well as a long lasting comforting existence, because they were used for sticking up in the window notices of lost keys and gloves, and trunks and their contents. The shop also sold coloured wools, knitting needles, and stationery, which was not all in the window, but some on shelves, and of course there was the ordinary book trade, for cash over the counter, for acquisitives, people who had to possess books. Indeed for a good many months in the year a steady small stream, of small monies mostly, came into that shop, and dropped into the till with a hollow distant startling sound, in the morning, but with a cheerful "move up there, here comes another, smack 'em-and-rattle 'em man" every evening. Later on, when she closed the shop, Miss Dunaven counted the money, made a little note of the sum in a small note-book, copied it on to a small piece of paper, and put the small piece of paper and the money into a shiney pink linen bag tied with many windings of string, put the pink bag into a large leather letter bag with a brass lock, which she locked, and then carried the bag up the street to the office of Josiah Oldbain, her employer. He was a Painting and Decorating Contractor, who had acquired the book and newspaper shop for a bad debt. He was a very deep-chested man with a brown beard, he was about 50, a widower, with two daughters, one eighteen and the other nineteen, and a strange unkempt-looking boy, Rex, of sixteen. The two daughters were often warned to keep a watch on the father, or he would be bringing a stepmother home. They would have been much more interested in bringing a couple of sons-in-law home, but nothing came of their interest. Beaux never grew serious, or perhaps it was because all the beaux were serious-minded, and were doubtful about Oldbain's financial state. They needn't have been, he was quite comfortably off, but the idea of his unstability came from the fact that he was radical in his talk and read a good deal too many old books, people thought, Victor Hugo and all that, and which might mean plough shares beaten into swords and barricades. A barricade in Main Street would have interfered very much with business, and anything like that would frighten away the invalids. "What people who come here want is peace, and not high falutin." But Oldbain was bustling with opposition, and that was why he engaged Miss Dunaven to manage the book shop, because she was a Catholic, and he being a free-thinker was in opposition to the Established Church, and even more so to the Dissenters, and there being no other Catholic living nearer than Oults, a market town, four miles away, by train, and seven by road, Miss Dunaven seemed to him to stand for defiance, and at the same time he knew she had just been left with little more than her two hands for fortune, as her father had been an improvident pawnbroker, who for the last few years of his life had taken nothing but unredeemable pledges, and when a few years after his death, her mother followed, she left her daughter her good thoughts to float about her, and the unredeemable pledges.

Oldbain's daughters need have had no anxiety as to their papa marrying again. It's true he might have enjoyed dressing up a little new wife in furbelows, of his own choosing. His daughters were far too fond of their own opinion in such matters to let him choose their clothes, and he gave them each a small allowance which they found just as exciting as, they knew, was good for them.

But Oldbain had an object for the lavishment of his taste. He repapered and repainted the book and newspaper shop every year, during the season when the invalids had flown away. The first time this happened Miss Dunaven was amused and rather thrilled, but the second, and the third, fourth, and fifth redecorating was just a plain exercise in forbearance, all the contents of the shop under old sacks and sheets in the centre of the shop and on the counters, and then all put back again. She was glad she never had to do that to the unredeemed pledges, for which she had, after everything was said and done, a kind of affection, for in the end they had turned up trumps, small trumps. They were sold off at auction by a most conservative and established churchman's auctioneer, acting under the instruction of Mr. Oldbain. And the unredeemable were actually bought, in many cases, by the original owners. But they still held their name of the unredeemable, for in the case of each the price it knocked down at was often grossly over, or excruciatingly under, the original sum lent. A dangerous smoothing iron, which, owing to a loose handle, was liable to fall on your foot, went to the original owner for sixpence. She carried it away in her bosom like a recovered pet.

Josiah Oldbain was a landscape lover and painter. He would go out on hill-sides, by running brooks, and sometimes by marshes. He liked marshes, and set up a small sketching easel and painted a tiny picture with sable brushes which he washed beautifully as soon as he got home, and before he ate, or drank his two evening glasses, at the "Carter's Rest." No Carters rested there, the railway had come too near. But several petty-minded old Gaffers used to sit there drinking and thinking, no doubt of butter-cups and daisies, and giggling at the extraordinary things Josiah Oldbain would say about Kings, Emperors, Principalities, and Powers.

Miss Annette gazed at O'Malley with the widest eyes she had ever looked at anything with, and then dropped the lids over those eyes. O'Malley was deeply moved. He had never, as he hadn't eyes in the back of his head, seen himself looked at in such a way. After a few general, vague, happy-go-lucky remarks about the beautiful climate and surroundings, Jasper walked him out of the book and newspaper shop. Miss Annette never understood what he said, she only received and absorbed the buttery richness of a brogue, which she had got all wrong when reading her "Charles O'Malley."

Jasper and O'Malley strolled about all the rest of the day, Jasper voluble, O'Malley pensive, but not so bothered with pensivity as not to doze in the sunniest corner of the mouldy old billiard room of the hotel in the late afternoon, while Jasper made some harness, horse, and vehicle calculations in a small twopenny note-book with a red basil cover.

The next day was Sunday. At three o'clock Jasper had O'Malley planted in what might be called the pleasure gardens of the place, beside him on a rustic iron seat, date 1851, Great Exhibition, ornate, but left so long unpainted, that now its rust drank paint like a thirsty desert, when, just before the first invalid came tottering into town, it got its annual lick. The first invalids were soonest benefited by the marvellous air, and life-giving waters, because they were met everywhere by "Wet Paint" notices, all the letters in capitals, but the 'i', which was always dotted, and therefore of course they could not sit down, and so got a great deal of healthy exercise. Camp stools were not on sale in the town at that time, indeed no one but a spendthrift invalid would buy a chair to sit on, and if there had been camp stools the name "camp" would not have appealed to those sick visitors. "Camp" meant only the Camp of Wars, and though, in the Crimea, soldiers sat on many strange seats, still it was hard to picture a bearded officer in the Guards smoking a meerschaum pipe, while he sat on a thing like two pairs of scissors tied together with a towel. The word "camp" suggested war, and not peace, and peppermint lozenges and respirators.

At five minutes past three Miss Dunaven came nicely along, putting one foot in front of the other, as if she could keep on doing it for ever, when, as a matter of fact, having been by train to Oults, to mass and back again, she had had an early Sunday dinner, by arrangement, with a former client of her late father's—if it is of any real interest to anyone to know, it was the owner of the unredeemable smoothing iron. All the railway journeying and walking was a weariness to Miss Dunaven's toes, at any rate when encased in Sunday shoes, so when Jasper sprang up to one, and O'Malley to the other side, she was glad, after a certain amount of canary-like hoppings and peckings about, to sink on the seat between the match-maker and the match made, well as good as made. Jasper started at once: "Miss Dunaven, you're looking, you'll excuse me, as fresh as the flowers in May, and the bold O'Malley, all from the Irish shore, like a wild Irish violet a-blowing and a-growing on the hill top." Thady, what was that poetry you were giving me about your ancestors Pat Loughlin, the Earl, and all the rest? O'Malley denied that they were his ancestors, but he had an instinctive feeling that he had an audience to appreciate his rolling, tolling voice, so once again it was his grief that Patrick Loughlin was not Earl

of Irrul still, and that Brian Duff no longer ruled as Lord
upon the hill. There was a small cliff behind him which acted
as a sounding board, and carried his voice as far as the
hobbling string of invalids who passed by between our friends
and the rustic fence, which made an edge to a miniature
glen, where an appearance of unknown depths was cleverly
suggested by dark ferns, and a tinkle of a stream sounded
very far away just now, but on any day, from November to
March, the tinkle was quite likely to be gone, replaced by a
snoring, groaning, hard-breathing brown flood, which seemed
as if it would never stop until it had sucked the big ferns out
of the ground. But the ferns would stand and the flood fall
away to delight the ducks a mile away on the flat lands.

The invalids on the sticks did not know what O'Malley
was saying, neither did Annette, but she liked the sound of
his voice so obviously, that now, Jasper decided, "is the
moment for me to make a clever excuse to leave the lovers."
He was in a great hurry to call them "lovers." His idea of an
excuse was to throw a black kid glove, spoil from a funeral
of some years ago, behind the after-guard of the hobblers—
the slowest. They were all now making for their lodgings, for
their Sunday frettings over their cures, and the difficulty in
getting a really satisfactory Sunday nap away from their own
homes. As soon as the glove fell Jasper sprang up, darted on
the glove and picking it up, followed the invalid off round the

cliff's edge to the right. Jasper believed that his throwing of
the glove was quite lost on O'Malley and Annette, and he
was half right, not that he cared, an excuse was with him, an
excuse, where it was practical or not. The glove was refused,
reluctantly, by the last of the hobblers, but the introduction
was made, ice broken. "Break his damned old neck I would
on any other day of the year," Jasper said to himself. But to
the last of the hobblers he produced symptoms, aches, shoot-
ing, and gnawing, also revolving, which were exactly the same
as the hobblers only of course much milder. An amateur actor
he was compared to the fully armed rasping voiced, rasping
minded professor of pains, who he was making his excuse
with. He walked all the way, the longest way, into the town,
with the professor. When pains got squeezed dry as a subject
he got him on to his relations. For that he pushed him down
on the last seat there was, before the outskirts of the town,
and a bloodthirsty lot of relations that man had. At last the
relations were all driven into the ground, and the invalid was
actually beginning to tire, and so moved away, and to his
lodgings. At the door, Jasper, out of the kindness of his heart,
rang the bell for him, and watched until the door was opened,
and then, with that curious touch of the master of finality,
caught the knob of the door himself, and so slammed it shut.
And then away he plodded to the hotel, where he tried to
doze in the billiard room, but, getting restless, dragged the
linen cover off the table, and tried a few shots, with a great
deal of screw on, then gave it up, and went out into the hotel
yard, where still a small, but dying, posting business was
carried on. There was a large brake, a gig, three very weather-
worn barouches, and a remarkable looking mongrel, between
a gig and a phaeton, the invention of some local wheelwright.
If it had had three wheels it could not have been odder
looking. Jasper, by ferreting about, found, in a sleepy after-
dinner condition, the ostler, the last of the postboys of those
parts. He moved about always as though bending forward in
a saddle, tip-tipping along a bad road, he was a folded man,
had never stood up straight, you would say, for forty years,
yet, not ten years before he was as straight as you or I, and
far nicer-looking, just nicer, because people looked nicer at
that time than now. Ten years before the time Jasper woke
him from his sleepiness on that Sunday long ago, ten years

before he was but twenty-five years of age. That made him but thirty-five when he blinked his eyes at Jasper. Jasper gave him a cigar, which he lighted, but hated, and the two went round the living poor remains of a posting yard, two uncommonly cute-looking horses, one old, and the other not young, but youngish, mother and daughter. Jasper was appreciative and respectful to these. He never spoke with anything less than respect of anyone's horses. But in the harness-room he cheapened the array of strong-smelling old tacklings, some with crests, of families grand, or doubtful grand, from three different counties, and all from far away.

Then the carriages were looked at with pity. Then Jasper gave the ostler a shilling, which shot into his pocket like a single shooting star, where once they tumbled over each other, so that he jingled while he tip-tipped on his postboy's saddle long ago. Jasper turned out into the street, and the ostler turned into the harness-room, where he sat on a stool with his head resting against the wall, between traces that hung on each side of his head, and a collar just above it, with dried hair and sweat on it, that had never been replenished for three or four years, or since the railway came. A little canary-coloured sunlight crept along the dirty white-washed wall until it rested on the ostler's neck. Then, thinking about a horse he once knew, the ostler slept.

Jasper turned out towards the path from the pleasure gardens, and at the last gate, where the path finally was left for the prosaic road. There he saw coming towards him Annette, leaning gracefully on the arm of Thady, and Thady looking very proud and unusual. They both were very pleased with their surroundings, which they thought they enhanced. When they sighted Jasper, they slowed down their pace to a very stately moving over the ground, as though drawn on some invisible trolley. Jasper almost trotted towards them, turning his toes out as he went and throwing away his cigar stump.

He swept his hat off and bowed. At that moment O'Malley disengaged his arm from supporting Annette, gave her glove a little pat, stood off to the left, gazed at her, and said in a clear and high voice, "Mr. Newbiggin, allow me to have the honour and pleasure of introducing you to the future Mrs. O'Malley, the future Queen of Mayo."

from
THE
AMARANTHERS

THE LIVES OF JAMES GILFOYLE

It was one evening. It was O'Connell Bridge. It was many years before the Amaranthers came to the sky-scraper. But not so many as to have the evening sunk completely away into history. A small young man stood on the bridge and looked up the River Liffey towards the ragged sky. The small man's name, one of his names, was James Gilfoyle, his mother was Irish by birth, and came from an Irish family of old, his father was born, perhaps, in Liverpool. James was older looking than he was. He was pale of eye and hair. He was thin and beginning to feel hungry. He was aware fully of where he was and of his surroundings. He knew that there was a time when the bridge he stood on was called Carlisle Bridge, and White Horse Bridge too, for there never was supposed to be a time, during the busy hours, he supposed, when a white horse couldn't be seen crossing it. He looked about him now and in the tram-car there was a grey horse alongside the bay, but that wasn't white, and there, sure enough, tackled to a sidecar came a white horse, fat and long-coated. James was looking about him in a merry way, perhaps that was the reason a ballad-singer, walking home with a bundle of ballads flittering in his hands, took one ballad from the bundle and put it in James' crumpled short left hand, the ballad-singer waited for no money, but went pattering on his way. James sidled towards the parapet of the bridge, and turned his right cheek to the west so that, holding the ballad close to his face, he could make out the opening verse by the failing light. It was a verse of passion, of a kind that chilled James' forgotten stomach. It was what he called political, but he was reading on and leaning more upon the beam of light that came to him, when some eddy of wind up from under the bridge, heavy with the smell of sewage meeting sea water, caught the ballad, plucked it out of his hand and threw it on the ebbing tide. James looked stupidly at his empty left hand. Then he turned his face up the river and took into his glare the advertisements that flanked the crescent bridge: Dog and Cat Advertisements. And he knew there was a train that left a station in the city every evening to the cry of "This train stops nowhere" and he knew some old jarvey tales, he saw photographs of drawings illustrating the jarvey jokes "the twelve apostles. Some of them counting the letters," and "English time before Irish time, niver hooroo." He knew there was a place called the Strawberry Beds, and he'd heard of Waxey's Dargle. He didn't know what it meant. If it was something to drink, he believed it was a cheap drink suitable to the "hoi polloi" of which he was one.

He looked up to the zenith, full of racing angry clouds and dark patches of blue. If he was ignorant of how the wind flew now, the vane on the top of a building in front of him soon told him that he would have a fair wind, for he was crossing the Irish Sea again by that night's boat.

The sidewalks were moving with men going home in every direction, but a few heavy men with full moustaches, and lanky lads with small whimsy moustaches, were coming into the city for their amusement. Across the roadway at its greatest width, down a step from the pavement, along a dark-panelled passage, meeting the smells of gravy, gas, and frying fat and grilling lean, James strolled, jingling a few coins in his pocket. He was going to feed himself with forethought and he was going to enjoy his grub.

He remembered as he ate that there was a county called Kildare not so far away, and that in it a lovely colleen did dwell. He'd sung in a chorus about her, and he knew for nearly every county there was a sweet colleen, and he knew there were lovely lakes with green islands and ruined castles, everywhere. And when he would be sheltering himself by the side of a boat on the steamer's deck that night he'd think kindly of them all. But he wished his mother's sisters had been able to find it in their best interests to support him in idleness a little longer, for in idleness he believed his best plans came to him. Now, since he left the little Eagle house, where his aunts lived, with his Gladstone-bag in his hand, he hadn't been idle, he'd been walking about, first leaving his bag down by the Quay side, walking about trying to get a hint from shop windows which might suggest a career for himself. But nothing came of it until he sat down, ate. Then reclining idly on the cushions, immediately plans came to him for starting in England as

> An Actor
> A Sailor
> A Stockbroker
> A Waiter
> A Punch and Judy Man
> A Reporter
> A Show Man
> A Circus Clown
> A Manager to a Singer
> A Bus Driver.

When he was selling boot-laces a few weeks later, on a Saturday night, in a market street on the outer edge of London, he had extraordinary good luck. Several people broke their old laces, close to him, and came to him at once for new ones. But next Saturday the luck was gone on somewhere else.

He saw a handsome man in a fringed-coat taking away the sticks from rheumatic men, and then having his assistants rub away the pains with a patent oil. He thought of offering himself as an assistant, but he did not think he had the necessary strength of arms. So he wandered about in the crowd crying his boot-laces. It was many weeks before he got rid of the last of his stock. He tried market after market. He even tried to sell them outside the Stock Exchange. He'd forgotten by now that he intended to be a Stockbroker himself. The laces went off, one pair at a time, but he was determined to give the boot-lace-seller business every chance. He believed, at that time, in the principle of leaving no stone unturned. He might have got rid of his stock for a song to some beginner, but he had never heard the cry of "Cut your losses." He struggled to the end and when he had finished with boot-laces he had finished for ever. He was one of the first to sell nougat. He sold many oranges "like wine." He ate a great quantity of them himself, he liked oranges. He had a vague idea of finding some trade on which he could feed himself as he went along. He dreamt of owning a small house, sub-letting part, or all but a small corner, and so living rent free. Then selling food, variety for different days in the week, and even drinks, of course temperance drinks, consuming, himself, any part of the stock he wanted at wholesale prices. But every trade must be no larger than he could carry on a tray in front of him, or in a basket on his arm. He thought even of selling clothes, but two or three suits for sale, and one on, would take up more capital than he could get his hands on at that time. His capital was never at any moment more than a very few shillings. The aunts by Dublin Bay sent a postal-order occasionally, but they had an idea that there were no postal-orders printed for more than five shillings. And when the postal-orders came they were made payable at the General Post Office and crossed. The envelopes they came in were tied about with thread and sealed with sealing-wax impressed in an oval and the words "I love you," and that was not especially for James, it was the only seal they had. James thought that if they didn't mean it the seal did, which just showed how vague his thoughts were at that time.

After three years of petty trading he was thinner, harder, hungrier at times, but alive, though every now and again there were days when, though he had eaten very little he was not so hungry. He didn't enjoy the feeling, it made him nervous. He tried to imagine himself owning a comfortable circus, and touring a daisy country through the long summer. But no picture came up before his eyes of the spirit. He didn't understand that, for he had read how men dying of hunger and thirst at sea dream of palmy shores with fruits falling from the tree, and tables, heavy with splendid food laid out, and spilling drinks, with a velvet chair, waiting for the dreamer to sit down and enjoy himself. He tried to raise the circus, the happy circus, with the piebald horses whinnying at the circus people in mufti, half-mufti, sitting on the back steps of their caravans, singing carols of the road and passing the bottle up and down the column. When he tried to raise this strolling vision of the roads he was standing wistfully by the kerb with lumps of camphor on a tray before him and he was looking down the long bazaar of a market street on a Saturday night, and at the far end of the street away, away, how far away, he saw the red streaks of sunset. Under that failing sunlight he thought to take his circus, but nothing would come up before him, and he looked disdainfully down on the little tiles of camphor laid out on blue paper, and he remembered that they could have nothing to do with his supporting of himself in kind, unless he had a new suit to preserve with a lump. He crossed the bridge soon after that and in Villiers Street he sold a lump to an intoxicated young man who liked the smell of it.

The next day he took all that remained of his stock of camphor, and getting a lift on the road, got to a half-suburban race-course. There at the gate he got rid of the last lump. It was, anyone could have told him, an absurd place to sell camphor, but he could not rest until he got rid of it, as he could use none of it for himself. It was absurd, and that was how it was sold. A bookmaker bought a piece for luck, and a professional backer bought the next piece for luck. In a twinkling they were all gone. In the silver ring that day in every lull, the men of chance sniffed about and said, "a bit mothy here, ain't it?"

He felt worried about himself, he had fed himself so often on fancy, and now no fancy came. So, getting rides to the race-courses gave him the idea. He stole a ride on a train, a hidden place on the steamer, and he made the port of Dublin. One of his aunts was dead, the second was dying, there in the little crumbling house with the Eagle, yellow and lobsided, over the portico.

She died in a few days. At the funeral, a friend of the aunts, seeing the worn-looking nephew standing there, opened his purse, surreptitiously, and under cover of a handkerchief, with a black border, passed a sovereign into James' hand.

Because he had the sovereign in his pocket James was much more nervous stowing away and stealing his journey back into England, than he was when he came with his resources much lower. He was timid because he felt he was worth striking. He discovered that, for himself, lying thinking in the dust, under the seat in the train from Holyhead. Being nervous he only attempted to get part-way across England before he slipped out among men. He was in a town that might yield something to a pedlar. He bought seven small meat pies on Saturday night when they were being sold off. He ate one for supper, and one for breakfast, the rest he sold to people who came in early Sunday morning on an excursion.

He was feeding himself and putting a little money in his pocket. So, riding free and feeding free, he got back to London and across it into the easterly side. His lodging had cost him nothing, for he had always travelled by night. He had never been with eel jelly, or hot chestnuts, or roasted potatoes, because they had too much paraphernalia for him, anyway it wasn't the season for chestnuts or potatoes. But about this time he found a baker who was agreeable to selling slightly burnt, or unsightly, jam puffs and small sausage rolls, at a price to the dozen, which gave a handsome profit. He did well several nights running, on one side of the river, then he went under the river along a deep shining tunnel, up the other side he found a corner by the entrance of a street with meat and vegetable stalls. He'd only been there a few moments when a quick little pony and trap turned out of the main road, not very handily driven, and entered the street of stalls.

It just happened that a butcher-stall man had a flare-lamp on the ground, prodding at it, and it began to make a roar just as the pony came abreast of it. That was a horrible-looking thing under a pony's feet. The pony threw himself towards the kerb. There were empty fish cases lying about, the scene was set for an accident, the cobble-stone sparks flew as the pony struck with his hind hoofs. James, obeying the traditions of the lonely street trader, turned his tray to safety,

he hoped, over on his right side, and then caught the pony's
head. The pony reared and then came down, but James' feet
were on the cobbles first and the pony found himself standing
upright unhurt, but shivering all through his body. James
Gilfoyle had done what the streets would expect of him. He'd
had bad luck with his pastry, most of it was scattered in the
dusty unkempt roadway. He had been quick, determined and
skilful, as the men of his order should be. He had the knowl-
edge of horses from the kerb-man's school. He had never
touched a horse in a stable or a field. He hardly knew what
they fed on. The traditional next move was that he should
turn again to his trade, without any seeking of reward or any
spoken thanks. But it happened this time that the two people
in the trap were not conscious of any tradition in these stray
accidents of the cobble-stones. They were a stout, pale, hand-
some woman, and a stout, handsome, but bronzed, man.
They were both in early middle age and very much alike.
They saw at once the dreadful state of the pastry. They were
very glad that nothing more than a shaking had happened to
the pony or themselves. They were in no hurry to be off.
They were glad to talk to any bystanders, and they were very
much impressed with the dignity with which James settled
the few saleable pastries left on his tray. After a time they
opened the little back door of the pony trap and James
stepped in and sat down with his tray in front of him, and
the three drove back along the main road. The pony wiser
than when he came. Chatting pleasantly they drove a mile
or so in a south-easterly direction, turned up a narrow street
shaded with trees, on the right. Fifty yards from the main
road, a laneway led to the back of the three small houses. At
the back of the second one a stable and a small trap-house,
had been packed in a very ship-shaped manner. The pony
and the trap were housed for the night, the owner of the pony
doing everything in a kind of hesitating urgency, like a man
who could manage better if he wasn't overlooked.

The woman had gone round to the front and let herself in.
The pony soothed, important, and comfortable, the two men
walked up the short garden to the back of the house, and
James Gilfoyle was soon sitting down to supper with Ayleen
and her brother John. This was not such an Arabian night
entertainment as it might sound, for the meal was eaten in

the small kitchen, because there was no servant and brother and sister both liked their food hot from the stove.

They were people who had been able almost always to do what they liked, and they had an idea that they would like to give James supper. He on his part was alive to the good business in a supper hot from the stove as against cold sausage rolls and a jam puff. He had taken the liberty of putting his tray and his bag out of sight on the top of a cupboard. So, sitting there with his back to the stove, looking carefully from under his eyes at his host and hostess, he looked like a not-too-well-off Bohemian among acquaintances. After the supper was half eaten they were all looking quite cheerfully at each other. The host was doing what talking there was. There was no trotting out of the pedlar, who, when the small quantity of light beer was being topped off with some undeniably honest brandy, was as much at his ease, as ever he had been, in company, before. He thought of the night outside without any misgivings, though he knew he was a long way from his lodging on the other side of the river. He knew that the police might question him with his tray and bag, but the pastry inside would show them he was honest and he had his pedlar's licence, and he believed he looked honest.

John was a sailor, a captain on a small steamer in the cross-Channel trade. His sister looked after the house. This seemed to James, at first, a dangerous thing to tell an unknown pedlar, who had been clever stopping an accident from happening. He might have been one of these Don Juans. But he remembered he looked honest and the lady might have another brother not in the sea trades, who might protect the lady and the house during the absence of the sea captain.

The Captain said he might be able to get James some sort of light work to do by the river side at the wharf.

The next day James found him by the wharf, but there was nothing to be had. After another couple of days, when he was to call again, John had a plan, that James, being good at horses, it appeared, should be a sort of stable-man and gard-en-man for a few hours a day, look after the pony and get more money than it was to be supposed there was in the kerb pastry trade.

James had never groomed or bedded a horse in his life, but the intelligent pony, Billy, by the winking of a nostril and a glance of a full eye, showed James the order of his toilette. There was a skilled stable-man in another laneway at the opposite side of the road, and from him, the wiley pedlar in James extracted information as he required it.

By a lucky chance John's clothes were too big to offer James. So James never wore a cast-off suit of his employer's. James bought a very neat suit himself, the funeral pound, which he had kept against such a spending, was there in time.

The third day of James' stable work showed him nice and presentable. The story of the three lives rushed on. James had a supper aboard the Captain's steamer with the Captain and his sister, the steward made no insulting sniffing when offering James the biscuits and the cheese.

James had been half a year a stable-man when the brother and sister took a new house, the same size and style as the old one, with a pony stable and coach house; the same rent, but in a neighbourhood a few miles further east.

James became a friend of the family, took a room close at hand, and all his meals with the family, a duenna, widow of a stevedore, who had died with money in the bank, being always present when the Captain was away.

James, to the neighbours, was a delicate relative, with a little pony of his own and a fondness for horses.

James' wages were small, but sufficient, and the arrange-ments settled themselves well, along days that varied very little. A fortnight of housekeeping and occasional shopping adventures, for the women, and the garden and the pony for James. Ayleen drove Billy herself generally, except on the shopping excursions, when James was there to stand by the pony while the women were buying, quickly, the things they

didn't want, and looking gloatingly and long on the things
they very much wanted. Indoors after supper an occasional
game of cards. But, as a rule, if the evening was fine, James
was taking busman's holiday down streets of stalls speckled
with pedlars. None of the pedlars he saw seemed to have his
plan of a support trade, consuming and using stock. A man
would be selling notebooks one night, nougat the next, and
then perhaps furry small dancing monkeys on strings. Even
the nougat couldn't be eaten in any quantity by a pedlar.

Every third week John the Captain was home and for a
few days the four friends went to music-halls and theatres
and came home to social suppers. The stevedore's widow was
a fine upstanding woman and could always show a festive
corsage, for she had a great quantity of silver ornaments,
lockets, chains and brooches and, on her brown wrists, brace-
lets that rattled and clanked, the rest only moved up and
down as she breathed. James Gilfoyle had learnt early in his
business not to ask too many questions unless they referred
to the readings of the ordinary signs of the road. And it was
a long while before it was revealed to him by the others that
Captain John had a way of making money unknown in several
senses, fraternal, legal, artistic, to the owners of his ship. He
ran a great many bottles of duty-free liquors, not every trip,
but constantly throughout the year. His owners were well
served by him for he was an almost perfect seaman. But his
other self, the dabbler in contraband, ran risks, threw care
away, played up his luck, and laughed a great deal, while
Captain John on the bridge had an unsmiling face.

Ashore, at supper, and sitting round the fire in the winter,
or in the little summer-house that clung about the French
window, an arch of communicating, the scent of freshly-
watered flowers floating in, the smell of a sweet light cigar
floating out, he was talkative and gay. In the summer-house
the hint of contraband was never on the tongue, little garden
walls have ears. It was round the fire the story came out bit
by bit. It was not shocking to James. He drank his very good
brandy punch with an air, and the burgundy—he got knowing
about that. The whole four of them were judges. There was
very little port even in the cupboard. The brother and sister
were against it on principle. It would make them too fat, but
the brandy and the burgundy they never stinted for the

widow, James, and themselves. Before long it was James who began to go slow and he was leading the most active life, for he saw that brother and sister and the stevedore's widow were going too fast. He knew how they'd held that course a long while. Not that either the brother or sister ever showed a hint of being even mildly tipsy. The stevedore's widow did. She stiffened, and if she was wearing her silver it clanked with a dungeon clank, getting on towards midnight. The widow was the first to break. She became very ill. It was then that Ayleen took herself in hand and it was then that, in the presence of the propped-up widow at her chair by the fire, she proposed marriage to James. James was not expecting this, though he had a great liking for both the brother and the sister. He was quick at making up his mind, without a twitter or a twist of his mouth, inside the count of five he accepted, and Ayleen immediately kissed him very soundly. And the widow, as sober as a judge, but giddy from the unexpected, applauded.

When John was home he was as pleased, though he was surprised himself.

Then, defeated by the contraband trade, for that was it, the trade did it, the orderliness of feeling bound to consume unplaced stock, ruined her health. The stevedore's widow died.

James and Ayleen were married, but her health, too, was undermined. In a year she was dead. In a year and a month John was dead. James buried them in graves near each other in a large cemetery on a hill. He gave up the house. He sold the pony into a good home with a well-to-do publican. As long as the pony lived, he was young when James first knew him, and he lived to a good age, the publican, when he met James, would say, "Billy was asking after you."

James found himself left the brother's and sister's savings, all in railways in a far country. He had an adequate income for a man living by himself in lodgings. He need not work ever again. So he became, what he thought was, a philosopher. He walked about and rode in public conveyances and observed the people, and wondered how they occupied their hours of leisure and at what they made their livings. He spoke very little unless he was spoken to, when he embarrassed the hearer, for he gave away his ideas, which he was engaged in forming, gave them away very slowly, slowly because the knowledge on which the foundations of his ideas were laid had been absorbed very slowly, at a walking pace. His later knowledge, gained on wheels, had come to him much more speedily. The whole central years of his life were spent in the same lodgings. His landlady, who first found him such a quiet responsible-looking, and easily-satisfied lodger, died of old age, and was succeeded by a daughter, married to a man connected with the Customs and Excise. James smiled every time he met his landlord in the hall, as he thought of how much his throat, in the old days, had kept from this man's employers. Starting from the dark corner on the right of the window in the sitting-room, and continuing with the sun, past the fireplace, into the corner, over the sideboard, into the hall, then up the stairs, to his bedroom, were the walls known best by James in all the world. The wallpaper was cleaned every spring, but never changed, the pictures were put back in their old places. He could not describe the wallpaper, away from it, except that in the sitting-room it was a yellowy-grey with a falling design, and on the stairs the paper was an orange-brown with a large weaving pattern in blue. But the pictures he knew as if they were his brothers, first a soft black lithograph, after an engraving, blurred, it showed a water party in a small body, a lady, a fine man and two small children, the man fishing, the lady fanning herself. There were distant hills wooded. The next picture was an oil-painting, a portrait of a man in a blue coat, with a black stock, a purple waistcoat, and round cuffs. He had a face that Sir Joshua Reynolds would have liked to have painted, but the portrait was not by Reynolds, it was not a family portrait, it had just been bought at an auction when some other landlady was retiring. Next lay flat against the wall a handsome miniature frame, and in it a picture-postcard of a seaside pier with a bandstand and poorly registered flags flapping. Over the shallow-looking glass above the chimney there was a bright-coloured lithograph, of a scene in Germany, water gushing, pigeons cooing, goats prancing, and a young man with ribbons playing a fiddle. In the distance were mountains. The next picture was a gay memorial card, a white tomb-stone on black, the name on it had no connection with anyone in the house. Some owner had made the little picture gay, by sticking little rosebud scraps, each with a tender green leaf, all round the glass, a frame within a frame, and there receding into the artificial distance was the tomb.

Over the sideboard there was a pair of pictures taken from an illustrated periodical. One was of some great glass-house with palms growing to the roof, this picture had been coloured by a careful child, originally it had been folded in the middle and still the faint white line at the fold fell like a sword of light through the centre of the picture. The companion, over the sideboard, was of the opening of some dark dock, sailing vessels in the background, a steamer with large paddle-boxes in front. This was also coloured by a child of thoughtfulness, a sunset suggested in the distance behind the furthest masts. All the pictures were framed in brown walnut, or black and gold frames, except the portrait, which was in a very well-coloured heavy gold leaf frame. By the door a tall narrow picture with trees, and lovers from the seventeenth century, a gaily-coloured print.

In the hall on the right of the door a large pale picture of a faded sea, a water-colour, with a fishing smack on the horizon, where an indigo sky was falling down on it, in the foreground the strong sepia was holding its own among the nautical litter of a pebbled beach. The stairs were on the right of the hall, so there the gallery of pictures turned against the sun. Three pictures looked down on James' shoulder as he climbed. The first a small oil-painting of a wild sea, the next an oval print showing a girl in a blue sun-bonnet, standing by a well, "A Wishing Well." The title was clear, the date would be of a long time ago. The last picture James saw before he turned into his room was a photograph of a steamer. It must have been recognised by anyone who had sailed her, it was so clear. But though James tried with a magnifying glass he could not make out the name.

He knew every corner of these pictures, he had examined them on his first coming to the house, and had, year by year, added to his knowledge of them until now it was complete. They were photographed lightly in his memory. But there was another picture in his memory, the wild tattered arch of sky over the bridge in Dublin, and his left hand holding the ballad there before him, and the first four passionate lines, and the smudgy print, with the stain of oil from it, soaked into the rough paper, and then away like a bird from his hand. This picture in his mind had never yielded its place to fresher viewing of the first scenes. He stood on that bridge three or four times after that first time, three or four times in his life, each with an interval of years, and though the horse-trams were long gone, and the noise about him was changed, and the acrid smell gone from the water, still he saw the same arching madness of the sky, at least once again. But no nail could drive out the nail of that day in his youth so long ago.

From philosophy to explanations of the universe. Number Seven, four horses with two passengers and one man driving. Symbolism! Splendid! Four spots for the four walls of a house, and the three spots, pyramid fashion, for the roof, the eaves and the roof tree. He had a fancy that there might be some-thing symbolical in Eves occurring there. But he realised that kind of thing was too vague for explanation by numbers. There should have been Adams coming in somewhere. Anyway puns would have to be barred from the first. They were too easy and it was obvious that they could not be universal. He thought if he had had a more general education he might be able to hit on some universal punnery. But he never thought of Esperanto. He never considered it in any way. It might have been about him. The man in the next house might have been singing in it as he rushed down the garden path in front of the house to catch the bus for the city.

He had an idea of improving his education at the Public Library, and he did read there from time to time, when his own machinery of thought seemed to work unhardily, or he thought he was living too much within. The Number "Two," entranced him, with its simplicity, for a time. He was most unfair in his dealing: two hands, two ears, two nostrils; what about five fingers? No, four fingers (twice two) on each hand, two thumbs. Black and white, good and bad. Oh, it was too simple, it was getting ridiculous, so he gave up numbers. At that time he had no disciple, or listener, and later, when he had one who would have been delighted with the twos, he had forgotten most of the corroborations.

He thought of bread, water, and salt as symbols, separate and together. If he had known at the moment the composite of petrol he would have forced it into a design, using petrol as an open sesame, and a currency of grease spots, his laugh-other-self put into his ear. He often ran a healthy-looking idea to a little tin-can terminus, and left it there bitterly. He thought his laugh-other-self was of this earth. He quoted "The Good Book," and when he was away among The Good Books, he was erratic. He had in the past called "The Good Books" any books in a public building. "The Good Book" doesn't say much about laughter up aloft above the Bright Blue Sky. The winner sets the laugh—that shows that in the Promised Land there will be no winners. No last laugh. He will not require laughs there. And the disciple—it was in his early days when he thought it necessary to say something— said, "I'll miss my laughs; I like a good laugh." James took the trouble to explain to the disciple. He used one finger to make himself as clear as possible to the little insipid mind, as a watch-mender might explain the working of a watch to a customer. He explained that it seemed improbable to every-one but the disciple himself, that he would be the same in the Beyond as in the near, and he might as well say he'd miss the little stripey pullover he pulled down to keep his little belly warm.

The disciple was a clerk in a booking-office at a railway station, where there was little or no business through the mid hours of the day; just the heavy busy rushes early in the morning and at evening time. It was a dark, scattered station, high up on black trestles. All the centre of the day could be given to thought, it might be occupied by studying the life adventures of Galloping Horses. But the disciple had lost fifteen shillings, one after the other, and he was through with the gambler's life. So he required, he thirsted for, something to think about.

He had, looking through his office trap-door, asked James some simple question. It was just off the actual worn track of "fine day," "poor day." It was a wondering question— wondering what made the day so dark when the wind wasn't blowing from the smokey corner of the city. "Dark days" was just the wide subject for James to kick about before him, all around the booking-room. The disciple had to lean his face as much through the trap-window as he could, to hear. After James was gone he tried to recall some of the philosopher's remarks, and to attach them along some line, but found it very difficult.

After another questioning of James, the disciple made notes immediately after the philosopher had gone. This became his practice for as long as he was able to remain in disciplehood. That was several years: for most of them he was a visitor, at least one evening a week, to James' lodgings, where there was always a large cup of coffee and a wild-looking cake, made first by the old landlady and then by her daughter—the receipt being a family one. The cake was shaded from a pink to a canary yellow and had citron through it.

These notes filled several small black notebooks, and were written in a blue ink which will fade a little, but never disappear. Those books were well made and well handled, and so having an appearance of value, they will never be destroyed. Wherever they are they are intact.

The disciple may be in his promised land, not missing his laugh or his pullover, or he may be alive, sitting thinking of how well his first grandchild took his christening. He married, that was what brought his discipleship, as far as James was its prophet, to an end. On one of the evenings when he had nothing new of James' to think about, having just finished filling in his notes from memory, of the philosopher's last button mushroom of wisdom, he met a fine young woman. He had heard about her before from an old cousin, who always ran young women through the fingers of her mind, when she saw young men who had steady jobs.

The young woman was taken on a Sunday afternoon to meet James at tea, under trees, in a restaurant, near a public garden. In such a landscape everything was against James making a good showing of himself before grey female eyes.

The young woman distrusted James; she took away his disciple. James was as well without him. She, when handed the wonderful notebooks, was almost disgusted with the want of intelligence of two grown men. She was to be excused, for the notes were in the disciple's own shorthand. When he tried to supplement them with his explanation, they both found themselves at sea. She was the worse off, for she felt as if a black helmet was being forced down on her head.

James suffered no permanent loss when his disciple slipped

away, but for a few weeks he missed his foolish listener. He knew he would never take the trouble to hunt out another, and this one was already out of his time. A memory of the old days, when the tide had come up to such a street, when there was snipe in this district; for the disciple had been born and reared in a cul-de-sac. James' talk had been so much of the prairies beyond the ether that the disciple, when he left his hand, was as conservative as the first time he looked on James from his trap-window. Now his wife had him trotting out into a New World.

James went on a walking tour through the ups and downs of England and the shores of Wales. He had a great many different tastings, of bread and cheese meals in road-side inns, on roads as far away from the motor traffic as could be found; and to each inn as he left it he bowed, and said "tomorrow you may be gone." He thought that on this tour some new idea for a key to unlock the sideboard tantalus of Whither and Why-so would be won. But nothing came his way except the smell of fresh-grown hedges, and many-flavoured beers, and an affectionate respect for the air he breathed.

Then in a moment he longed for his bridge and the sky over it and away from it. He crossed the Irish Sea once more. He stood and looked up the river, the same sun time as when he first stood there, and he felt there, fanned out within the reach of a long arm, stood all the round towers, the green hills, the mountains, the monuments, the little lakes, the little colleens by the lakes, the sea bays, the sea islands, the lake islands, the fiddles, the dancing floors, the shamrocks of the fields, the leaping salmon in the rivers. A warm sea of fancies loved, lapped so close that he could dabble the fingers of the hands of his long arms in the little waves breaking among the infant sedges. He could have taken a train away into that heaving place of his own heart, but he wavered. A motor-'bus came by with names on its sides, the names of towns he longed to see. But the longing cowed something in him. He turned away with timid steps, and in a little while the large street growing chill in the evening air, he turned into a cinema. And he saw clouds racing behind round towers, and he heard music—happy, mournful, glycerine music that quickly caught the clouds' spirit and chased them away, rolling from nowhere to nowhere. And he heard a man's voice, rich with indiscriminate charity, cry of love. Himself knowing well the love he sings is of the Ocean which never rises in a mist to condense into rain and rivulets, to tumble round its course back again. So it swims ever unchanged.

from
THE
CHARMED
LIFE

ON THE ROAD WITH BOWSIE

Now we are on the road again—the land ahead is flatter than yesterday's land. But in the distance we can see the green rise where just hidden by a fold is the Pride. The sky circling over us in every colour that is, and silky, a tinker twisted withy tent. The old tunnel shape and we two, like tinker fleas, skipping on the tent floor. Great energy in our thighs. Three large flat-shored bland bays lie on our southerly hand. Short green grass, or sand, is all about our way, and the road is built on stones brought from a distance. It is a road that waves up and down, too short the rise and fall to give it the name of undulating. It is a dancing road, a singing road, and Bowsie sings, just a "lal, lal, lal, lal, lal, lallity". And I don't feel in any way irritated by his voice, any more than I feel irritated with a bird which tells me the same fine thing over and over again.

A thin stooped man comes up a little green path on our right, and falls into step by us. He nods his head in time to

Bowsie's lal, lalling. Then he says "It's a pleasant, and a natural day to be walking this road." He joins us, of course, from the land side, and at first he stayed by me. I was in the middle of the road, and Bowsie on the left by the sea. But after a few paces, this new passenger moves round behind us, and comes up on Bowsie's left, between him and the sea. Observing these bays: "The sea never did me any harm," he says "and I don't believe I ever did it any harm unless it was an insult to throw a bucket of potato peelings on the surface of it. You would notice that potatoes are peeled at sea. There was a time when there were darn few potatoes going on the long voyages, but that's neither here nor there. I am the man that never misses anything on this shore. If it was an empty box, it makes its presence known to me. A wild bird of the ocean laid an egg just above high water spring, among the stones that were like eggs on the point beyond. I walked straight to it, here from where we were standing. I never touched the egg. But she never came back. I think it was a foolish egg to make me look foolish. But if that was her idea she failed on me for a man that is so much by the brink of the sea as I am. I could never be made look foolish by its brink. It was a bird that was long on the wind, and swift, and had no very important knowledge of shores. There are places along those bays where there are little farms of shells that would delight your heart to look down on, and to lie among, very sweet and clean. There is no contamination on these three bays. The draining from Hayden's Hotel sink into the ground. I spoke to Hayden and him building the place. He agreed, as soon as I moved the word from my lips, that no house of his would contaminate the whiteness of the strands. Wasn't it a grand thing that a man would have so much respect for the sea's lips that he would not annoy them. He's full of songs sometimes. Like our friend here. He thinks it does the air good to ventilate it here and there, with the voice of man, singing praises on himself. You'll forgive me speaking so openly and 'foolishly', you might say, if you didn't understand the respect I have for you both. Of the two of you, our songster here has the more understanding." Bowsie goes on with his "lallity", either from toughness of hide, which makes him not notice a personal appraisement, or from the oil on his old duck's back of individuality, or just general and panelled vaguenesses produced into perspective until they meet in a point.

Sea-gulls are flying about us far more than we noticed along our ways yesterday. Sea-gulls have the gift of changing their shape, and size, at will. One type of gull will in an hour look as all types. And a herring gull can hang in the air close to your face, his jeering cry still, and be for a time an albatross. In mist he can draw the grey gauze round him and disappear behind its curtain, and he comes back a pierrot of the first melancholy type, cringing at Pierrette's door. Then with a flirt of his tail, he can stand up into the sky a whitewashed tabernacle. I look over at the passenger on Bowsie's left, and he looks to me like a white-washed tabernacle. He is so cleanly shaved—so sea clean. Clean in his blood; he looks as if he lived on spring water, and the leaves of the ground. His whitewash is of that pure variety that hides nothing, but whitewash beneath. I suspect him for an instant of being a martyr of some kind. But then, I know he is not. He has a springing defiant walk, as a man carrying no other man's load; but bringing his own along, held up by the end of his finger, with a conjuring trick, which has taught that finger to lift, and convey, a heavy package, by pressing its tip against the package's upper side. As I think about him, wondering, he turns his face towards me, and a smile beginning on the forehead, and sweeping down to the chin, shows me he eavesdropped on my thought. He looks to me, this moment, as small as wood sorrel. But this one, he looks to me like Downpatrick Head in a gale of wind. We are walking in step, at about three miles an hour; a nice pace, the legs swinging steadily on, while the body, from the hips, can twist about as it likes. Three gyroscopes nicely balancing, in that better society, where three are company, and none compromises. Nobody passes us by. If they did, they would just see three benign looking men, who must, they'd say, have lately fed well. As a matter of fact, all of us are hard set. Bowsie and I forgot to eat, even a biscuit of lunch. And the passenger eats when he rises at dawn, and again immediately after the sun has set. He allows the sun to rise him up, but he, in return, tucks him into the hay at night, and often, at this time of year, the sun does go down under a fiery bunch of hay clouds. In the early days of magic lantern, an exhibitor would simulate a dissolving view with a wisp of hay, moved up and down, between the slides. But the passenger thinks nothing of magic lanterns. He is old enough to remember when they were a novelty in far-away valleys, and he has sat in little halls, in distant lands, watching the bright, and gloomy, pictures on their white sheet. If he was in a position, at the time, that gave him a right to be close to the engine, then he would stand behind the lantern, and view the slides in his hand, before they were pushed into the lantern, to be enlarged into jellyness. Especially he liked the bright-coloured ones, he liked to see them in his hand, and to hold them up against the small back light of the lantern. Then he could be ready to hand the wanted one to the exhibitor, the lanternist. Once as a young sailor he got a full night of entertainment, when, because the sheet was set up clear of the walls, he was able to get to the back of it away from the spectators, and so see the other side of the picture that they saw. He knew there was little difference between the two pictures to the ordinary gross eye. But with him, and his eye, the people and the houses, and the trees, were in a world, a third world, in a ciotogact world. There was first the event, then the slide made from the photograph of it and shown to those in front. Then the inner side of the second world, and that belonged to him—all that evening. He was the last out. Indeed, the care-taker, who smelt of cedar, was in the roadway pulling the door to after him. When, out of the dark building stept our young sailor-man tripping on his toes, but too wrapt up in himself to give away his soft breaths in talking to the care-taker. He just said "farewell". He is like a man, to me, now, that is constantly saying farewell—tipping a past over the side. As he walks with us, I have a sense that he is making a prolonged farewell with us, because it happens that his freakish plans take him along our way. He has only a blow-away interest in us, and why should he have more. We are unable to see the grain of the material of his memories as he is hoisting them into the deep blue sea. We neither get the pictures of his old mind in the detail, or in the broad swing. We get something, and before we pass it along the wooden cash holder, and the stringy wires, to our own cashier's perch of the brain, we try to make out a bill for it, in some striking

little language of our own, flippant when it ought to be pranc-
ing, and buoyant when it ought to be sunk.

But this man is a great man; I can tell it by his way of
walking and his leaning on the greatness about him; for what-
ever way our values have moved, up and down, and round
about, one side for correspondence, the other for address and
stamp, like a foreign-going post-card, everyone alive allows
the sky is great and this man knows that.

If I let my imagination pull me about, I will be seeing wild
things, wilder than I ever saw them. Just now this man steps
off the roadway to walk by its side, where a long strip of
emerald grass, short as the fur on a young seal's back, lies
by the road. And I could think that before each footfall the
little blades of grass made themselves into a little pattern, to
take the tread of his foot. Just now he is silent, his arms
hanging lightly by his side, except when he lifts one hand, or
the other, to, with his finger tips, move back a lock of his
brown hair, which hangs before an ear. It is as though he
likes to let his ears think they can listen to all he hears.

But now he is talking to me directly, his chin on his right
shoulder, as he paces along, and he does not seem to look on
the path he treads, even with a glance through his fringed
eyes. There are white stones here and there along it, but he
never stubs his toe on them.

I listen to him talking, but my eyes are watching his feet—
their careful "rise and fall". I would say only that I know
they are not under the governance of the eyes in the head
above them. They are very neat feet in boots of thin leather,
old boots, but well cut and sewn together, long ago. Hand-
some boots and handsome is that handsome goes, they walk
handsomely. We are moving along slowly, but I know by
these swinging steps that these feet would eat a road before
them as fast as any man, short of a champion, very short of
a champion, could cover the ground.

This man tells me of birds he has seen in foreign lands. So
small that one perched on a high swell's necktie. "People
standing about, at the edge of the wood, on a summer evening,
shaking the sweat out of their hats, thought the bird was a
stick-pin head. Like a jewel, you'd say—yes, a jewel on a
finger, finger ring perching, a jewelled ring. They said, some
of the ladies, fine ladies, stylish, would put a bit of honey on

the tip of the ear. So the bird would perch, ornamental ear-
ring, jewel hanging, one on each ear, ruby you'd say, this
side, sapphire that side, biting the lady's ear—all in the dusk
of evening. Darting out of the trees, to throw themselves
around in the last bit of sun, when it was sinking very strong,
long strokes of it maybe split round a rock point on the
horizon, and coming up to you, where you stood, like a gold
corridor. Some say the shine of snow is very fine. I have never
seen snow. I was never on a winter day in the land when
snow was on the ground. Snow doesn't like me. It melts
before I come. I was in a seaport, where the town streets
were torn up with the melted snow. But the last lump was
carried down a gutter to the sea before I landed, a day before
I landed. I don't mind thinking of it—I'm not afraid of it.
There are few men who move about but have seen snow, if
it was only on the top of one of the great high mountains,
where it never melts. But I never saw one of these mountains.
I was off a coast where there was a high scattering of moun-
tains just within the coast.

"We came round a headland, and the men got me up out
of the bunk to see snow. I was in my stockinged feet, but
there was a roll of mist all along the mountaintops, and the
boys said to me 'There's where it is anyway, behind that
curtain hanging down'. That night we were blown off the
coast, and I never saw my snow that was waiting for me
behind the curtain. Now, I don't care about it—I didn't care
then, but the crew they wanted me to see it. They were
always talking about it, snowballing when they were children
'nothing like it. Makes you laugh. And snowballing girls and
it goes down their necks.' There was one man, he was the
oldest of the lot, he said he got cross because a girl said there
was too much snow down her neck, and this man, just a child
then—Joe was the name I knew him by—'Joe Boots' because
he had a fine new pair of sea boots, very big for him, but
padded with old rags when he had time. This man, then man-
child, hit the boy that threw most snow at the girl, and the
boy, when he got the blow, he caught it in the chest. He went
down into the snow, into a soft drift, and all the little boys
and girls ran away, and there was Joe digging at the drift
with his hands, to get the boy he hit, out. The drift was deep
enough, but by the sides of it, there were two pieces of drift,

like little cliffs, and they fell down. Only one child stayed with Joe, and that was the girl that complained that she got too much snow. She stood behind Joe, just the two there, and the darkness falling down. And Joe scratching at the heap. He did get the boy out. He didn't seem to be breathing. The girl she kissed the boy's face, and then, Joe said, she kissed him. And then the two, Joe and the girl, dragged the snow-bound boy away about a mile, and they got him into a little house, where a shoemaker lived, he and his old wife, and they got hot cloths on the boy, and kept taking him out of one hot blanket, and putting him in another. They had all his own clothes off him. And, Joe said, when that snowed boy, quivered an eyelid, and came up alive, he felt grand, and he sat down flat on the hearth, by the old woman, with his back against her knee, and went asleep like that. But the girl when the boy came alive ran out of the house and cried loud. Joe heard her going away towards her own house getting farther and farther away as he fell off asleep. Joe said he'd seen all the snow he wanted that night, and though he'd often seen it since, he didn't want to, and what's more, he didn't want me to be looking at snow."

As this passenger along the roads by my side talks of the past, he loses his stoop and comes upright. But in a little while he stoops again, and then for a little he is silent. His eyes are now looking straight forward along the road, and presently, far away over a hillock, I see a figure of a man riding a bicycle. I know it must be a postman for I can see a bag hanging about the man's side. He comes very slowly nearer, for his way of riding is to pedal quick, and hard, up any little hillock, and take his feet off, going down. On the level he plods so slowly as to be little better than under steerage way. Come abreast of us, he salutes the passenger, by beating his left hand to his breast. To Bowsie, and myself, he gives a quizzical nod, and, by way of delaying the time in its flight, he rummages his bag as if he expected to find letters for us.

By the aloof smile of the passenger, I know he expects no letters, and neither Bowsie, nor myself, left any address for forwarding of letters to. So it is not within the fence of possibility, post office possibility, that there should be anything for us. The postman is a middle-sized man with sandy and grey side whiskers, clipped close to the cheeks, and covering them to the line of the mouth, below which the face was close shaven, three days ago. The man has grey-blue unquenchable eyes, and it is not by the laws of chance he became mercury to this flat hand of country laid down on the Atlantic edge. He is a man who knows everything that is written on any post-card, and in every sealed envelope, and parcel he carries, not because he reads with these eyes of his, the post-cards, nor by experiences and deduction, makes the covers of the rest translucent. It is simply, that he doesn't care, and so the messages inside screech to him to give them the importance of a habitation in his mind. Now he empties, out on the grass, the contents of his bag, about a dozen letters, and post-cards, half a dozen circulars and newspapers, and one, badly tied, parcel. He shakes the bag well holding it upside down. He goes a little way from us to do this. I think it is to remember the secrecy of the post. But, in a moment, I see that it wasn't. Starlings have come from, God knows, the old ruin inland. They settle with commotions on the shakings of the bag, and the postman, coming back to us, explains—the parings and sweatings of wedding cake coming out of the little boxes last night. A flat stone or so has kept the letters and papers from any sudden blast of wind. Now, the postman picks them up, and drops them back in his bag. He stands with us watching the audacious starlings lunching on the sod. They are quite fearless before our feet. The postman's voice speaking to us has given us a proper standing with the starlings. The postman sighs, re-mounts his bicycle, and goes slowly pedalling away in the direction from which we have come. It was on a dead level piece of road we met. So he must pedal, as demurely as he is capable of, until he meets a little rise and makes his scuttling effort for the fall beyond. The man walking with us spreads his hand out over the horizon from sou'-west to nor'-east and he says: "That man goes through this country every day, and will so continue until he goes out on his pension, and yet he doesn't know the first thing about it, and he is as well off. His friends are just over it, those birds and the like, if he had wings on his feet, he would just stay hovering, and perhaps, by the time he's out of his time, you'll be able to get wing seed and grow wings on your heels, good luck to him anyway. And you two men look jaded. You can

see the winning post now." He is pointing to the far huddle
of houses where the Pride Hotel stands up against a yellow
sun. He turns short to the right, and passes behind us down
a little dell among the bushes on the land side, and on a
rabbit path, he passes on inland. "We meet again," he calls,
and, with our faces set on a course, we plough along our way.
"Jaded," he said. Bowsie's untidy clothes, now look jaded.
Am I jaded? I didn't think I was until that man spoke. Do I
look jaded? But isn't that a permanent look on many of us?
Bowsie does not turn his face towards me to appraise my
appearance. That might mean politeness, or it might mean
that my appearance has been obviously jaded for several miles
past. I wish a bird would sing, a lark climbing up his song
into the sky, would cheer us both up. But some more sugary
song than a lark's, would be better just now. The lark is so
clear, and so full of joy unattainable to me on an ordinary
day, at this hour unattainable to Bowsie too, I believe.
Squelch, squelch, squelch, squelch. Neither of us had noticed
that a little stream, dammed up on the sea side of the road,
had spread over the road for a space of five or six feet. Half
an inch to an inch deep. However, our boots were water-tight
to that, at any rate, and we escape to the higher grass by the
roadside. Bowsie says, "It's a good road anyway, and that
flash wasn't the road's fault, but the fault of some careless-
in-honour contractor who scamped the dab of cement which
should have given the entrance to the pipe below the road, a
smooth curve, which would have made the stopping up of the
pipe's mouth, with floating sticks and sods, not so easy." So
Bowsie stooping down and prodding here and kicking his heel
there, is beginning a breaking up of the dam. Now, I am
helping, I have a beautiful lump of a sod—just under my
foot, and am just going to move it on one side, and exult
myself, as the exulting water rushes forward—unbound. But
something in Bowsie's eyes is so wistful, I turn away and
move to some meanly secondary, obstruction of short twigs
and straw, and a wisp of sheep's wool. I know Bowsie breathes
thanks to me for my generous holding back. And now, his
work on the pipe's mouth finished, he comes up to my fine
sod, and, waiting a second or two so that the flood may be
held up as high as possible, to the very top of the sod, Bowsie
pushes the sod away and the flood curled, like a dolphin's

forehead, plunges to the pipe head, and gurgling in its pride, rushes under the road to spread on the land side, a little kite-shaped patch of sand, sticks, and straws.

I think to myself, if Bowsie would only listen intelligently to me I would say—now we gather the skirts of our togas about us, and leave the highway of utility for the highway of romance. Some link is rattling in my brain between Romans making aqueducts and ourselves directing the gutter flow. And it comes to me, in a flash, that those voluminous long and baggy double kilts, one time called plus fours, appeal to so many men, because they flop about them like toga ends, and I believe that those, to whom these flappings appeal most, are those who do not feel within themselves that noble pride, which remembers that "The noblest Roman of all" is dead. Anyway, I am not going to say any of these nonsensical mistings of words to Bowsie, for I am not sure, whether he is for the wide, and ankle long floppings or against, and as we go wandering on jaded, "jaded," he said, we are not either of us in the humour to stand an argument in pure aesthetics; for neither of us, I know, would, even at the last pinch, and cornered, introduce any material values in such a case. Jaded we may be, but at least we are of a kind fit to meet on a field of honour, no matter how long, how short, or how shivery we make our stay there. On we go—plod. I think if I turned my head and looked back, it might make the way we have yet to go seem a mere bagatelle—to gaze away in comparison to the long distance behind us, to our sleeping-place last night. A huddle of specks just breaking the edge of the green grass, a grey sand line of distance, only faintly silhouetted, against a pale blue, pencil scratch of the day before's starting hill. But I'm not turning my head; I am facing the last lap, breasting the storm of fatigue that seems to press down towards us, loth to let us win our way gaily up the road, down the road, over the bridge, running water very trying on frayed tempers, up the rise to the glass house door of the Pride. This bit of road is sacred to fatigue. On it when Bianconi was in his prime, ahead, where the Pride now stands, was a long stone cottage with stables for tired horses, and a space in front where the fresh team waited. The fatigued legs of horses came along this last bit of road. But, ah, they were brave legs, and they made an effort—where? here? No, not yet. Now? No, a

little further, Bowsie. Ah, it's you, Bowsie, who have ever the
bolder heart, and the wish to jump into your collar. But now,
my boy, you have your chance. Down this short dip. Scatter
the gravel. Up the hill—we're carried under on our steam
down again. Up over the ridge of the bridge. The rhyming
bridge. Now, stride more handsomely, up, up, up. Three ups.
Three efforts. Now, down into a sloping stroll, to bring the
battering hearts to quietness, and we are in the Pride's mouth.
Successful wanderers from no prosaic shore.

from

AND
TO YOU ALSO

MARS IN HIS GLORY

One day we will be so wise about our possessions that we won't want to wear them all at once, and so we may be able to contemplate pugilists fighting for glory and soft cash without any idea of having them filmed as they fight. The substitution of the celluloid memory of an event for a chancy human and private memory weakens the event itself, and presently you have a visual entertainment that is more than a quarter ballet—like Association football. And when it's seventy-five per cent ballet it still won't be straight ballet. And about that time a trap-door will open in the middle of the playing-field and the referee squealing on his whistle will disappear down below followed by the players. Cricket being a minuet, and dignified with its great age before the films came along, may last longer, and also because the minuet is such a particularly up-stage sort of dance. If Cricket had ever been linked to the cotillion it would have been different, even so "the smart cotillion unsuited to the million" would have remained unsullied by the flickings of the screen. And yet the screen didn't mean to do any one any harm only to make some money for the sportsmen connected with the screen, and when the last word is spoken it is the fast shutter which is the real cause of the spoiling of a game. When I see "a still" in a newspaper of Mother's Boy popping straight up into the air to meet a football with his round head and bounce it, while his friends and foes make little harlequinade posturing right and left. When I see this I wish I had never opened that newspaper.

Boxing when I first saw it was for those who appreciated, at least the appearance of, an olden day. The cunningly knotted handkerchief round the waist. The fighting small clothes coming well down below the calf of the leg. The light high-lows. Often the fighter in the ring might have slid from the coloured print of the old-timer hung on the wall, and

among the ringsiders your eye would rest awhile with affec-
tionate interest on a coachman-looking overcoat, double sewn
and overlapped at all the seams, and almost every part would
be of a kind peculiar to the feeling of the nob it covered. The
low-crowned billycock with the curly brim side by side with
the high-domed wide and flat-brimmed built of as hard a felt
as the billycock. A few broadly checked caps were beginning
to creep about worn very markedly over the eyes, to shade
eagle glances from the yellow flaring gas jets up above the
world so high. Yellow gaslight made the old roped magic
circle hum and brim with excitement for me, an excitement
which never got me by the breast and shook me so well under
the white light. For one thing, under the gaslight the men's
bodies took a more fighting colour and their shed blood took
a more Burgundian tinge.

> The dark Burgundian wine
> That would make a fool divine.

Every good colour was thrown down for the fighting men and

> In Eighteen-eighty-nine
> Upon an emerald plain
> John L. Sullivan,
> The Strong Boy of Boston,
> Fought seventy-five red rounds
> With Jake Kilrain.

By quotation, you may remember the heroic history best. But
by quotation we surely do live in it best.

Mutt: "How old is Hortense?"
Jeff: "She was playing Camille in Sacramento the night
    Corbett fought Chyonskie on the barge."

I saw a young boxer once beautifully turned out with a pair
of lovely fighting boots given him by his sweetheart. After
three rounds of gentle glove flapping he sat in his corner and
he was laughing. When the second pushed him through the
ropes towards the dressing-room he said to him, "Don't ever
come here again". He was too well turned out to make history.
Costume must not be too well chosen. The fortune of the stars,
the weather, and the hour must decide, and that perhaps at
the last moment, between the cobble-stones and the sawdust.

Carton in his slippers wouldn't have the power to worry our
old hearts as Carton in his cold top boots on the ladder, one
rung up one rung down, can do every time we see Frederick
Barnard's drawing of him in a dingy old junk shop window.
Clothes don't make the man. But they give the man a chance.
I do not put everything on the boots, it was the long-skirted
coat that clothed the Revolution which helped the boots to
swing about the stage. Nothing lasts but for a time. Still
Irving's hop-and-go constant walk suited those boots and that
long coat so well that, with better luck, a great block of drama
might have lived about them even to this day and beyond it.
As soon as we get a good carrying costume somebody has to
come along and change it. Perhaps it's just shop-keeping and
the costumiers want to sell something new instead of hiring
out the old all the time. Ah well, I hope we don't always get
what we deserve. I hope we're not as bad as all that, not as
bad as all we get. No man on earth was so bad as some of
the hotel table d'hotes he would be liable to have slapped
down before him. Still it must be a great moment, a pulling
back from the craggy brink, when the weary pugilist, weary
of wandering round inside ropes which never befriend him,
to see after some lucky punch, where his lucky angel pushed
out his fist, his opposite warrior lying broad on his back,
satisfied to be beat to the wide, with no intention of opening
his eye while the one, two, three, four, five, six, seven, eight,
nine, ten simple multiplication is breathing up the air. What
a moment—old troubles forgotten for a little while. How
peaceful the avenue of our futures would look if we count out
all our too vitiating care in a count of ten. "You're out,"
"you're out," "you're out," go home to your noisome ten-
ement and let me always circle away from it. And how that
lathy coachman in his long black Newmarket, with the crim-
son carnation in the lapel, how he circled away round the big
pond in the park, on the Sunday before Chestnut Sunday,
with his four dark bays rattling to their beckoning nose-bags,
and their stables, as did he himself. He smiled down on me
in gentle pity as I sat beside him on the box. He was sighing
to himself lightly in his middle throat, and leaning his chin
down into the comforting folds of his white four-in-hand
cravat with its splinter-bar pin. He was as happy then as ever
he was though he lived into more exciting moments. And now

he's old, doubled up, like a horseshoe twisted by a professional strong man, and breathing like a fish in an aquarium, but if he was to hear a horse whinnying in a field he would rub a finger down the side of his nose and then pinch his old knees and wish for sleep. I saw him once again, once only to know him, though I may often have passed him changed with the passing years. I do not want to think of those coaching curls before the ears with silver lines among the raven's feathers. But perhaps he has had sense enough to give them something out of a bottle like the young man in the song. The second time I saw him he had been a passenger, urbane, uncritical, driven down to Epsom Downs by an amateur and there'd been a spill. No one, man or beast, got more than a shaking. But the amateur coachman was sad about it and apologetic. Sad, for it was his off day, or the off day for the watcher of his luck. The inn he had brought his professional whip to was uneven, profuse in the wrong place, on the tables everywhere were large glass flat dishes full of piccalilli. Perhaps the owner was an old East-ender, who thought every one must think our earthly paradise is surely scented with fried fish, piccalilli and paregoric, like the New Cut in the days of old when we were boys, and gave an atmosphere as he would have it for himself. But the long bar of the Criterion did not smell of piccalilli, and the amateur whip knew that and knew that the professional couldn't appreciate the New Cut. The amateur was low in himself. It was perhaps the cruelty of the buck in the ever season of the deer park, but my professional whip was bland and graceful. He stood over me where I lunched soberly and he admired himself in the looking-glass on the coffee-room chimney-piece, and he pulled his tie straight; it was a stiff long-ended silver grey bow, not the billowy four-in-hand of his working hours, and he sang softly, but not so softly that I did not hear.

> She loves me,
> I know that she loves me.

Ah, Mars in his glory rattling a song in his gold helmet. Saturn registering disdain. I saw him but a few hours ago in a point-to-point in the county of Dublin. Sleet on the hills, mud and water on the course, he was finishing fourth. Orange jacket, green cap, aloft on a musical comedy queen named after music, and she was blowing hard; they were a long way fourth, drenched and muddy. He may perhaps himself have helped her to get even as near as she did to a place for his name carried wings. But he was unimpressed with that day in February of this year, and six lengths from the post, and the Judge in his cart, he lent away and blew his nose as Adam blew his, with his fingers—a farewell to point-to-point.

Of all the gifts my Fairy Godmother gave me I cannot tell myself which I am most thankful for. But there is one I have loved long, and though sometimes my love cooled, I found it at my heart and throat again. It is that gift of the gab, and because I love it so, I think it a golden gift, and because I have had it for my use I think it very large and fine. But I think now I will offer it, not wittily saying "I'm not looking a gift in the mouth", back to my Fairy Godmother so that she can give it to some one younger in talking. And if she says, "Well, take something else, some other gift in exchange", if she says that, I'll be dumb, for I don't know what to ask for except fortune, and I am half afraid Fairy Godmothers don't give those sort of gifts.

from
THE SILENCER

HARTIGAN TALKING

HARTIGAN I haven't been in London for years and it's changed. Every place changes as soon as your back is turned. I wouldn't know Cork, I suppose, if I saw it now.

MALONEY As the saying is, I never saw Cork, but I often saw drawings of it.... (*imitates the popping of a cork and slaps his cheek to represent the liquor running out of a bottle. All laugh.*)

HARTIGAN Wonderful drawings the Chinese used to do of ships. You couldn't always recognize the ship, but the curley sea was always magnificent. Curious thing how fond old sailors were of having a picture painted of their ships. They were very particular, too. Everything had to be just so. I suppose where every moment of a man's life at sea depends on exactness, it affects him in every way for ever. But all the old sailors I ever knew gave as good as they got. Exact they were and exacting. In the face of the overwhelming and embittering forces of rock, air and sea those old boys stood up to all their troubles. They lived and died game. I saw an old sailor man one time a good way down in the Antarctic. He stripped himself, put an iron billaying pin in his mouth and he said "Iron to iron", and he stood up on the deck facing sleet and snow and bare to the buff, and he shouted out loud "I'll split the wind or my breast bone", and he was slapping his old chest all the time and then stretching out his eight old fingers and his thumbs, as if he could scratch the venom out of a hurricane. It took three of us to pull him down and throw him into his bunk and sluice him well with rum. The old man sent his steward down with it—a whole bottle full. Ah, those were the days. The days of old, the days that are no more.

JOHNSON Well, I never saw anything like that in all my life.

CURTIS I saw the other day in one of the illustrated papers a photo of one of the last of the windjammers. It looked very old.

HILDERBRAND Extraordinary.

HARTIGAN I knew a cowboy once, one of the old school! He had absolutely golden hair, long straight golden hair hanging down to his shoulders. He was six foot two and rawboned. He had blue eyes. He was a very nice man except when he was full of old rye and then he was nice too — to his friend. But he didn't always know his friend when the old rye was well up between his eyes. And the worst of it was that one time in the gay old days of old some travelling quack oculist told him his sight was in danger if he didn't get a pair of glasses at once. So old Charlie Weston got a pair of gold mounted nose nips and wore them on a string from his neck. But he never used them until the Old Rye was in command. Then he would fix the glasses on his nose, take a six shooter in each hand, and go look for his friends so as to locate them before shooting up his enemies. It was serious work having him squint in your face seeing if he could recognize you while he pushed your stomach in with his six shooters.

JOHNSON What a life these men lead.

MARSHALL That's nothing to the individuals he'll tell you about. How he existed with them, I don't know. It's beyond me. But I suppose it takes all sorts to make a world.

HILDERBRAND Go on. Tell me about the parrots in the trees.

HARTIGAN Ah, they all flew away, and I followed after in a canoe, and where they settled I became Counsellor to the King of the Palm Tree Palaces, Palatzio el Palm Oil. Ah, nothing doing! They couldn't palm anything on me. This man wanted little here below but a singlet, a pair of ducks and a belt to hold 'em up. So after Royalty had told me all he could remember of the Arabian Nights learnt out of a copy he got from a flying Mish (he told them to me as the legends of his Nation), then I started in and told him Gulliver's Travels with additions. He was tickled to death almost. He liked anything I could tell him, and tales of adventure by sea he loved best of all. He had an old State Canoe of his own, but he never was in it since he was a child. The State Canoe had a two foot beam and the old Bold Boy himself was very nearly four in a cross section. Once in the shallow end of home lagoon he made an effort, and with a couple of stately chiefs up to their waists on the port and starboard hand, he got a little way. But, well, he looked to me like a man trying to ride a Tishy full blown. I don't mean the fleshy Tishy of the days that are gone, but the india-rubber one the boys used to take in bathing with them.

HILDERBRAND (*stops and listens, looking towards door on left*) Some-one coming. This'll be Tyler. I'll see him in five minutes. But don't forget you've got to tell me more about that fat old King.

(*Goes quickly in through door right and shuts it quietly after him. Shadow appears on glass of door left; handle turned and enter* TYLER, *nondescript, pert business man.*)

TYLER I have an appointment with Hilderbrand this morning.

HARTIGAN Yes sir, Mr Hilderbrand is expecting you. He's held up for a moment. Won't you sit down.

TYLER No, thank you. I prefer to stand. I'm rather pressed for time. Mr Hilderbrand has to settle a matter with me, then I'm off.

HARTIGAN You're rushed for time! I've seen a man rushed for time; I knew him, a racing cyclist of pedalling days. His name was Spare and they called him Spare-neck for short. He was very short when I saw him—short of cash. He'd got to get to a coast track to win a race. He couldn't steal a ride because he'd done it too often. He tried to tie his machine to the end car but they cast him adrift. However, he darted in behind her, got the suction and held his own for two hundred and fifty miles.

(TYLER *sits down, drawing chair nearer to desk.*)

Hopping over the ties. The sleepers' sleepers! He didn't sleep himself for a month. Bumpity, bumpity, bumpity, bump! He made the coast all right and won his race and offered to compensate the Railway Company for loss of Dignity, so they gave him a free pass for life. So he got fatty legs and never raced again. So it comes, so it goes.

And have you ever noticed the way the luck always plays from the sleeve! I believe, and I believe you, sir, believe the same, that Pandora's Box——

(*Bell rings on desk.*)

HARTIGAN (*takes up telephone*) Yes, sir. Mr Tyler is here, sir. Will you go in, Mr Tyler?

TYLER What about Pandora's Box?

HARTIGAN It's got a false bottom.

(*Exit* TYLER *through door on right. As he goes through door he says very cheerily*—"Hello, Hilderbrand!")

(*Murmur of pleasant voices from inner room or a laugh or two.* HARTIGAN *tidies up desk, gets up, moves about, straightens engraving on wall, puts chair back in place. Opens drawers of desk, looks in, closes them, generally busies himself. Enter* RAN-SOME. *Tall, liverish-looking man, heavy black moustache, in long black top coat, dark grey trousers, black soft felt hat, bright blue neck tie.*)

RANSOME Is Mr Hilderbrand to be seen this morning?

HARTIGAN I'm sure he'll see you, Mr Ransome, but he's engaged at the moment. I'll tell him you're here. (*Takes up telephone*) Mr Ransome, sir, would be glad if you could see—yes. . . . five? . . . ten? fifteen? Three, very good sir. (*to* RANSOME) Just a moment and Mr Hilderbrand will see you. Won't you sit down? (*Gets up and gets chair for* RANSOME *who sits down restlessly*) Ah, Mr Ransome, how are the Chilterns looking? Very blue and beautiful I have no doubt these mornings. I hope you have a view from your breakfast room; a breakfast with a view is worth seven breakfasts with a dead wall out-look. Of course in a sense everything is a view, a point of view. Take a breakfast room with a dead wall view with a view to suicide. (RANSOME *glares at him gloomily: telephone bell rings*) Yes, sir; at once. With a view to a more circumscribed horizon, but a more cheerful one for old friends; take a cheerful view yourself and put off suicide, for Hilderbrand will see you now. (*Rises, opens inner door for* RANSOME *who sighs deeply and goes in, passing* MR TYLER *who is going out.*)

TYLER Goodbye, my boy!

HILDERBRAND Goodbye, Wat.

(*Murmur of low voices if possible.* HARTIGAN *continues tidying up desk, changes position of note books, ink stand, etc. Tears a letter or two from pocket and puts them in waste paper basket. Takes novel with staring jacket from drawer. No particular novel jacket, just bright dabs and streaks of colour. Tries to read from beginning then skips a lot of pages, looks at end, back to beginning, closes sadly and puts novel back in drawer, folds arms tightly on breast and looks straight before him for some time. Door bursts open. Enter* CHARLES TORNBY, *short, blooming golden-haired young man, clean shaven, very smart, light clothes, bright tweed overcoat, flower in button hole, gloves, white spats, brown boots very shiny, smoking long cigar.*)

TORNBY I've got an appointment for 12.45 with Mr Hilderbrand. (*Looks at wrist watch*) It's just a few minutes short of that.

HARTIGAN I'll tell Mr Hilderbrand you're here. (*Fiddles about a little and takes up telephone*) Mr Tornby to see you. Yes. Yes. Yes. Yes. Yes, sir. (*looks attentive*) Yes. (*Puts back receiver*) Mr Hilderbrand will be a minute or two, but he won't keep you. He has an old family friend in with him now, very difficult to get rid of, but he'll move him on in a moment. These family friends can be a tiresomeness sir.

TORNBY I am an orphan.

HARTIGAN Sad, sad. But wasn't there some story about orphans braving storms, though I suppose it cuts both ways, as the sailor said when the wind backed, and the snows of yesterday came again. And I tell you that a topsil yard is a poor perch for snow gambolling and a snow-ball fight in the ship boy's eyes is a poor substitute for eiderdown quilts, footwarmers and hot grog. And there's no use telling me that if you fall overboard the temperature of the sea will seem warm and comfortable in comparison with a frozen deck. Contrast isn't everything.

TORNBY I don't quite follow you, but you interest me exceedingly.

HARTIGAN Don't try to follow; it's of no consequence. Sailors on frozen decks have to walk very Agagishly. I saw

miners, genuine miners—all of them had red shirts—
playing with a frozen deck of cards. When they prised
them apart with their jack knives, they put each card on
the knife point and simmered it in front of the fire a
while to thaw it; but it was interesting, too, because those
miners had useful memories for faces and back views and
each knew the cards he himself had toasted. After a
dozen hands had been played, the game became too
physiological, and they turned it into Snatch, snatch, run
and shoot; or shoot, snatch and run; or shoot, shoot,
shoot. I was having a bird's eye view from a bird's
nest of this battle. I was comfortable enough but I was
nervous, for I got afraid that the owner of the nest might
come home at any moment to his eyrie. I don't know
what bird he was, but I feared him. By the size of his
nest he must have been about as big as a calf.

TORNBY Splendid!

HARTIGAN Big and splendid I could handle, but you see he
might have been big and punctilious and petty and it
was getting toward two o'clock in the morning, when,
you remember Napoleon said, the best sort of courage
manifests itself. But suppose that old bird had it and I
hadn't; what then? But there was a lull down around the
fire, so I slid down my tree and approached the boys
very carefully, and as I went I said: "What about a game
of forfeits?" They were a terrible tough crew. They'd had
none of the benefits of a Home Life, and when I explained
the game of forfeits to them they were delighted. They
began at once sharpening up their knives on stones. (*Door
in distance inside inner room, is heard to bang*) That's Mr
Hilderbrand's old family friend gone, I expect. (*Bell rings*)
Yes. Now. Quite so. Now, Mr Tornby, Mr Hilderbrand
is quite ready for you. (*Jumps up and goes toward door to
open it.* TORNBY *rises but stops and comes towards* HARTIGAN.)

TORNBY You can't leave it like that. Your miner friends were
sharpening their knives——

HARTIGAN Sharp knives are sometimes better than sharp ton-
gues. That's a moral remark. But just then my late host—
if a host can be a host in Absentia—came home with a
sharp tongue and a jag on. I never actually saw him
because I was busy watching my step at the time. But

he darkened the sky and my miners must have taken it as an omen, and they began looking regretfully at the knives and putting them back in the sheaths. But man is but a changing arrow of the sky; a turnspit on a tower, ever wavering, ever trying to catch the wind by running before it, ever spinning on a high heel. Mister-face-all-round with a knife, one moment nestling in a pigskin sheath and next in between some human ribs. So I sailed out of camp. I got five seconds start, and my boys in the red shirts had high miners' boots on while I wore dancing pumps. So I went away doing three yards to their one. They fired a few shots, but wide. Then one of them accidentally hit his friend's hip pocket, with its pocket pistol made of glass, and all the Old Rye was spilt on the earth again; produced by the earth, it went back to the earth again. The miners stopped hunting me instantly. They felt the occasion was romantic. Like all men dressed in fancy dress, they were fanciful.

from

THE
CARELESS
FLOWER

THE EMPLOYMENT OF
OLIVER JAMES GAW

PART ONE

The beginning of winter, a middle-heighted man clothed in
a meagre suit of tweed, a knickerbocker suit, moved on the
cobblestones along a cloudy street parallel with a murky river,
which flowed scummy, black, sulphurous and crowded to the
sea on the North-West coast of England. The man was seen
by many people, because as he strode that uneven street he
hit in the shoulder, with his shoulder, on the belly, with his
belly, the men in dungaree and pilot coats, who did not give
him his road. He wanted a clear road to the ferry landing
place which lay on his right, the entrance to which was
through a tall dark shaft, between two warehouses. The dark-
ness of the shaft would be intensified by a lamp, a gas lamp,
with its flame ever streaming, one way or the other, in the
wind, which came along up or down the black shaft from the
river.

The man was in a hurry, this Oliver James Gaw. Business
called him, business, pressing business, more pressing than
any that had ever called him in his whole store of years. An
offer of a job, a whole winter's job, a desperate job to get, a
splendid job to hold, palms, parrots, dames, fair dames. Oh,
no more of that fancy business. Just to have them hanging
on your words. Words, that was where the desperation came
in, words, words, words. He had his store of them always
ready. But these would be special words, strung together
properly, and backed by facts, *facts*, facts; "The facts in the
fire and I wish to God they'd stay there."

In the man's breast a folded paper lay, close to the left
nipple of that hairy façade. It was in that inner pocket of
his waistcoat, made once to hold gold and notes, and in
imagination, that Midas mystery of the fairy bells, a circular

letter, and a large bond, payable to bearer. But this morning, when he scraped out that secret pocket with a pencil end, all that came out was dust, not gold dust, just grey woolly dust. The folded paper, unfolded, was as full of promise as a circus poster:

GOOD-BYE FOG
WELCOME SUNNY SKIES, SUNNY BOYS, AND SUNNY GIRLS,
AND MIDDLE-AGED SUN LOVERS TOO
BASK UNDER THE PALMS
SEE THE ORCHID'S HOME
SEE THE KOKER-NUT IN FLOWER
SEE THE BURIED CITIES OF ANCIENT DAYS
SCRUTINEER
10,000 TONS
WITH INSTRUCTIVE HISTORICAL LECTURES
SAILS FOR THE SEAS OF SUN AND GLORY ON
NOVEMBER 15th
For further particulars apply:—JOS. WEBSTER,
14, Quay Street,
Alberwide

Gaw had known Jos. Webster many a day ago. They had both been scholars at the Grammar School in Choughport. But Gaw, starting his career by hard work at his books, had first considered seriously the medical profession, then engineering, then banking, and had, at that last, failed to pass the examination for a desk in the rather romantic sound-ing bank he had thought of as suitable for the employment of his talent. So he had drifted, if his departure with a solid leather portmanteau, bought in a second-hand trunk shop near the docks for thirty-five shillings could be called drifting. The portmanteau was a fine, imposing, and very heavy piece of workmanship, made by the stitching together of the halves of two distinct portmanteaux. What had become of the other halves, who can tell? But there was Oliver James Gaw stand-ing on the station platform with O. J. G. in fresh white paint on the portmanteau side. And grouped around him were his "parents and guardians," well, one parent, his mother, a pinkly faded woman with a kind of curving complacency of manner, and a way like Lordtown Noddy of laughing at everything and everybody. But she laughed her last many years ago, and all the guardians were gone to their long accounts before Gaw went hurrying, that November day, for his own particular ferry, to carry him to Alberwide.

Drifting, or dragging, he had gone to Liverpool and entered an office near the docks, where no previous examination was necessary to win a high stool.

Liverpool and other towns and cities up above the waist-belt of England, had found him bread and butter. But now the bread had crumbled in his fingers, and the butter had melted into other people's mouths, and at fifty, looking sixty, in that November evening light, he found himself so embarrassed for hard cash, that, if there had been no other way of getting to Alberwide, he was prepared to, in the spirit, if necessary, swim down the sulphur river.

But the ferry landing place was reached, just on the lucky tick of time. The *Prairie Bird*, the little steam ferry, was just alongside the small grimy jetty that stood to the west'ard of the ferry steps. The captain was holding her to the jetty with a loop of rope. There were half a dozen passengers when Gaw leapt on board, down on to the deck, for it was half tide, and the little vessel was below the boarding of the pier.

The *Prairie Bird* was a narrow streak of dirty grey with a funnel which the captain considered a light puce. The passengers sat, back to back, on a seat which ran like the knife board on old omnibuses, fore and aft. And the *Bird* was as old as those old omnibuses. The six passengers were evenly distributed, three a-side. And when Gaw sprang down on the deck he had to make up his mind quickly which was the safer side for him to put his body's weight. If he had placed himself foolishly, the Engineer, Jamesey, very black and hook-nosed, would have screeched at him, and Gaw's nerves were too on edge to stand screeching. The Engineer was watching the river, the sky, the *Bird*, the passengers, and the captain. The captain was as nothing to him, a mere loblolly boy. But the passengers, all passengers, he looked at with his piercing eyes into the black coaly rims. If he had seen a passenger before he always spat over the side. If he had seen the passenger before, and could not remember where, he spat twice, once over the side and once down into his engine room.

Oliver Gaw had journeyed that river on the *Bird* when the engineer was Jamesey's father, and he knew how important it was to balance cargo nicely. For once in that long ago time, after many narrow escapes of rolling over and sinking, there was an affair of the deep, or at any rate of a ship and the salt water, for the salt tide ran strongly in the river, even though they had to meet and grapple the noisome droppings from the river-side factories. The accident of the *Bird* came through her passengers, a full complement of twenty she carried, on that bright day. And thinking something that floated fast down to them with the ebbing tide was a corpse with its face upwards to the sky, they had rushed over to the port side. Luckily, or unluckily, the *Bird*, for some avoidance of the current's greatest strength, was hugging the shores at a long bank of mud, and at the moment that the twenty passengers heeled her over with themselves, they saw that their corpse, as it floated in a few feet widths of water between the vessel and the mud, was only a blown-out paper bag, an empty sack and a tomato tin so cunningly arranged by the vagaries of the curling eddies of the river, into the appearance of the very dead. At that moment they hurled themselves all but four on to the mud bank. The four had been on the outskirts of the crowd, and so escaped a bath of mud, but as the *Bird* sprang back, recoiling to her starboard hand, she carefully, and cattishly, threw the four into the water.

They were rescued by the Captain and Jamesey's father, a genial man who enjoyed a joke, quite unlike his son. When the *Bird* had sprung from side to side in this wallowing roll the captain had hung to his wheel. But even without the wheel the wooden sort of hobby-horse, which he sat astride of, was never able to unseat him. He had a knee grip and a balancing seat which would have made him a man to ride a bucking mustang. These thoughts came into Gaw's mind as he sat watching the warehouses slide by, or towards him, as the little vessel crossed the river from side to side, from jetty to jetty, curling her way round the coming and going steamers and lighters, taking on and leaving passengers. The passengers came and went. Sometimes as many as ten were aboard, sometimes as few as four, three often, and himself; all were men. As Gaw sat there, with his hands clasped together in front of him, he thought with idleness, to rest himself. He thought that, perhaps, the first riders of bucking mustangs were sailors, who rode the ponies as they rode the yards in a gale. He thought how unsailorlike was the riding in London in Rotten Row, which he had seen. And then, suddenly, he was in a green and shiny park with great distances, and a gold sky, and a large house like a palace, sometimes on one side of the picture, and sometimes on the other, and sometimes replaced by a huge aviary full of many coloured birds, all with their beaks open to sing.

When he opened his eyes he was looking down on the grimy deck, his chin had fallen, he had slept. He came slowly, well, in a second, or two or three, to realise where he was, and why there. He looked about him, the passengers were the same, none had gone, none had come. He looked back up the river and saw the last landing stage they had called at, the passenger next him had not turned the newspaper he was reading. He had been reading, Gaw could tell from the way the paper was folded, the gossip column of a Liverpool paper, and he was still reading it. So, unless he too had slept Gaw's sleep was but a losing of his surroundings, and substituting of others, for a few stale moments.

The last landing place of all, down by the river mouth, almost at the open sea, was by the quay at Alberwide. The river there was almost clear, and seaweed grew there, with a brown and yellow gloss, and a purple sheen. Seaweed grew right up by the town of Choughport, close to the Town Hall, but a sewage-nurtured and chemical-eating seaweed which no fish ever smelt but with disdain. Alberwide, on the south bank of the river, had its quay and one narrow, long row of houses, bleached, pinched, cropped about the ears, with door-knockers green with verdigris, and daring grass growing among the cobble stones about their doors. It was the last pushing out towards the sea by men on the southerly side of the river. Beyond were clinker-strewed sand and low sandhills.

On the northerly side of the river was Arbour Hotel Point. It had another name in ancient days; but the "Arbour Hotel" had won its right to give the Point a name. There was a railway station half a mile away, two trains each way a day. There was a bunch of buckthorn to shelter a sandy pit which might have been a garden. There were three or four wooden sheds bound to the sands with wire ropes. And built on and into a rock, the only rock above sand within ten miles, the

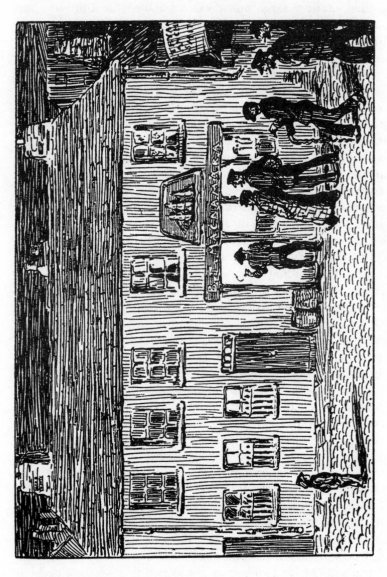

SAILORS COME ASHORE

"Arbour Hotel." A long low rakish-looking building, with the Arbour leaning against it to the easterly side, and in front of the Arbour a piece of hard-bitten, do-or-die, green-grey sod. There were ten windows in the front of the hotel facing south and to the river, and in front of five of those windows was a glass verandah eighteen feet wide. Well built that verandah was, well built, well stood. A blue-jerseyed ex-fisherman, the last on that coast, with putty and paint, nursed that glass box through winter storm, and drying perishing suns. It never leaked. And any day in any month of a year you might find yourself baking gently in a golden glow, which unbuttoned the waistcoat, sweated the face, and gave a merry thirst, which only fire water could quench. Among the five glass-boxed windows was one broad door, and before that door, fanned out a bar, shining with gay bottles, which were constantly emptying and always refilling. Rum with the sailor label and old "Puss Puss Tom Gin," caught the eye. But there were plenty more labels and even the softer sirens of the bottle, the raspberry cordials, which horrid men sometimes put into beer, and limes embowered in green topic leaves. There were cigars in a glass darkly Colorado Madura, others in boxes, splendid ladies, jewelled, magnificent as the cigars they smiled over when the box was opened, with the half-moon of the plug tobacco cutter forced under the front of the lid. Up came the lip with its one thin spike of a nail tooth still in it, up with a gentle pop. The picture flap, like the frontispiece of a book, after a glance, would be turned back, and the fingers of the buyer of the cigars and the fingers of the guest, who was to be entertained with far away Havana, would both begin to tingle and twist to be about their cigar's middle.

Behind the bar, rather high, and above the top-most tier of bottles, hung three frames. In one was the oleograph of a full-rigged ship, flamboyant, useless looking, the artist having more love for dashing waves than dashing ships. Another frame held the middle place, and in it, tacked and stretched flat, was a cotton handkerchief with the flags of all nations; some of those flags were obsolete, but there behind the bar they stood their ground. The third frame had in it a large engraving from some old illustrated paper of years before; it showed a large railway station, full of girders, and a glass roof arched high, and little lady-like figures down below, in crinolines, and stately little gentlemen figures in tall hats, with policemen in taller hats still. The whole had been coloured by a child with a rich blue and a yellow ochre, which after, perhaps long after, the small cherub had gone aloft, still held its own down here on earth, nailed to a hotel wall, bound to a rock, beside a river mouth, where dreams may always begin.

The bar was governed all day by a tall, slim woman in the late thirties, pale, and of a refined appearance, long-shaped eyes, straight brows, and a high forehead. Her natural teeth had been large and irregular, but the artificial ones she had possessed for some time now, had altered the character of her mouth, and any old customer of the "Arbour Hotel" who had known her with her own teeth, would now find her changed. She found herself changed when she looked at herself in the brandy advertising looking-glass on the shelf behind the bar. This looking-glass was tilted, so that she had to look down into it, and so she always saw herself with sky and flying seagulls as her head's canopy. She did not care for this, for she so thoroughly disliked the sea; as for seagulls, she had a feeling that the sea was theirs, and that they were responsible for it, and gloried in it. She also very much disliked their laughing cry, she had an idea they laughed at her, a thing, certainly, no human being had ever done. Miss Annie Malcarn had easily got her position as the queen of "Arbour Hotel" against all comers. The owner of the hotel also owned the "Commercial Corner Hotel" in Choughport. He had had enough connection with the sea, at an early date in his career, he called his years a career, and he had a right to, if ups and downs make a career, to distrust it. And so, when having interviewed twelve fair, hard, soft, flint-eyed or fish-eyed, young women, who thought the bar at the "Arbour Hotel" would suit them, he saw Miss Malcarn, he said to himself, "she shall have it, she looks more like a half-tide rock than any I ever saw." The salary was comfortable and Miss Malcarn was able to rent two small rooms in Choughport, and leave Hotel Point every evening and catch the eight o'clock, the second and last, up train, at Goul Dock Station. Her employer being now at the apex of his career, a director of the Thron Dock Railway Company, she was presented with a season ticket, first-class. There was only one first-class compartment, so any that travelled so grandly, travelled with Miss Malcarn. These were, her employer, or some other of the directors, or the ticket collector who joined the train at First Ferry Station, and sat down on the deep blue cushioned seat opposite her, and passed any news there was to pass, and gazed out of the window against the grey walls of store-houses in the summer, and against the black nights in winter, and picked his teeth with the tickets.

Miss Malcarn looked on the ticket collector as part of the railway, but she did not admire him, though she thought—if the idle movements of her brain could be called thought—of him as a piece of superior humanity to the directors. The news the ticket collector gave her she absorbed, which she might as well do, for she never bought a newspaper but once, and that was when she saw a muddy urchin with a broken cap too large for him, and she thought he looked like Jackie Coogan (she *had* been to the cinema), if it wasn't that he was very pinched and had a screaming voice. The boy carried an evening paper under his arm, a newsvendor's poster fluttering about him like a kilt:

LOCAL
HOTEL
BURNT OUT

She bought one of his papers, dreaded to open it, but did so near a shop window, and by its light saw it was not the "Arbour Hotel," which she had only left an hour or so ago, but an absolutely irrelevant little, tumble-down alehouse on the top of the hill, on the edge of the town, where the turnpike gate once stood.

The customers at the hotel during her hours of duty were almost all regulars, and all within a certain fairly wide circle of the respectabilities. They all wore collars. Later on in the evening the man in the blue jersey stood behind the bar, assisted sometimes by his wife, broad, buxom and smiling, who kept house for herself and Blue Jersey in the kitchen and rooms behind the bar. They had plenty of space, much of it full of driftwood, very good driftwood too, for it kept the stove hot in the winter, in the bar.

The hotel made no provision for putting up people. Once a fog-bound, or storm-bound, or leg-lost, captain had spent the night on two chairs in the bar. But Blue Jersey had to watch the captain, and the contents of the bar. The captain had a revolver, that was the trouble, the fact was not discovered till other customers had gone, and Blue Jersey and his wife were not able to get the revolver from the captain, who held it even in sleep, and in his hip pocket, with a drunken man's grip, the barrel of the revolver sunk in his pocket, the haft in his hairy fist. It made his position for sleep uncomfortable.

So Blue Jersey watched. He was not afraid of the captain shooting anyone, but he gathered from the conversation he had heard with the others, that the captain was romantic, and he had seen romantic sons of the sea shooting at bottles in a bar, that was all. It was illegal, he was pretty sure, for the captain to be in the bar all night. But the revolver would show that he was holding his position by force of arms. He had no fear that the captain would drink up the store, he knew by the signs in the fluttering eyes, before he slept, that the captain would not seek alcohol again until morning was well advanced.

The captain was an unusual type of customer for Blue Jersey's hours of command. His were the hoarse-voiced mahogany-faced quay workers, left from Thron Dock, after discharging some big steamer of her grain. Before turning back into the narrow streets about the dock, where they lived, these men, with the specklings and dust of their work on them, would walk the half-mile to the "Arbour Hotel," because that glass house was to them romance. Then at closing time back again and home.

Indeed it was a few minutes before closing time they would begin to move about stiffly, and fill their pipes, with the strong tobacco they used, for one last homeward bound "drink of the pipe." These men, there were seldom more than a dozen of them together in the hotel on one night, were of a different type from the other quay workers. They lived in one or two streets about the docks, while other men and their families were seated over a wide area of small mean houses, and large tottering ones, divided into tenements. The cheek bones of these men were higher, their eyes deeper set, and though their surnames were often the same as those of the rest of the crowd of strong men who lifted cargoes out of ships by Thron Docks, they had three names which were only borne by themselves in all this company of the dock-side, Gallen, Gown and Broon.

As they walked to or from the "Arbour Hotel" they marched always, strong of foot, in a loosely military formation, and they never laughed in a roadway.

They sometimes arrived in their homes what is called "merry," but never truly drunken, and never did one of these marching men stop to lean against a battered lamp-post and vomit, as some thoughtless drinkers in that neighbourhood often did (you would think some dark corner would suffice, but no, nothing would do these thoughtless but the lamp-post and its spot-light), as men lean for comfort against a shaft:

A Broken Shaft
For the Half Daft

But each of our marching men broke the ranks, sturdy and steady, at his own door. Inside, his wife and his family, either in bed in little cots, or sitting by the fire in quiet conversation, welcomed the master of the house as a shipmaster, fresh from a harbour that he knew of, and knew of well.

The same dozen were not at the "Arbour Hotel" every night. The individuals varied from night to night, but the air about them was always the same. The conversation was of ships and cargoes, and the places ships came from, and captains of water, and politics, and of strange beliefs held by strange people far away. Their conversation was always woven as though some standing strands were constant, and unaffected by any tossing of the hand which threw the shuttle across and across, they were not the company of a clan, or three clans. Loose and open, light and airy, they were but laced together with a seriousness, like men who march a jungle in the night.

The customers of the hotel during Miss Malcarn's hours were clerks from Custom House and Warehouse, and from ship-brokers' offices, and there was a doctor who talked too much, and one or two ambiguous salt-water, bailiff-looking people, their clothes too thick and their faces too sour. Some of the idler prated of the tally clerks, thought, that if these men could be entranced with liquor they could reveal secrets, queer goings about, either on the river edge or in the dark docks. They took their drink as though it was theirs by right, and when they paid always threw their money on the bar top, in front of Miss Malcarn. They rarely asked for change, but if they had not counted with perfect surety, what they owed, asked, and when told made up the sum exactly and banged it on the bar. But they almost always knew what they owed. If they had to ask they always used the same phrase "what's the damage?" Just the old cant words; by them they meant that in taking their quantity of drink from the bottle or china barrel they had wounded, and that they would not heal the wound if they could, but would pay.

Occasionally, as it would have seemed odd not to, someone would stand them a drink, and at intervals one of them would stand a round of drinks to all in the bar. When it was drunk, or before the last man had finished, they would stamp their way to the door and move away. As they left they always took off their hats to Miss Malcarn, the only piece of graceful-ness, if it could be called such, so hardly was it done, they ever offered the bright bar of the "Arbour Hotel."

One of them once, in a moment of what was almost child-ishness, gave Miss Malcarn a double tomb-stoned smile. Miss Malcarn was startled, she spread one strong white hand on her stomach as if some hard elbow had struck her there in a dark crowd. But when some callow cadet of the office stools tried to be pleasant about the smile, Miss Malcarn was not in a laughing humour. She caught the smile, indeed every man in the bar saw it as it went out of the door like the tail of a comet. Not that Miss Malcarn was ever in a laughing humour in the bar. If she had had a laughing nature she would have felt her position too much to indulge it. She really was too tall for a barmaid, or for that particular bar, because the floor behind the counter was higher than before it, and so the customer, even if over the middle height had to leave himself exposed to the too downward glance from bacchante. A putty nose, a frayed neck-tie, and a dusky shirt stand up poorly to a bird's eye view. However, there it was, take it or leave it, Miss Annie ruled that domain. They were used to her rule. She was used to them too. They admired her because she never allowed herself or her bar to get untidy. She had only once been seen outside the ring of her bar, and in the bar-room itself. It was once, when the place was full of cus-tomers, some stupid elbow had upset a long drink, and some other stupider one had upset an ash-tray into the puddle, and the mess was too much for everyone. Blue Jersey was out at the moment hunting his driftwood, so Miss Annie herself lifted the flap of the bar, and came out with a swab and a duster, and the customers stood away and made room for her and gazed at her with astonishment, holding their glasses and tumblers in their hands. Many of them must have at some time seen her away from the hotel walking like an ordinary being to the railway station, or in the streets of Cloughtown. But now she was a wonder to them, there in the bar-room, like a seal on dry land, or a blackbird strolling on a pulpit. In a moment or two she was back again behind her bar, the incident was closed, and men supped up their drinks once more. Miss Malcarn did not admire any of her customers. She was very nearly impartial in her attendance on their wants. There was just this difference. There were two of the hotel drinkers she disliked; a tall, dark man, an insurance agent, had once walked into the bar, after a long walk on wet sand by the river mouth, out to where it met the sea, and he had not properly cleaned the sand from his boots, and after a time it dried and fell about and he walked in the dry sand and made a crunching noise which irritated Miss Annie. It was not that she usually had nerves, that was all the more reason for her to dislike the man who had irritated her that one day of all the year, when she was aware of having an incipient hint of nerves. The other drinker whom she found unpleasant was a square, very fair haired man who was an electricity engineer; when slightly tipsy the man had insisted on singing. It was nothing to her that he sang "Annie Laurie" with feeling hardly marred by liquor.

There was no singing tolerated in her bar. These two, the dark and the fair, knew perfectly well that they were permanently in a class apart.

Miss Malcarn never forgot the regular tastes of all her customers, but these two each time had to tell her theirs. But "Arbour Bar" was a happy place. If, on account of Miss Annie's aloofness, it could not be called "one happy family" at least it was a limited party of good acquaintances. They were knit together absolutely on one thing, both behind the counter, and before it. They had no difficulty in clearly making the difference between the "Arbour Bar" and a "Harbour Bar," a mistake often fallen into by the tongue of some strangers from some soft, more southerly part of the country. And if such a stranger tried a funny verbal skipping between "Arbour" and "Harbour," a pitying silence was all he got for his fun.

Miss Malcarn was interested, passionately interested, in one man in all the world, the porter at Thron Dock Station. There was a stationmaster much above him in pay and station, a widower too, "no encumbrances," either; an earnest worried man darting out on the platform, and back, into his office, always with his hands full of fluttering dockets, invoices, and waybills. But it was the porter who was all to her taste. It was a hopeless passion, he had a wife and a family of four. But he was the miracle of man to Miss Malcarn. He was stocky, deep-chested, broad-shouldered, with a head of bristling ginger and grey tufts, all standing every way, so that his peaked cap had to cling to whatever side it could. He had a tough, bristling moustache, and his voice could roll, bark or roar. He ever moved about his platform in whirls of energy, as though to the music of his own voice. He twisted milk cans to his will. There was a Palais de Danse up in Choughtown, where the porter had once appeared, unafraid. Those who had seen him wheel a milk can in the matter of his duty, if such a roaring trade as his could be called a duty, now saw him whirl a billowy fair one. At the dance's end he whirled her, gasping, to a form against the wall, fought his way to the buffet, brought her a cup of coffee, and a stick of chocolate biscuit, bowed to her stiffly from the hips and rolled himself out of the dance house.

Annie Malcarn loved the platform he walked on. He was the roaring monarch of his domain. She was only the silent one of hers.

Among the regulars, not so regular as the most regular, not in daily attendance, but once a week, Wednesday was the day, early closing in the outer fringe of Choughport, three elderly men always sat in the afternoon, in the bar of the "Arbour Hotel." In the fine months, as much in the sun as possible, in the cold months, close to the stove, two were grey, the third should have been, but being entirely bald, he wore an intelligent-looking wig of russet tint. A wit, the only professional wit ever functioning in that bar, had said he ought to change the tint with the changing year, spring buds and summer flowerings, not always sad autumn, or what about "winter snow to crown the year on the pate?" But the wit was a visitor only, washed down by the tide on the *Prairie Bird*, a journalist, a reporter, to report on life on the ocean's brim, and the proposed new dock on the Alberwide side in opposition to Thron first in the field, first in the mud, or first in the water, to give a "write up" in the *Choughport Telegraph*.

But personal remarks were taboo in that shining bar. That is why the two greys and the bay were called by the other regulars "the old salts." Well, they carried their names, they were pickled in the brine of all oceans—in imagination. As far as one could read another, in all that bar of regulars with their encrusted, moulded minds, they were the only ones with minds turned towards imagination's living gates, and perhaps they only turned them so once a week—on early closing day.

This is a sample of the beginning of one of their conversations. Said the first grey to the second grey, better call him the "rusty grey," there was that difference, "I'd sooner be here than on the West Coast this very evening." This would be the month of July, hot and stuffy. The west coast he talked of was the African coast. None of the three had ever been there, nor had they sons or even relations out there; that would have spoilt illusion. That would have soured romance with realism. These three friends had begun their building of hectic places, through one buying a magazine which made adventures under Palms and on hot ocean beaches its mainstay and its enticement. He lent his magazine to the others. Then from magazine to books and back again, they built a back-cloth of cut and come again, never say die, green waves slapping high, close-hauled, crack on all, what she can't carry she must drag, and sunny lands for all. In front "the short sharp bark of derringers" the upwards slash of the long knife, Hey for it, High for it, He for it still. But never above or below the surcingles of the temperate zones. What they loved was adventure under the sun, or the burning stars. Sometimes a "bit of calico" was saved from a crocodile's jaws or a worse fate, but seldom. It was man's world. The bay had a good atlas, but even he liked it best with plenty of scope "somewhere west of Mozambique" or "down south in the old 'fifteens" or "nosing around the Caribbean." There was a

telescope at the back of the bar and Miss Annie would hand
it out as if it was a loaded gun, and generally wrong way
forwarded. With it you could sweep the view to seaward.
Once the three old salts, they had the bar-room to themselves,
at the time, opened the window and steadied the telescope
and saw *Mark Anthony*, an ocean tug, coming back out of
storm, beaten to her meat by a Glasgow tug. She had gone
out down the Irish Sea and away for a broken-down grain
boat from the far aways. But Glasgow's ancient toon was
first. Now *Mark Anthony* was coming home miserable, nose
out of joint.

"Ah," number one Old Salt cried out above the wind which
was coming through the open window, "she looks to me as
if she'd had a pretty tough dusting out in the Western Ocean,
that's not child's play, they haven't got the guts for tug men.
What they want to do is to get up to windward of her and
let sweep down, buoy out the tow rope on the waves and
snoose her with it; I've seen it done a——" "A score of times"
he was going to say, when he remembered he'd never seen
anything done on the ocean deep, indeed neither he nor Rusty
Grey, nor the Bay, had ever been further away by salt water
than the Isle of Man, one summer with their families and
once, the three alone, keeping the deck all night, to the Port
of Dublin. Even on the dry they had journeyed a very little
way from home. The Bay, before he had got the wig, had
gone on holidays as far as Ilfracombe. He spoke of the visit
sometimes. After two or three glasses of rum, from the bottle
with the sailor on it, standing by the coiled rope, he would
say, "nice soft name that 'Ilkrafoam,' nice people, nice place,
Ilkrafoam."

The three friends did not talk much when there were many
others in the bar, they listened and were always adding some-
thing to the collected nautical material, which lined their
memories.

They were perfect friends, they never corrected each other
when a technical term was wrongly used; later on they took
an occasion to use it rightly themselves. In the pellucid atmos-
phere in which they met a jarring correction would have
fallen like a piece of faulty masonry in an edifice of fairyland.

And they never sang. Even under very much rum, the Bay
had never sung. Miss Malcarn liked the old salts, perhaps as

well as any of the regulars, partly because she only saw them once a week, and partly because they never looked as if they were going to sing.

This strong feeling against singing in her bar was curious, because she had once sung herself in a scene which could hardly have been more public, in the material sense.

It was winter and pantomime time. "What do you think of our Panto?" the citizens asked of one another, in Market Street, Choughtown. That year's Panto was "Cinderella" and Miss Malcarn knew the story. She had, as a child, a little twopenny picture-book with a shining lithograph picture, and a strong smell of the ink and the glossing. But the last two pages were gone, early, while she owned the book, and, though she had been told the end of the story, she wanted to see it for herself. She was interested in Cinderella, not that she thought herself anything of a Cinderella. She had her coach, her first-class carriage lined with blue, from almost the beginning. But she longed to see Cinderella and the six white ponies and her glory. The eight o'clock train would of course get to town too late, the only road was by the river and the *Prairie Bird*. She could, many times, had she wished it, have left earlier than the train at eight, but she was a stickler for time, and also she disliked the river for its salt tides and its ships.

All the change made was that Blue Jersey came on duty an hour earlier. It was quite a change though for the regular customers to have a man drawing their drinks and dashing them their sodas. Not that the regulars got out of hand, in any way, during Miss Malcarn's absence. They all waved to her as she went down the gravelly path to the little jetty, and after she was gone they were more than usually careful not to spill drink or pipe ash about the floor. Though her body went up the river on the *Prairie Bird* her soul ruled its domain, you'd say.

The *Prairie Bird* went up with the flood tide. The only other passenger was a greasy, fat, battered, travelling melodeon player. And so they sailed away up the river in the dark trough between the walls of warehouses, he, at intervals, pressed the melodeon, as it lay upon his knees, and it would give a crooning moan. Steamers and lighters were passing the ferry steamer continually. Miss Annie had got used to them, and was admiring the port and starboard light of the *Prairie Bird*, and she had got used to the looming passing steamers, when the loblolly boy captain, perhaps, through letting his spirit sink into quietude, as he heard the melodeon croon, careless, let the strong tide carry the *Prairie Bird* under the bows of a bustling steamer outward bound. A terrible hobgoblin voice from above roared. Jamesey came up out of his engines, too enraged to spit, the loblolly boy came to life, a part of his wheel's life, and *Prairie Bird* snorted away to the nor'ard. So swiftly did she answer her helm that she threw her engineer's thin back against an iron rail. He went down into his engine room. The Travelling Music, who had been sitting by the stern, pressed his melodeon's side. The danger was passed.

But Annie Malcarn was deeply moved, the momentary nearness of death in black hated water, the dark blue sky above, with its starry rivers, the warehouses on either hand, and the low cry of the melodeon, all affected her and washed her under a wave of emotion, which caught her in its clasp so suddenly, that her whole length rang with a desire to express from herself the power of the moment. She lifted her head, stood up, grasped the rail that protected the entrance to the engine room, and sang, clear and bell-like, up, up, up, hoping to clear the shadows of the warehouses, and reach the under arching of the sky. She sang the only verses she knew perfectly, she sang, "There is a Green Hill Far Away." The captain drooped by his wheel, Jamesey stood by his engine, with a new piece of waste running slowly through his hands, and the wandering melodeon player, in his seat nearest to the waters, smiled sadly, and waited his time to bring his poor cottage door music to lift to the song its cry of "With you" "With you" "With you."

Miss Malcarn had learnt to sing the hymn in her days of Sunday School going. She had never heard it sung in a church, indeed of late years she had attended church very seldom. The song finished, the singer sat down again with her hands in her lap. A quarter of an hour later she was stepping on to the quay almost in the centre of Choughport, and only a few minutes walk from the Choughport "Globe." She thoroughly enjoyed every moment of "Cinderella." She heard the orchestra tune up, and she was the last spectator to leave the theatre, walking just ahead of the attendant, who was carrying the tide's leavings—a black kid glove with white stitching, a brooch of diamond effect, and a chocolate box with a faint rattle in it, which might be a chocolate. Presently she would make certain, and if it was a chocolate in the box it would be rattled in front of the theatre watch-dog, a yellow and white, bushy-haired terrier, who hated the rattling fussing of mice, but pounced on a chocolate box with a rattle inside, worked the lid off with his clever nose, and crunched the chocolate with a careless rush, which never changed to a nursing of a luxury, a making of it last, tasting before crunching.

When Miss Malcarn got home to her lodgings she was absolutely satisfied with the ending of Cinderella's story.

As Oliver James Gaw, now awake, on that November evening, looked about him from the deck of the *Prairie Bird*, he saw the last three passengers left were of about an age, one grey-headed, one a sandy grey, and one with a red-coloured wig. He was the one who read the newspaper. Gaw was at once in a sweat of nervousness, these three men must be bound for Alberwide. Ah, but perhaps they might be going to the north bank. Gaw always thought of the sides of the river as north and south, as if it ran straight from east to west, whereas it turned almost round about on the gully of its bed. To think correctly he should have thought of left bank, Alberwide, and right bank, Throndock, and the "Arbour Hotel." "That's it, these three old beaux must, they must be bound for the 'Arbour Hotel.'" The hotel had its own jetty, shaky, but holding its own against the tides. And the *Prairie Bird*'s captain was authorised to land passengers there at their own risk. Gaw didn't care where the three went as long as they kept away from Alberwide for five minutes. He had a die to cast, a coin to toss, a chance to take, win or lose, if this fails what next? No next, this wins. Think only of victory, Napoleon, in his little boots, never thought of anything else but victory, on his going days. Here I am, the landing place of Alberwide. If they attempt to land I'll throw them from me into the mucky waters.

But the three made no move, they did not even mention to the loblolly boy captain that they were going further, evidently they were regular known passengers. They were the Three Salts bound for the "Arbour Bar."

Gaw sprang to the landing stage, hurried up the steps, and strode along the face of Quay Street, searching for No. 14. That must be it, where a motor stands by the kerb.

As there was no one standing between him and the door, Gaw thought he might safely slow down and pull himself together. The moments which made up the prologue to the drama in which he expected to fill the leading part, on the stage of Webster's office, flitted through his mind.

In Liverpool he had picked up from an office hall, where it had fallen from the letter-box, the advertisement in red on a yellow ground of the *Scrutineer*'s coming voyage under the sunny skies. He dropped it on the floor, after a glance, and then went out into the street, at that moment a newsboy rushing by stopped, thinking Gaw signalled for a paper, so he bought one, did not look at the news, but automatically turned to "Situations Vacant."

There he read that a Geographical and Historical Lecturer was required immediately for an Instruction Voyage, Salary ample, all found, apply to Jos. Webster, 14, Quay Street, Alberwide.

He became suffused with excitement, turned quickly on his track, jumped back into the hall, snatched the yellow advertisement from the floor and read it carefully through by the uneasy light of the dying day, which came into that hall. He read the advertisement to the end, apply to Jos. Webster, 14, Quay Street, Alberwide.

Into the street, so pressed for time that he did not stop to pull out his watch, up the street he knew there was a watchmaker's perfect clock, timed to Greenwich. This clock was on his road for Lime Street. At three-thirty there was a train away which would give him a connection for Chough-port. He knew the time well, an old engagement never altered. As he ran by the clock he said, "seven minutes to do it in." He had once done it from that very watchmaker's window in five—some years ago. "Never mind, pick up your feet, the good God will put them down again, it's picking them up that does it, swing them low, crouch to it. Slide the traffic at an angle, don't try and zig-zag it, whish, that was near, these motorists don't care, like the sailors in the songs. But this is fate, that yellow bill, the paper just out, that advertisement never came out before, I'd never have missed it. Did it in five, oh glory, I had a return ticket then, now I've got to get a ticket; oh, mangy legs, do your work, come on, come on, I got to be first in the field this time, old Jos. Webster's my bird. This is written, the bill, the paper, the train, all in a chain, my legs chained. Ironed, oh iron, iron, iron, iron, irony. Oh, loose its chain, cometh up like a flower in the midst of life we are in death, oh, stick it, stick it, stick it, old son of the roads, oh God, no more clocks, running blind, second wind, second leg, turn again Whittington, Whit, Whit, Whit, ing, Ton. Oh, come on. If some mug cried 'stop thief' now that'd start a hunt, like a spur to me, if I had an electric prodder now I'd get another ounce or two out of me, come on Chicago or bust, stand clear of the gates, nothing can live with me, nothing can. That boy gave me space, John Gilpin, he had a horse, if I had a horse today I'd jump ahead of him, and let him catch who can. There she is dead ahead, Lime, Lime, Lime, Lime Street. The clock, the fuzzy clock, four minutes and a half I done it. Two and a half minutes to go, steadily now, the fare, the ticket observe, the ticket clerk, easy job, but no palm trees in the wind's eye, tired-looking ticket puncturer. My old fist is shaking the ticket up and down, his business is to hold the ticket to let his puncher bite it. Passengers don't punch their own tickets. Hope the carriage'll be nice and warm, if I get one to myself, I may if I'm lucky, I'll walk up and down it, cool down, must mind if there's any funny opening window business, to keep out of the draught, don't want to start influenza or some shakings. I'm lathered right down into my boots."

He did not get a carriage all to himself, but one in which there was only one other passenger, a man of the tramping tradesman type. He had beside him on the seat a shredded suitcase, which might have held the needles, threads, buttons and scissors of a tailor, the razor, soap brush and scissors of a barber, and the small saw, large hammer, bits of genuine copper wire, paint brush, and pencil stump, of the general handy, general contractor. He did not look the kind of traveller who would want a lot of fussy business about opening windows. He was a man of sense, he had other plans. He noticed Gaw's jacket open. He saw the steamy lather he was in. He signed to him to button up his jacket, even with closed windows that railway carriage was a chilly place, the heat was only coming slowly on. The tramp tradesman pointed to Gaw's newspaper, which he still held in his hand, told him to fold it, and shove it down between his waistcoat and his shirt. "The bit extra does it, this isn't the right time of year to get a chill, boss."

Gaw did everything he was told, and presently he rose up and paced the carriage centre, and stamped and took care of himself. "That's the way," the tramp tradesman said, "you and I, sir, are about of an age to take a bit of care, we want to always have a bit left up our sleeves. Some of these young jokers can hop it out twice running. But, without offence, I'd say that you and I have got to watch out when the hinges creak, a drop of oil, next time running sweet and easy, that's the way it's done, I talk, but tomorrow might be my Waterloo."

At the Junction Gaw got out and the tramp tradesman said, "Plenty good luck, I can't say fairer than that."

"And the same to you."

Gaw gave him the merry wave of the hand, and the tramp tradesman went on further into the land, where at some wayside station he would start once again some campaign of tussling for money in villages and hamlets, where a conservative air and a sententious voice, another voice from that which he used when helping Gaw with his roadster's advice, must win him his way.

At the Junction, cheer of cheers, the Refreshment Room still existed, for Gaw was beginning to feel very wan and cold. Ten minutes wait for the train for Choughport. Hot coffee, one small rum in it, cheer of cheers, glow of glows. But Gaw took no chances. Five minutes before the train started for Choughport he was in a carriage, this time all to himself, and smoking warm and stuffy, and full of other men's tobacco left swimming in the air.

As soon as the train started out came the red and yellow bill. He read it three times, then folded it carefully and put it in that secret pocket. After that he took the crushed newspaper from his chest and cut, with his sharp penknife, the advertisement for the Geographical and Historical Lecturer, and put that inside the small pocket of a little black notebook which he carried in his hip-pocket. It was one of those little notebooks which cost very few pence, and have, sheathed at their side, pencils with lead of a kind only capable of making the most ghostly marks.

Oliver James Gaw had made no particular study since he left school of either history or geography. But that was beside the point at the moment. The matter was this, Jos Webster was an old schoolfellow of his, a year or two younger, never seen since school days, but then a looker-up to Gaw, as to a superior column carrying a brain far above his own. Gaw knew that during the years he had himself grown down into himself, and was even a little meagre for his years, in courage. But then time may not have given Webster any advantage. Gaw argued that, Secretary to a Sunny Sea prospect which had to advertise in an evening paper for a Lecturer in Geography and History, wasn't likely to be a very magnificent person, and he, with the coffee and the rum, and also having taken half a minute off the station race, felt he had a fighting chance of putting Jos Webster where he wanted him. When he got out of the station at Choughport he looked well at the handful of passengers who came away with him, and none looked in the least like men after the Lectureship of the Seas. Nevertheless he lost no time in hurrying to the ferry landing-place, and was happy to be the only one who boarded the *Prairie Bird* at that place. He felt almost certain then that no one could have got ahead of him. The field was before him. He was on a tip-toe of excitement, and that's why he allowed himself to lose himself a moment in sleep to silence his nerves, to steady himself for the tussle ahead. Old schoolboys never meet on level terms, one or other must give away weight.

On the door of Number 14, when he slowly reached it, Gaw read: JOS. WEBSTER, AUCTIONEER. The door was an outer door, ajar. Gaw pushed it in and on his right, in a small room with an open door, and the cheerful pink smile of a portable electric heater, stood a large table, on the right side of which was a pile of envelopes and a yellow stack of the "Good-bye Fog, Welcome Sunny Skies" advertisement. A rough spreading of addressed and stamped envelopes occupied the middle of the table. On the left was a blotting pad, a small basin with a sponge in it, and a metal machine from whose mouth had been drawn a long green ribbon of halfpenny stamps.

Open, face downwards in the middle of the blotting pad, with a fountain pen thrown carelessly beside it, lay a bright paper-covered book, and even though it was upside down to him Gaw was able to read the title *Sunflower Sam of Shanandoa.* Gaw was glad the book was still circulating. Even if he had not been able to read the title he knew the bright picture that the cover made.

At the moment the book's latest reader was sitting sideways in his great office chair, in a brown study, gazing unseeing out of the dusty window, and musing on Sam and those days that are no more. It was the office boy of the house of Webster who sat so. With a turn of his glance, but without a shade of impertinence he took in the fact that business had begun again, and that the figure in the not too grand clothes, was taking a card from the pocket in his little black notebook, and holding it out, "If Mr. Webster is in his office give him that. I'll wait."

The office boy threw himself—he was fair, very young, wide-faced, and heavily built—into a stride such as Sunflower Sam himself might have used, went into the hall, climbed up the stairs to Jos Webster's private office. Presently he returned. As his feet came down the stairs Gaw could hear in the room above dragging of furniture from this side to that.

"Mr. Webster will see you at once. Floor above. Oh Kay."

"Oh Kay nothing," Gaw muttered to himself as he set his teeth, and treading firmly on every creaking step of the stairs went up. "No Oh Kay funny business with me, no old school-fellow-well-met, if the job's not fixed I'll have it, or I'll beat him up."

As soon as Gaw's feet reached the narrow landing, a door opened, and in the doorway, he saw standing, with his back to the light, the same Jos Webster of the school days: except that he was in every way more rotund, there was no difference. When Gaw followed him into the room, and the two stood looking into each other's faces, of course the years came down on Jos, but they stopped, at a point, perhaps twenty years, after he left school. He simply looked a very fullgrown up Jos of the school-room and the muddy football field. He was of course now dressed in clothes as unlike a grubby schoolboy's as imagination could build. He wore a festival costume of various shades from banana through cinnamon up to a rich

Burgundian handkerchief edging, with, in his lapel, a car-
nation one shade below.

He said, "You don't look more than forty, not a day. I'm
a lot more than that myself, of course we both are, well, there
it is, it's no use, the years keep coming along, what with one
thing and another. Here, sit down, sit down, squatty vous."

Gaw said, "I see you're busy, but I won't keep you long,"
and he looked over at a large table with a large ledger propped
up against two very worn-looking volumes, one an earlier
volume of the *Illustrated London News*, the other, which at first
Gaw thought was a family Bible, was Volume VII of an
Encyclopaedia of an Early Victorian date.

Mr. Webster motioned Gaw to a deep green leather arm-
chair, now holding a really commanding position in the centre
of the floor, facing a very large, heaped fire. The room reached
right across the house from north to south, it was thirty-five
feet long and had been the drawing-room, sixty years ago, of
a ship owner, a small ship owner, he only owned two ships,
but they carried no insurance, and he and his family, banking
on their luck, or he banking on his luck, and his family
landing on him, they slept sound and lived in comfort.

Jos sat down on his office chair and, dropping one white
hand on the ledger in front of him, and placing the other
under his chin, where he could feel how satinly he had shaved
that morning, gazed at Gaw with the bright allure of friend-
ship.

Gaw sank into the cosy green chair, found himself falling
too far back into its warm recess, heaved himself forward,
then stood up, and reaching down into his hip-pocket, pulled
out the little black notebook case, fingered out the advertise-
ment for the Lecturer, walked over to Jos, and put the scrap
of newspaper on the ledger face in front of him, with his two
strong thumbs holding it down, and said, "I'm after that
position."

Jos allowed his bright eyes to close slightly and let little
wrinkles round their edges play their little dancing game a
moment, then he said, "You want it, do you?"

Gaw said, "Yes, Jos, and I'm going to have it."

"Why, of course you can have it, old Gee Gaw. It's only
twelve pounds a month, you know. Of course there's no

outings for you, grub and all that. Let's fix it now. I write you a letter, Gaw, you write me a letter accepting."

"When does the work begin?"

"Right now, she's sailing before the month's out. I'd ante-date it if I could but the advertisement's only just out now, now we'll start right."

He opened a drawer and took out some paper with not only a business heading, a business border like an ornamental handkerchief, but lithographies in bright colours, palms and blue seas as bright as the cover of *Sunflower Sam*. Then, reaching over to the far side of the table, where a fountain pen stood upright to hand in a jade holder, wrote, reading out as he did so, "November eleventh — Dear Doctor? Professor? Got any title? No, well:

> " 'Dear Mr. Gaw, I am delighted to think that you feel you can get away for our "Good-bye Fog Cruise," and will help us with your valued services, the salary we offer is twelve pounds per month from home to home, and of course all found. I will be very glad to get an early reply from you, accepting our offer. I am, yours truly, Jos Webster.' "

The letter finished he handed it to Gaw who folded it and put it in the breast-pocket of his jacket. He rooted about in the drawer until he found some plain paper, got up and vacated his chair in favour of Gaw, to whom he dictated, "Now you write as following — Hold on, what's your address? All right, I know, I've got it on your card. Glass Barrel Corner, is it? No, no; better put 'Adelphi Hotel,' write 'Adelphi Hotel,' put the date November eleventh, no, date it tomorrow, November twelfth. 'Adelphi Hotel,' I don't know, doesn't look so good not writing on the hotel notepaper. No, looks all the better, professors don't swank, don't have to, that reminds me, I've got to put your address at the bottom of my letter to you, gimme."

Gaw gave him back the letter and he put on the address and returned it to Gaw.

> " 'Dear Sir, Yours of yesterday received, with offer, which I have pleasure in accepting. Yours faithfully, Oliver James Gaw, Lecturer.'

"Better put my name in the left-hand lower corner, 'Jos Webster, Shipping Agent, fourteen Quay Street, Alberwide.' Now I'll give you a month's pay in advance. It's the rule for the post. Just a moment, I'll pop down below and get the cash out of the safe."

Quickly he jumped it down the stairs, in four swift skips, with his hand on the banisters. In the office boy's room he quickly wrote a cheque for twelve pounds, pushed it into the boy's hand, and said, "Up the street now and tell Willy the Stiff to give you eleven in Treasuries and a pound in silver, quick now, see what you can do, you and the mustang."

The boy darted into the hall and from under the stairs dragged out a bicycle, a grim-looking weed with ancient cushion tyres. To spring from the doorstep into the saddle, and to clatter up the street on to the pavement flags on to the right was "the work," as the rider would have said "of a moment." And when galloping, such might any stretching imagination describe that cycle's action, into the bar of "The Old Cape," without dismounting, Willie Brown, "Bill Brown" to himself, the galloping office boy brought up all standing at the bar's edge, he flipped the cheque across the wood into the breast of "Willy the Stiff," a stout, dark man with wide brown eyes, and a magnificent moustache, its splendour enhanced by a clever use of what were really whiskers, to suggest that the ends of the moustache were hanging below the level of the chin. In a husky voice Bill Brown gave his order, "Eleven paper hangings and a quid in the white stuff, and gee, Stiff, move quick, or—" here he spoke in a much lower voice, almost to himself— "I'll let you have the contents of this." And with a whimsical look on his good round face, he hauled a repeating, pink cap pistol from his hip-pocket, pointed it at the floor and pulled the trigger. It failed to go off, a little adjusting had to be made, and then the pistol spat half a dozen vicious spits at the floor. By then the change was on the bar top. Bill Brown had it carefully counted into his palm, pushed it all, coins and paper, into his breast-pocket, gave a kick at the front of the bar, rode into the dark afterpart of the room, turned, rode out of the door with a muttered, "Keep a good look out," to Willy the Stiff, and hurled himself and his steed, back to Number 14 where Jos Webster was watching him.

The time occupied was within four minutes. Willy the Stiff murmured to himself, "Snappy" and turned again to his reading of "The Port of Liverpool Official Sailing List and Shipping Guide."

As Gaw sat in Jos's chair in the long room above, he could not help seeing, from the dates on the page open in front of him, that the ledger was an old one, long out of date and use. He thought to himself, "perhaps the whole thing's humbug; a bluff, a card house. Perhaps my coming so quickly has called the bluff, the bluff caller who didn't wish to find a bluff. Bluff King Hal. Bluff King Jos. Perhaps presently I will hear, the old sound of the pistol shot, the old fall of a body below, a scream and the game is up. A scribbled note, saying, 'I cannot face it, tell my wife and family, ask them to forgive, good-bye all.' " He looked on the floor, there was a scrap of paper with writing on it, not very far under the table, Gaw hooked it towards him with his foot and saw it was without tragic appearance, a small flimsy receipted bill from an outfitter in Choughport. Newlands, he remembered the name. Newlands sold a great variety of things. He put on his glasses, and crouching towards the bill on the floor, was able to read the single item "To one Yacht Cap, 15s. 6d."

"That's flight. The whole thing's gone queer, he's got his start. I sit here. I wait three-quarters of an hour, then I go below to ask Sunflower Sam what about it, he's gone, taken his reading with him. The door's open. I look out, see two sour-looking men coming along this side of the street, and another on the river side, all coming towards the door, and each of them has his right hand stuffed down in his topcoat pocket. I go upstairs and sit in his chair, with my face made out ready to say, 'What can I do for you gentlemen?' when they all jump into the room and cover me with their revolvers. I must remember to up my hands at once. After that the dungeon, a lot of talkee talkee in a mouldy-looking office, smelling of handcuffs, and then chucked out into wind and the rain, defeated." Just then there was a rush up the stairs of a pair of feet, the door opened, and in came Jos with the twelve pounds in his hand, which Gaw carefully pocketed, but with a cheerful air. The paper, rolled up, went into one trousers pocket, the silver dropped in the other.

Jos sat down in his office chair; Gaw sprang from it to the

room centre when he first caught the sound of the rushing feet coming up the stairs, and wrote a receipt on a half-sheet of paper which Gaw signed, producing the stamp from the pocket in the little black pocket-book.

"Now," said Jos, "sit down, boy."

"Yes," said Gaw, "but I don't understand how it comes you are ready to take me on like this, what do you know about me? I may have been leading a criminal life since you saw me last. I may be a ticket-of-leave man. I may be a dipsomaniac, anyway how do you know that I know any more geography and history of any place than when I left school?"

Jos raised his hand, "Crave silence for the great Employer of Labour. I would be sorry to think you were a criminal, or a drunkard, for your own sake, and because, from the firm way you walked up our palatial stairs, I would be prepared to bet, that you were neither the one nor the other, but the same old honest, straightforward, kind old, don't-let-you-down old Oliver James Gaw. As to history and geography, the particular kind you'll have to discourse on you can make it up at the public library, and bring a couple of two-bob books afloat with you. Your lecturing won't begin until the boat calls on some old Palmy Island with a ruined calabooza, be strong on the Spanish, Spanish Main, all that. But there's another side to the question, if the worst came to the worst, my bread's got butter on both sides. The captain, well he's a protégé of my father-in-law, he thinks he's Captain Kidd-Morgan-Kettle. He's about five-foot-two in my estimation. In his own he's a skyscraper. If you'd believe him, he's cracked more skulls with belaying pins than any skipper alive today, he's got a charmed life, bullets hop off him, bowie knives slide off him. But he's dumb, strong, silent, only barks short sharp ones. We've got a splendid mate, I chose him, about seven feet high and five feet across the chest. Of course, if Captain Lovell, that's his name, he can't help it, he says, 'but the end rhymes with hell,' got jumping around outside the laws of all nations, the mate could just smother him, and the rest of the officers'd see he got fair play. But little Lovell would never bring it to that, and anything short of that, Gaw, especially if you're a criminal dipsomaniac, plus your general knowledge, which I know you always possessed, and your gift of speech, why, you'd have him sleeping on the Dolphin striker, if the old *Scrutineer's* got such a thing, but you know what I mean, for peace and quiet. Well, I might as well make everything quite clear and then we'll understand each other. Here, cigarette, or pipe?—cigarette, see the monogram, the old man, princely style, didn't cost much, between you and me the monogram's better than the tobacco. You don't know I married a rich wife, well, she's the only daughter, only child, of a rich man. She was Adelaide Martin, and her father's Half-a-Quid Martin."

"Do you mean Alfred Quintan Martin, the music hall proprietor?"

"That's it, Half-a-Quid Martin, always on public occasions makes a speech about the first, and only theatrical engagement he ever had, 'played a week in a play called "Sarah's Young Man," and they gave me ten shillings and closed the account.' Music halls, theatres and public houses, the old man got them on strings, like beads. The old man thinks it the funniest thing ever was, that he, the great palatial music hall proprietor, should have been thought only worth ten bob one time. The old man don't see there's lots of people knocking around now, who, with ten shillings all good, on a Saturday night in their pocket, would walk him off the pavement outside of his own house. The old man's got no imagination, or if he ever had, it's gone, and yet he's got a good heart, good heart, no imagination, funny thing, isn't it. But I forgot, most important, excuse me, telephone," and Jos walked to the southerly end of the room, where a telephone stood on a gipsy table, sharing it with a brass Benares bucket, from which jutted up a tall thin palm. As Jos took up the telephone receiver, he frisked the palm's feather end with his left hand, "Under the palm local colour." He called up the office of the evening paper in which the Lecturer advertisement appeared, and Gaw heard him give instructions to countermand further advertisements for applicants, and to substitute an announcement that the position had been filled. Coming back to his chair, Jos said, "Just in time, that'll stem the rush a bit, another thing that delights me about you getting the job, shows you I'm thinking of myself all the time, you can lend me a hand. You might come down here tomorrow. It's not your job you know, but if you can spare the time, just run down about early afternoon, and help me chase them off.''

Gaw said, of course he was delighted to do anything.

"That reminds me, make out a list of all your expenses, the firm'll pay that, and you'll want a rig-out for the tropics, anything you're short of, light dinner-jacket, yachting cap, pair of horn-rimmed specs, just bring the bills to me. I can let you have a yachting cap, if it'll fit, bran new, but that's another story. Well, now, the father-in-law met this Captain Lovell in some sea-port town, I believe it was in the Tower at Blackpool, if you ask me, and Lovell told the governor that there was a great scheme with money in it, he had his eye on a steamship—the *Scrutineer*, lovely ship! the Spanish Main! new bits, not worked over by the regular runs. Buried cities not yet dug up. For a strong silent man he talked a good deal. When he heard who he was talking to he was overcome, you bet he was, thought he was just talking his mind to a worker like himself, didn't know, from Adam, that he was talking to the great, enterprising capitalist, Quintan Martin. Well, well, well, wonders will never cease. Never thought of the old man, photos sticking up of him all over everything. The old boy was greatly taken with the Captain and his voyage, chartered the ship, never asked me till it was all done. A surprise for me and my wife—that was the idea, I dare say it was. He's got no imagination that man, that's why he does these things. They're a substitute. He'd got the charter arranged so that he could extend it right on and on, until the sea dries up, if so desired. Well, the old man puts down money, but he must see accounts for everything; he knows the price of everything—going down every item, so I had to be given change, to carry out the old man's ideas. He thinks he plans revues and pantomimes; he thinks he's a planner. But what he wanted was all of us to go, my wife and myself and himself, sitting at the top of the table on the Captain's right, and the passengers were to be sweet girl graduates, and a few old professors and their ladies, and they'd all sing shanties every night, and no one would be able to down the old man, and they'd have fancy dress balls every week. That'd give the old man a chance to dress up. He's got a tartan dress, with red boots, specially made, fattest tartan I ever saw. The idea of having no time limit on the whole business was, that every passenger would be so delighted, that they'd just keep on extending the time. Of course the governor'd have to come home, every now and then, for a few days to keep everything on this side up to the knocker. For those who wanted something to write home he thought of you, well, of your host. A lecturer to keep the passengers thinking they weren't wasting their time. That man's got no imagination; he can't imagine anyone tiring of a sea voyage, anyway with him on board. It's want of imagination makes him constantly be having little operations on his inside, little snippets taken off," and Jos with the first and second fingers of his right hand, gave an imitation of a pair of scissors. "And now only two days ago he had the car round and had himself run down to the nursing home, more snipping, and of course he won't be fit to travel for a long time and, of course, Adelaide and myself will have to stay and see that the old tartar's all right when he comes out."

"I see," said Gaw. "Have you a big passenger list?"

"Not so very big—only about twenty so far, but they're coming in in dribs and drabs. A shipping agent in town books them, and several others scattered about the other towns, Liverpool, Manchester and the smaller places. I sit in the office up in town in the mornings, and give them any encouragement I can. You'll be able to give me a bit of help there in the mornings when you can spare the time. I've got my yachting cap there, I won't need it at once on account of staying to watch over my father-in-law; and later when we do start I can get another. It'll be a good thing for you to have around with you when interesting the prospective tourists. It gives people confidence, and I really believe it keeps people from being so sea-sick at first, if they've got used to looking at maritime fixings in good time, instead of having the whole ship tumbled on top of them all at once. If I have my way, no one'll see Captain Lovell until they are well away from land. One look at him, and some of them'd want the money back, and go back home ashore in the pilot's boat. Well, just wait till you see him. I come down here every afternoon to see about stores and all that."

"Where's the ship?"

"Oh, she's lying in the dock on the other side of the river. I've got a motor launch, I soon nip across. Some of the correspondence is done here. You saw Brown down below being busy sending off circulars. Now it's time to close down for today." He put his foot on an electric bell push under his table, and continuous buzzing went on in imitation of a factory closing whistle.

William Brown could be heard dragging the mustang to the hall door.

"Now I'll run you up to town in my car, and leave you anywhere."

And soon the two schoolfellows were making a fumbling course along a very bad road at the back of warehouses, and with a desolate swampy land lying on their right. After a little they turned towards the river, with a better surface, and between high grey buildings darted up to the town, across a bridge, and into the open space in front of the Town Hall, where Gaw got out. He said he'd put up at what used to be called White's "White Heather," "if it's still there. Till tomorrow afternoon then."

As Gaw turned away, he thought he walked on air, and was full of money. A little later while Gaw, in the coffee room of White's "White Heather," was finishing off a couple of grilled chops, well done, with chip potatoes, he got a telephone call. The box was in the hall, between the ornamental pots with ferns in them, raised in tiers on a wooden stand, and the mahogany and leather long seat where the knights of the road sat in summer and criticised many years ago now the calves of the feminine legs, which went twinkling by, beyond the proscenium of the hall door.

Gaw pulled the door of the telephone box to behind him, and heard the only, as yet, half-familiar voice of Jos, and the voice said, "Just been talking to the old man; they aren't going to operate for a few days. The old man's full of beans, but—this is good news—he called me up on purpose to say he'd been thinking and he'd come to the conclusion that you couldn't get a good lecturer for less than twenty a month. So I'll owe you eight pounds—I'll give it you tomorrow, and I'll re-write our letter to you, and send it up to you by hand in the morning, and I'll send you up your letter of acceptance. Then you copy it, date it day after tomorrow, and send it back to me at the office in town. Number four, Market Street, but it's on our note heading. My messenger'll take your letter, you'll want the morning to yourself. But I say, tomorrow early in the afternoon, down at Alberwide, you'll be there, won't you?"

"I'll be there—two o'clock, eh?"

"Two o'clock, fine. I'll have Willie Brown put a notice in the window and do his best. Glad for you this bit better stuff."

"Many thanks."

"Good-bye—goodnight."

"Good night."

The evening meal over, Gaw thought to stroll about his ancient town, when he remembered his day was not finished. There used to be a quarter past seven train, search a time-table, ah, still she goes, catch it easy. Back to the Junction, change again, back to Liverpool, a taxi, no less, to the lodgings, hurried throwing of clothes (a dictionary, a *Sporting Clarion Annual*, shaving machinery), into a couple of suitcases; an inspection of an overcoat, a rejection of it, thrown on the floor, leave it for the sweeper, a running downstairs to the time of:

> We're a-selling up the Happy Home
> We're a-popping up the few old sticks.

Then he paid his landlady, in the parlour off the hall. She was a plump, flat-faced, cheerful, middle-aged woman, with light straw hair, and looked pleasedly surprised whatever her lodgers did. The taxi, no less, engine still running; back to Lime Street, back to the Junction, back to Choughport. Then all settled, all moorings cut, Gaw strolled round the well-remembered corners and through the streets of the old town. In Market Street, where in his youth the noises at night were the rumbling of drays late about their work, and an occasional growler and a still rarer hansom cab, now the noises were the wails and shrieks of motor horns, and the back-firing of motor bicycles which, with their side-cars, were constantly coming and going. The people who used them—young men and young women—all seemed to scream louder than in his days. The noise underfoot was banished away; rubber tyres and rubber heels he thought musingly. But more noise above ground. He liked walking up and down the street treading his way through groups, and thinking, with a retrospective fear of the youth that he was, when he last lived in Chough-port, and he remembered some of the fanciful hopes he then encouraged. He sheltered in an archway from the steady air which was blowing up from the bridge and the river, to light his night-cap pipe. He was a slow filler and packer down of a pipe, and a slow, dry, smoker. In his jerky spasmodic, grown-man existence of hopes, which whistled in his ear, and left no memory behind—unrecallable whistles—he never hoped the same things twice. He was disillusioned on that hope. He paced the street twice again from end to end, then up once more and then he met the people coming from the cinema houses and from the theatre. The cinema people, he noted lazily, were all chatting, not about what they had seen but about themselves. The audience from the theatre were not speaking at all. But the motor horns and the back-firing soon screeched down every other sound, and it was the cinema people who climbed into the side-cars and crowded the motors even as far back as the dickey on some dust-laden old cus-tomers, from far down some country road. The theatre people soon thinned away, moving round dark corners into the town's further heart. Very few were carried away in motors or side-cars. Two tall men from the theatre (he was certain of that, because he saw they had the programmes in their hands), parted close to him, as he stood a moment watching the end of a November day's activities. One got into a heavy, open motor and the other, pushing his programme into his pocket, took out a latch-key and opened a door, a yellow and Indian red-grained door, beside an ironmonger's shop, sighed, and let himself in.

An old woman came out of a side street hoping for treasures (when the coast was clear) from some corporation bucket on sentry go at a kerb's edge. Two sailors, slightly humorous with liquor but cautious, were bargaining with a stolid taxi man to give them a passage to Thron Dock. The night was on, and Gaw turned towards his hotel. As he neared it, a daughter of the night, no longer young, and moving with a kind of tottering run towards Market Street, greeted him with "Good night, smileo." He returned to knock the ashes out of his pipe against the pillar of the door of the "White Heather," and put the pipe in his pocket. She turned her face over her shoulder towards him, and saw his face as he turned into the hotel. She made an unpleasant mouth at his back—and continued to totter up the narrow street with an imitation tipsyness of gait, which would not deceive either those in authority or those without any.

In the morning, as Gaw shaved by his window, he was glad to have the sun shining on the white cover of the dressing-table and presently on his face. There was no view, at first he thought from the window, as a few feet away was a grey stone wall with lichen and tufts of bright green grass. No view? Why a most comfortable, enclosed, and happy view for a man with money in his pocket. And two sparrows on a gutter, just arrived at that moment, to add cheering life to the scene. Just then one of them got something very good out of the side of a piece of lichen.

After breakfast—bacon sizzling (the kitchen not far from the coffee room), eggs strawed—better fried than boiled anyway. Boiled eggs for breakfast always made Gaw think of Jane Austen; he never stopped to know why. Buttered toast— not stiff *rigor mortis* toast—try and butter it with life yourself— but the real thing, dripping. Ask the waiter to get today's paper, *Daily Telegraph*. No local newspaper today, tomorrow; one tomorrow, he'd be an ocean citizen.

Gaw only skated over the crests of the paper's news. And "here it comes"—the message from Jos. Gaw opened it by the little writing table in the coffee room, first fishing out with delight (which proved the fairy story was still holding the board), eight new one-pound Treasury notes. And thoughtful Jos had sent a sheet of plain paper and a copy, from memory, of Gaw's original letter of acceptance. Evidently Jos preferred the look of the "Adelphi" to White's "White Heather." "Ah," mumbled Gaw to himself, as he wrote the new letter of accept-

ance, "a prophet in his own country." He pocketed the new letter, with the offer and its border of promise under the palms, put his acceptance in an envelope, went out to the hall, and gave it with a shilling to the messenger, an old soldier—sailor-tinker-tailor-looking customer, with a grey knitted muffler, knitted for him by his granddaughter aged ten, who loved him because he was neither soldier-sailor-tinker or tailor, but just an old retired quay-wall wiseacre. On his way back to the coffee room for a final lingering chaser of hot tea (in the "White Heather" coffee room they gave the guest a little battered, plated kettle with a spirit lamp). He met the waiter, and speaking from his heart to the tip of his tongue, said, "You tell Mr. White I find his place as good as the best and better—you tell him that."

"I will. I daresay," the waiter said, "he'd be glad to hear it; he's been in the cold ground a long while now. We've got a lady manageress, she does her best. The place belongs to the Ogdens, the drapers up in Market Street, that's why we've got so many 'fall-de-da-lalls' in the drawing-room. Ever seen the drawing-room? You ought to, don't miss it." And Gaw looked into the waiter's face and smiled, as man to man. He had only glimpsed the waiter either over his shoulder or for a moment in the passage, and he had thought him a young man. He now saw he was old and grained. Only a certain flat-footed, slowly waltzing way of swinging about his work and a resolute turn of freckled neck, had suggested the prime of life.

The whole fore-part of the day was taken up with shopping at Newlands, the outfitters; everything was in a state that was once called "ready made" now called "ready for service." Some things were called "a kit"—no, no, not a dinner "kit." But it amounted to that—the studs, the ties, the shirts. But a "kit" suggests one only of each part of the complete costume. A "kit," Gaw thought, must all be about the person at one time. He began, but gave it up, a conversation on the matter with the head of the department, who was then looking after him, and nursing him through this easy form of shopping, where all Gaw had to do was to see that he did not run the "Good-bye Fog Cruise" into too heavy preliminary expenses. The head of the department was a dry personage who feared fanciful conversation during a business interview.

He had once let himself go in conversation with a prospect, and then found he'd let the prospect go, his memory richer by two or three merry remarks and some clear thought too, but without having purchased so much as a shoe lace. Once the head had gone to a town not far away and found himself stranded there, and he'd jumped into a debate in a public forum there, and had poured away all the speech he'd pent up in business hours behind his vocal chords; anyway, he spoke entirely from the throat, *pro bono publico*, he knew there was no one in that room to whom, just then, he could sell anything.

After a time people said "bolshie" and went away. And he went on. He rang out a sentence and when he thought it was time for a verb, he slung a verb into it, and on he rolled, and more people went away. At last only one man knew what that department's head was saying, and it wasn't the department's head—it was a green-faced, black, and dark-haired wit, a hard felt hat drawn down over his eyes, which were red-rimmed. He knew what the Departmental Head was saying, because he always knew what everyone said. At last it was closing time for that parliament and only two of an audience remained—the understander of any speech and the caretaker of the parliament, who was waiting to lock up, but who did not mind himself how late the speech flowed on, for he slept (poorly) on the premises. But the time came when the man of one last speech paused for a moment, probably he had a feeling of emptiness in head and stomach. It was some hours since he ate and he had been using up his stored energy for a long time. Also he saw the door key, the symbol of farewell, in the caretaker's hand. The "Symbol of Farewell," or is it "The Gipsy's Warning," they call it? No, that can't be, for gipsies have nothing to do with door keys; they walk through hedges as if they were not there. But the long-time speaker had humanity. Pitiless with a counter in front of him, but loving with a long streak of greasy oil cloth between him and a night-watcher with the "Key of Night." So he ended and sat down, put on his overcoat. So exhausted was he, suddenly, that he dragged his overcoat on as he sat in that hard Windsor chair. Then he put his hat on. The caretaker took his cap out of his pocket and put it on his head; the session was indeed over. The tired speaker sat for a few moments, with his hands curved with the palms upwards, resting on his knees on his black overcoat. Then he stood up. Black felt hat and red eyes came over to him and shook hands; the caretaker, feeling that this was an occasion, shook hands also. No one spoke. And the head of the department went down the long stairs to the street, followed by red eyes, who at the door turned away into the darker end of the street while the victorious (it was a kind of victory) speaker went towards the lighter end. The caretaker locked the heavy door, drew a mug of cold water from a tap at the end of the hall, and with a lighted match held high, found his bedroom door at the far end of a cross passage, and with the last dimming spark of the match, lit a gas jet set in the middle of the wall over the fireplace, and began slowly taking off his boots.

The Departmental Head was right in not getting into a conversation with Gaw, not because there was any danger of he himself talking too much; he would never have got a look in, for Gaw was brimming full with the desire to talk. His jaws ached with the desire to be holding up a megaphone of talk, and he had his share of talking all his life while the outfitter had only had his one big night. Gaw was Vesuvius at his red work, as shown in those endearing pictures brought home by all sailors in the Mediterranean trade long ago. And the outfitter was an extinct volcano, an "unfortunate crater" as the Dublin wit in the voiceful crowd said, also long ago.

All purchases made, Gaw left the shop, and walked out into a flickering November sunshine, and the Outfitting Head looked at his back glumly, as a dog looks at an india-rubber imitation bone, not without a certain amount of empty interest.

A snack (that was the name they gave it), a snack of lunch in a bar, bread and cheese, and stout, and a careless extra savoury, two cold, once, hotly toasted, sardines on a toast, a toast "the toast of the regiment," "the toast of the town," and he thought of "the toast of the ship,"—Miss Reece, daughter of Captain Reece, and he thought of the old song and the poisoned bread, no not toast and "*It was eaten by MacDougal's daughter*," and he laughed sardonically to himself, the cheery brutality of the songs of other days! But it was time to be moving down the river, to help Jos Webster handle the appointment seekers.

The deck of the *Prairie Bird*, as Gaw stood amidship on it and balanced his weight to her erratic buoyancy, made him think of the deck of the ten-thousand tonner on which he would soon be tripping, or plodding, his way. Though he had never sailed on an ocean his stomach had found itself able to stand up well to coastal pitchings and tossings, and he had no fear that the professor of history and geography would be laid low. He was so much at his ease at the moment that he spoke to Jamesey and asked how his engines were standing out the years. Jamesey's reply was just a grunt, but he brandished an eye down at his engines and imagined they cowered, an understanding cowering, as between two affectionate beings.

At the Alberwide landing stage, Gaw hurried ashore. As he came down the river he was glad to see no crowd waiting at Number 14. "The next run of the *Bird* will bring them down," he thought.

Jos Webster was waiting for him in the lower office, and in his hand he had a number of soiled pieces of cardboard. He showed them to Gaw; on one side was a rubber stamp of Jos Webster's rococo signature. The lintel of the J, the cross to the T, and an underlining flourish were each a quarter of an inch wide of pure ink, got by some dexterous pressing down of the nib till it squeaked. This signature, when rubber-stamped, called for a constant refeeding of the ink pad. His other signature, the one he commonly used (the bank would gladly recognise either), was a very modest affair, and looked like a cheerful drake, followed by his little row of ducks, wandering down a water meadow in the cool of evening.

On the other side of the dingy cards was printed, in large black type, the word GROG. And Webster explained to Gaw that at one time it had been his business, from time to time, to auction the bent grass cut and bundled from the sandhills. Farmers came from a distance to buy the bundles for rough thatching and every buyer received, as an act of courtesy, a grog card redeemable at the "Arbour Hotel", for grog or its equivalent value. Even a small pork pie was in the orders of exchanging.

"What I want you to do, if these professors come down by the next boat, is to tell them the job's settled; take them down to the *Bird*, tell the skipper it's all right, let him take them across to the hotel landing, and give each of them a card; oh, hang it! if there ain't more than a dozen of 'em, give them a couple of cards each."

Standing by the table Webster was opening letters from inquirers about the "Sunny Skies Voyage." Now as the *Prairie Bird* would not be down at Alberwide for a little while, he and Gaw climbed up the stairs to the private office, and there they read through the inquiries. A few contained cheques, and one had a pre-paid wire, so anxious was the sunny boy— it was a boy, of age not known—to be certain that he was in time to book his berth. Other letters were asking as to the best sort of clothes to bring. Some asked if there would be facilities for sun-bathing; some asked that there should not be. Webster promised everyone everything. "So far there's twenty-two of them, and I am telling them the truth, for at the time of writing there's room enough almost for a couple of monarchs and a Soviet: and any old dictator can have a bathroom to himself. When my father-in-law gets here he expects to be the emperor, the Great Mogul Scrutineering. But when the passenger list really fills up, they'll all sift into their own little groups, we'll find. And as long as the mate comes well forward, and the skipper keeps well back, they'll be just as mild as milk. You're right," and Webster glanced at Gaw's hat which was tossed on a chair, "not to wear your yachting cap at first—well, not when you are explaining to the history professors. You'll look more human and humane to them without it. Later, for the passengers booking, that'll be the style." He looked at his watch. "Now if they come they come."

# IN SAND

CHARACTERS

ANTONY LARCSON   KITCHEN MAID

JOHN OLDGROVE   CHAUFFEUR

THE MAYOR   OLD SAILOR

EDITOR   VISITOR

TOWN COUNCILLOR   GOVERNOR

ALICE   HOTEL BOY

HER MOTHER   BROWN BOY

HER FATHER   BROWN GIRL

MAURICE

ACT ONE

TIME: *An Autumn evening many years ago.*

SCENE I: TONY LARCSON, *an elderly man, pale, clean-shaven, dark grey hair, is lying in bed (left of centre), slightly raised on pillows—white nightshirt.*

JOHN OLDGROVE, *a man about forty, with brown short whiskers and moustache, clean-shaven below the line of mouth, hair left above but clipped close. He is dressed in a brown jacket and waistcoat, blue trousers, black boots, half-Wellingtons, but trousers not stuffed into boot tops.*

There is a shaded lamp on the table, throwing very little light on LARCSON, *but illuminating* OLDGROVE. *The bed is a four-poster with dark green damask curtains and lining to back of bedhead. There is a glass-fronted book-case over drawers to the left—door to the right. Long, hanging bell-pull between door and bed foot.*

Right and left as they appear to the audience.

LARCSON (*in a low, clear voice*) Well, my boy, now is the accepted time. I accept it anyway, and you must accept it too.

(*He puts his right hand on the right hand of* OLDGROVE, *which is resting on the quilt.*)

I haven't got to be giving you hints, or beating about the bush with you. I haven't got to begin twisting the quilt edge or crying "hark" every time there's a ticking noise in the wainscoting. I suppose Catherine told you something of what the Doctor said a day ago. He did me the honour to make no bones about it. Indeed, I could have wished just at first that he wouldn't have honoured me as so brave. However, it's me that will have to make bones of myself. Oh, forgive me, John, the vanity of the joker. Joking to the last. All that need is dead for me, as between our two selves. Five or six days, Jack, if I keep on drawing lucky breaths, or maybe it might be only hours and one of five days has gone.

OLDGROVE But isn't there something in the strength of your constitution—a temperate life. . . .

LARCSON I asked about those things—first he used long words that I couldn't understand. When he was Hick Heck Hocking my mind was following my eyes out of the window. One time I would have *looked* as if I understood to save my face. But I thought a man with such a short tether needn't worry any more about whether he appeared to have any Latin or not, so I asked him for simpler words—and I'm satisfied.

OLDGROVE Mister Larcson, you have great courage. It gives me courage to see you so.

LARCSON No courage, just quietness. I'll tell you one good thing, the best of the news, no pain, no fussing, perhaps in my sleep. I often thought, when I thought of such things, that "in my sleep" would suit me best, and I don't suppose, all the same, that I was unique in that, and I wasn't unique I suppose either when I used, in the full of my health, to bury myself in style. I fancied going up to Glasnevin with two or three bands, but if only one, I wanted the Girl Pipers playing: "I know my love by his way of walking." When I planned my funeral I always floated above the procession myself, and I am telling you now, it was particularly grand to me to see that Pipe Major swinging up her baton in the air.

OLDGROVE You aren't tiring yourself talking to me, Larcson, my dear friend, is it good for you to give your mind to such things so much?

LARCSON It is good for what I am pleased to call my mind. I had another ending, dying on a quay wall after saving a beautiful little girl child from the dark waters, some of the people carrying the child to hospital and some of the people standing round me watching me gasping out a hero's death—no pain, no fuss, except a certain amount of friendly fuss—but I never could satisfy myself with my last words. There I go, Jack, teasing you again. I must give up teasing for evermore. It's right I should. I don't have to do any heroic actions now even if there was time, so I should stop all teasing. With God's help as long as this life lasts with me I'll tease no more.

OLDGROVE Would you like me to read anything to you?

LARCSON That is an idea. It reminds me of a plan I have had in my head the last few hours, turning it over gently now and then. It's a plan for a memorial to myself that'll hurt nobody.

OLDGROVE You never wanted to hurt anyone.

LARCSON More often than you thought, but I was lazy. In the book-shelf on the middle shelf there is an old green book of the Poems of Tom Hood. I read old poems in it soon after the Doctor and I had our talk. I could have waited until you came and asked you to read to me from it. But I remember what I want to remember—when I was a boy I was very fond of the poems of old Tom Hood and there was one "Forget me not". All sorts of forget-me-nots ending up with:

> "Six tons of sculptural marble
> As a small forget-me-not."

Well, now, that's not what I have in mind, but I have written out here, just roughly put it down in pencil, a plan I have that'll hurt nobody.

(*Takes folded paper from table, and with his left hand makes effort to pass it to* OLDGROVE. OLDGROVE *stands up and takes paper.*)

OLDGROVE Am I to read it now?

LARCSON No, not now. It's just a few notes. I'll tell you now what it is, and I want you to go to James and get him to write it out fair and legal and so that there can be no mistake about anything and then bring it round to me any time to-morrow in the afternoon before I get sleepy, and bring along James' old clerk, and the young one to witness it when I sign it, and also to be able to say I'm clear and able to know what I'm up to. It mightn't be necessary to have all this paraphernalia, as it's only a wish, a thing I would like to have carried out when I am gone, but it might as well be done well and strong, and it'll amuse the old clerk and the young one, to have a glimpse behind the scenes of an old oddity's last days. I won't have you witnessing my hand, because that mightn't be correct if this plan is considered part of the real will, because under that you get, you know John, your share of what there is.

OLDGROVE You are very good to me.

LARCSON And you. It isn't much. If the locust ate a many years, perhaps I ate the locust in the end, and there's precious little left now. So it's well that:

> I will not long delay
> for the corn,
> Or for the oil,
> Or the wine that maketh glad
> The heart of man.

OLDGROVE Wouldn't you like to rest a little now, and I'll leave this paper under your pillow and then I can come back in an hour's time, say, and you can tell me your plan.

LARCSON Oh, I'll have plenty of time to rest. Give me a sup of that stuff in the glass and I'll heave ahead.

(OLDGROVE *takes glass from table and puts it into* LARCSON's *hand.* LARCSON *drinks a little, slowly, waits, drinks a little more, hands glass back to* OLDGROVE.)

LARCSON He says it's twenty years old. He thinks that a great age, and so did I once but, just now it doesn't seem to me so extra old, though whiskey and men aren't the same thing, though they have many things in common, and though, I suppose, they punish each other. Still I don't have to worry about it now. When the bell rings for the last lap the egotist doesn't feel his egotism making either lead or feathers to his heels—and here is my plan—

—THE MEMORY OF ANTONY LARCSON—

I want you, or James, or both of you, between one month

and three months after I'm dead, sooner than that would
be a botheration, and longer might be too long, and
someone in the town might say: "And who was Antony
Larcson?", and that would be painful to the faithful and
the few. I want you to choose between you a nice little
girl of about ten years of age, born in the town, of parents
born in this town. You'll think my mind with Pipers'
Bands and everything is running on nice little girls, but
in this case a little girl is the only choice. A boy would
think the whole affair woman's work, beneath him, and
my memory would get a bad start. When you have found
your suitable little girl she is to go, with her people, and
James, or yourself, just after the last of the low water
spring tide, to the far strand and there just above the
water's edge she is to write with a stick in the sand:

TONY, WE HAVE THE GOOD THOUGHT FOR YOU STILL.

She's to wait there, and all of you are to wait, until the
water has flowed in over the writing, and then you are
to give the little girl a very large bag of very nice sweets,
and you are to, as soon as you get back to town, pay
into a Savings Bank ninety pounds to stay there in the
Bank for her till she is twenty-one years of age, accumu-
lating compound interest. I don't know what the money
should amount to by then, I never was any good at
arithmetic, anyway it'll be time enough. Do you under-
stand, is it clear enough?

OLDGROVE Clear enough. We'll have trouble, I'm thinking,
over our choice. The parents of the little girls who aren't
chosen, and me and James living on here catching the
black looks. It won't do James any good in his business.

LARCSON And I'm sure there must be lots of nice little girls
born of lovely parents themselves belonging to this town.
Maybe you'll have to draw lots among the little girls.

OLDGROVE It'll worry James. It'd be an awful come down for
a lawyer to have to draw lots. By nature they must
believe that everything can be done by argument. They
could make water run uphill by argument, they believe.

LARCSON They are great men of faith.

OLDGROVE I wouldn't like to be a lawyer, perhaps having to

act against your best friend. You could refuse, but if you were hard up you'd start thinking of your wife and family and how it's an unlucky thing to refuse good money.

LARCSON Well, Jack, you haven't got any wife or family to be bothering about. You'll be one not-so-old bachelor carrying out the wishes of a genuine old bachelor. This used to be a great town for bachelors long ago, it was full of them, but of late years they've been captured in numbers. I think the young women are advised by their aunts—that is if the aunts are settled and out of the running themselves—how to catch a husband. I believe they band themselves together as soon as a new eligible bachelor appears in from over the hills and far away. They band themselves together to all have a try for him, but they're under a bargain, as soon as he shows signs of wavering towards one of them, for all the others to stand clear until she either gaffs him or fails; in this case they all come back to their prey again.

OLDGROVE They're awful. I think, Tony, you mustn't be tiring yourself, now. You should try and rest a little. I'm thinking just now that when James and I have to choose the little girl for your money—but let us hope there is a mistake made by the doctor, they do make mistakes sometime; they'll tell you, some of them, that mistakes can be made, let us hope so, and you may be here with us for a while longer yet. . . . I'm thinking whenever we have to choose the young girl there'll be some scalded hearts among the fully-grown young women of this place. There'll be snorting in Gath and a publishing of it in Askelon. Can't you picture them, Tony, but you must be resting yourself now and not bothering yourself with such thoughts. James and I will be well able to take care of ourselves. You always, in the past, had grand ideas. Indeed, you often told me ideas and plans that would have shaken up all the old Bank Managers of this place, retired, and in active service. But you never put any of your plans into operation—you had too kind a heart to want to upset anyone. But I wouldn't have cared. If I had the ways and means I would have shaken this exquisite old town upside down, including their worships the Mayor and Councillors. I'd just love to take them on a marvellous grand picnic to the Island, and then to have the boatmen slip away with the boats and leave the city fathers to entertain themselves. They'd light a fire as a signal of distress and all round the shores I'd have the people lighting answering fires—as signals of joy. I wouldn't appear in it myself. I'd have an alibi. I'd manage to be seen somewhere else altogether at the time of the goings on. But I don't suppose any alibi would satisfy them unless I was in my grave at the time. Oh, it'd all be a lot of fun, of course, and nobody a bit the worse. As soon as they saw the joke, the Mayor and the Councillors would be laughing all the time thinking of each other keeping vigil on the Island. And I would not leave them in misery too long. I'd send out the boats to them pretty soon, and the makings of a bowl of punch in every boat just to warm them up. But I talk a lot and you must be resting, Tony. If I hadn't talked so much you would have been asleep by now.

LARCSON No, Jack, I like to hear you talking.

OLDGROVE I'll go now (*standing up*) and I'll come in to-morrow, with the paper all made out.

LARCSON Come to-morrow, yes, but don't bother about having the paper made out at all. You understand, I know, what I want done. It doesn't have to be tied up in any legal form for I know you will carry out—that's how they say it, "carry out"—my wishes. Good-bye, Jack, for the present.

OLDGROVE Until to-morrow. Have a little rest, now.

(LARCSON'S *eyes are already closed, as* OLDGROVE *lets himself out of the door, closing it gently*.)

LARCSON No pain, no fuss, "perhaps in my sleep," he said.

Slow Curtain

SCENE 2: *Sand by sea, low rocky point with sea mark, on right. Sky overcast, it is raining. Distant hills.* THE EDITOR *of the town's weekly newspaper, with spectacles, wearing pepper and salt suit, and small cloth cap.* THE MAYOR—*tall hat, frock coat, white*

waistcoat, grey trousers, ends roughly turned up, light dust over-
coat. OLDGROVE *as before, with low-crowned derby hat, carrying*
bouquet of Michaelmas daisies and roses, also pointed stick with
bunch of many coloured ribbons on it, and a large bright blue,
plush-covered box of sweets. OLDGROVE *has an umbrella which*
he holds over the MAYOR. *Three* TOWN COUNCILLORS, *wearing*
overcoats. One has a walking stick, and one has an umbrella,
with which he tries to shelter the other Councillors, in turn.

EDITOR *on extreme left behind* MAYOR. OLDGROVE *on* MAYOR'S
left, the COUNCILLORS *grouped on his left.*

THE MAYOR The young lady is already claiming woman's
privilege by keeping us waiting. Ah (*looking off, away*
right) I see three figures now emerging from the village.
One of them is quite small, Miss Alice, no doubt. The
others will be the parents. They'll be drenched before
they get here if they have not come properly prepared.
These al fresco affairs should take place in the summer
months. Not that our summers have been very magnifi-
cent lately. I think, with your permission, Mr Oldgrove,
and my Councillors, owing to the inclemency prevailing,
it would be an act of unkindness to ask this child and
her papa and mama to allow themselves to be detained
here a moment longer than necessary for the carrying
out of the wishes of our departed brother—I think I may
call him brother. So with your permission, I say, I will
read some few words I have jotted down here, which
will, I trust, put us *au fait* with the matter now in hand.
(*Puts on pince-nez, takes papers from breast pocket and reads*)
We, my friends, citizens and indeed I may say citizen-
esses, are gathered here to-day on the shores of the wide
ocean, so gentle in summer, when the zephyrs epitomise
the character of the all too fleeting moments, so rude,
rough and boisterous in winter though (*looking up from*
the paper and turning towards OLDGROVE *and the* COUNCIL-
LORS) I'm not sure that the equinoctial gales aren't the
worst time of the year, and if this isn't the first of them
threatening now I'll be agreeably surprised. First comes
the rain, I've noticed, and then the wind clears away the
rain and the sun comes out and you think it's going to

veer to a good hard quarter, and then it backs and the wind and rain come howling down on you and the slates and the chimney pots go flying through the sky (*continues reading*) and boisterous in winter ... gathered here to carry out the last wishes of a distinguished member of our community—Mr Antony Larcson—who was taken from us but a bare six weeks ago. He has gone to his eternal rewards, where we must all go in God's good time. For some of us that day cannot be very far off. For some of us the long vista of the years which stretch before us gives me the thought and the hope that they may be years full of sunshine and the singing of the little birds who bring only messages of gladness.

1ST COUNCILLOR Hear, hear!

(*The* MAYOR *turns his face towards the* EDITOR *who makes a mark in his notebook.*)

THE MAYOR While for some of us The Autumn of the sere and yellow leaves is approaching with no uncertain tread, for others, for one other at least, the primrose bud is unfolding itself in the ambient airs of hope and promise. A certain politician, I have been informed, has preempted the primrose for himself and his admirers. I do not mention the flower in any political connection, pro or con. The primrose flourished before the politician was drawing his first breath of life, not to say cutting his first tooth.

2ND COUNCILLOR Very true.

(*The* MAYOR *turns his face towards the* EDITOR *who makes a mark in his notebook.*)

THE MAYOR Dear friends, and fellow citizens, Antony Larcson was ever a lover of the old town. Its interests were ever in his thoughts. When he burnt the midnight oil of study, in nine times out of ten the study was earmarked to, in some subtle way perhaps hardly observable to less brilliant intellects than his, earmarked to the advantage of all humanity and therefore, as the most human spot he knew, to the advantage of the old town. He, when he

heard the first notes of the Last Post, the first rattling of
the curtain rings which presage the final drawing of that
dark curtain which hides from all human eyes, if not from
all memory, a frail and tottering human being leaving the
stony pastures for, we hope, a bright and gladsome land
beyond the veil.

When he heard that bugle call, our noble friend set
himself like a classic hero of old with his back to the tall
pillar, and did bend all his senses to the supreme effort
of the survey of all the tombs and memorials of all the
ages, from the pyramids of the far desert to the lonely,
small cross of boards driven into the earth above a
narrow space, shouldered in among a crowded concourse
of the dead on some mountain eyrie of those who, in
spite of all the savants, cling still to the Immortality of
the Soul.

Our friend, I have no doubt, considered all forms of
remembrance, everlasting flowers, feasts of honour — men
remember much in gratitude when in their cups, the
ancient heroes tell us. He gave a passing thought, no
doubt to the ringing of bells once a year for ever and
always. But belfrys rot and tumble down in decay. Or
men's ears grow heavy and sluggish to the sound of oft
repeated bells — "Who was that for?" "I don't know who,
some old fellow that died in the old days long ago." "It's
a pity they wouldn't put the price I suppose he left for
the ringing to some better purpose." That's the sort of
talk the ringing of bells gives cause to after the passing
of many years. Our friend, no doubt, could have had a
posthumous portrait painted of himself from a photo-
graph. I have in my possession myself an excellent Carte
de Visite which, though executed some years ago, is
unfaded and gives a very fine impression of this friend
of ours. Should a portrait in oils have been his wish, it
would have been hung within the Mayor's Parlour,
where it would have been an incentive to the young men
of our ancient land when on the threshold of their careers.
But "simplicity" and not "excelsior" was the word
emblazoned on the banner, which our late citizen carried
in his strong right hand. There is a something in sim-
plicity that appeals to us all, perhaps. (*Lifts his head from*

reading paper, which he holds in his hand, but does not read again.) Perhaps it is that there is so much of the child even in the hardest of us all, and we know that it is only the hard who have survived the last generation in our town. Whatever may have gone on in other places, you know, as I know, here it has been tooth and nail. Get a good hold and never shift it till you get a better. It has been down, or be downed. I never killed a man, even in thought, though maybe I let a sinking man go down the third time. No, I have many things I'll suffer for in my last hours—but no—I might have seen them go twice, but before the third time I held out a hand—that is all I can say for myself, and I hope it will be accepted when I'm moaning on the hinges of the door. Maybe it would have been better if this man, whose wishes we are following out today, had never decided to leave these wishes which are in a sense a criticism of our bad old ways, and a criticism I say on even the best of our ways.

What he left for this purpose would hardly pay for a new pump up on the Mail Coach road, but a pump would have shown he appreciated the goodness and the virtue of cleanliness. The ways of men, and especially men on their death-beds, are strange ways, and not to be understood by those who stand in their full health, not thinking of their last hours, but of the hours which keep coming towards them like waves of the sea, some with crests of glistening foam on them and some dark as blood, no two waves alike. I speak out of my heart, and I don't care who hears me, and if it wasn't for the hope that I may keep my chin up above the on-coming waves, with the help of God who made me, if it wasn't for that I tell you, I would raise my hands above my head and let my cursed old body sink into the depths. (*The sky is getting lighter.*) But here comes the sunlight in time to welcome this little maid. She and her fond and proud—proud they should be—parents, are almost upon us.

(*The* EDITOR *comes forward and takes the manuscript of the* MAYOR'S *speech from his listless hand.*)

But there is another group of people coming into the

green land now at this moment, as I am a living man, 'tis the woman pipers' band. (*He turns his face towards* OLDGROVE.) I see the hand of young Oldgrove in this, and I know what they are playing.

(*Pipers' Band heard, far off, playing: 'I know my love by his way of walking'. All the time coming slowly nearer. The sunlight is gathering strength, and shines on* ALICE *and her mother and father, as they enter right.* ALICE, *a girl of almost nine years of age, nicely dressed, small slip of paper in her hand.* MOTHER, *woman in the thirties, well and pleasantly dressed.* FATHER, *not very tall, wearing waterproof and carrying umbrella and* ALICE'S *waterproof. Band playing all the time, coming always nearer.* MAYOR, COUNCILLORS, OLDGROVE *and* EDITOR, *take off hats.* ALICE *and* MOTHER *bow.* FATHER *takes off hat.* OLDGROVE *moves forward and hands* ALICE *ribboned stick.*)

THE MAYOR You are welcome, Miss Alice, to the far strand by the Ocean Shore and the sun shining in the sky welcomes you. Come now, down to the tide's edge and let you write those kind words you have, I believe, in your little hand this moment.

(*Drum Major and one or more of band now appear on right, as they finish tune.* MAYOR, EDITOR, *and* COUNCILLORS *make way for* ALICE *as she walks to edge of sea.* ALICE *saying each word clearly and separately, reading from paper as she writes.*)

ALICE   TONY—WE—HAVE—THE—GOOD—THOUGHT—FOR—YOU—STILL.

(OLDGROVE *hands her the box of sweets—and to her Mother the bouquet. Box has picture on it of a cottage covered with roses.*)

THE MAYOR Do I get a kiss?

(ALICE *puts stick and box of sweets on sand, goes to* MAYOR, *who stoops. She puts her arms round his neck and gives him a kiss, takes the* MAYOR'S *chain in her hand and looks at it.*)
(*The* EDITOR *takes out his handkerchief and unobtrusively wipes his eyes.*)

THE MAYOR Now we must wait until the tide flows over your calligraphy, Miss Alice.

(*All turn faces towards the sea, silently, then, after a time, all file off right. The band waits a few moments, then playing 'The girl I left behind me', follows. Sound receding. Empty stage for a space of time, then*)

Curtain

ACT TWO

TIME: *Twelve years later.*

SCENE 1: *By a bay, on left summer-house of an Hotel, gaily painted. A flower bed, a white balustrade, suggestion of arbutus tree on right.* ALICE *and* MAURICE *enter left along shore.*

MAURICE Alice, you are very kind to let me call you Alice, so very kind to a man twenty years older than you.

ALICE Why not, Maurice?

MAURICE Why not, indeed, "why not" you say "this old man might be my father," and surely you think a few weeks acquaintance in a tourist hotel should warrant a short name for such a one. But, Alice, I put my cards on the table, win or lose, and should there be no one else, no young man near your home, in which case I am too proud to fight against a young man for your love. But if there is no other, then, as my heart was my own till I met you . . . then I ask you to marry me.

(ALICE *says nothing, but walking along the beach begins writing on the sand.*)

MAURICE Oh, why do you keep me waiting for my answer? But I must have patience, and what is that you write upon the sand?

ALICE I write TONY—WE—HAVE—THE—GOOD—THOUGHT—FOR—YOU—STILL.

MAURICE Then there's another, and Tony is his name.

ALICE Tony is dead long ago.

MAURICE But still you remember him. But you are too young
to spend a life mourning. I ask not that I should supplant
Tony in your heart, I will only ask a hearing for my love.

ALICE Tony died when I was a child, Maurice.

MAURICE Then take good time to consider, I won't rush you.
I could say that I could give you a life of comfort, and
perhaps I might even say of luxury, though perhaps not
so luxurious as you have with your own people. I will
get a motor car, though it may not be so well turned out,
nor the chauffeur so well trained as your own. My own
coachman is strong and intelligent and, if I ask him, he
will learn to drive a motor car for you. I have no secrets.
I am a fairly wealthy man. My grandfather and my
father were carriage builders and I, an only son, inherited
the business. It is an honourable and ancient trade, but
if it is too ancient for a youthful age and, if the motor
car drives the horses from the roads, then we must fit
engines into our carriages. I am not an old fogey but still
I will always love the sound of horses' hooves on a road.
My dear creature, I have nothing to hide.

ALICE I have something to hide, or something that perhaps I
should hide. I should perhaps say only "good-bye" and
then after I leave tomorrow, we would never meet again.

MAURICE Wait! Oh, wait! Think, think, don't say anything yet.

ALICE I have something to hide. I am a fraudulent visitor of a few short sunny days. That motor and that chauffeur are not mine. I pay for these by the week. And now my holiday is over I pack my clothes, look how new they are (*she holds her arm up towards him*) and I will never wear them again in an hotel like this one. I will go back to my work. I work in an office and I keep some of the accounts and type-write the important letters. But (*looking down on the sand*) TONY—WE—HAVE—THE—GOOD—THOUGHT—FOR—YOU—STILL.

MAURICE What fraud is there in all that? If, to test me, you had told me you were a forger you would have found me stand the test. Try me how you will I am a determined man. Test me as you will.

ALICE It is Tony's own fault. When I was a child, an old gentleman called Antony Larcson died, and I don't think I had ever seen him, but, if I did, I never knew him. I often saw old gentlemen walking along the pavements in the old town, but I knew the names of few of them, and this Mr Larcson, I don't believe he ever knew I was in the land of the living. No, I was chosen by two other people. You see, he left a sum of money to be paid to a nice little girl born in the town, of town-born parents, who, after he was dead, had to write on the strand: "TONY—WE—HAVE—THE—GOOD—THOUGHT—FOR—YOU—STILL". And the nice little girl had to be chosen by Mr Oldgrove—a friend of Mr Larcson and his solicitor—and they chose me. Perhaps they put my name in a hat with a lot of other nice little girls. And anyway I was chosen, and with my mother and father, and the Mayor and some Councillors, and a band of girl pipers, and Mr Oldgrove, I went down to the far strand and wrote: "TONY—WE—HAVE—THE—GOOD—THOUGHT—FOR—YOU—STILL" and I was given a lovely box of sweets, the biggest I had ever seen. We waited till the sea came in again and covered my writing. And whenever I find myself on a sea strand for all the years that have gone by I write to encourage Tony. I looked on him as a good friend—didn't he give me that great box of sweets, and the money—I didn't think such a lot about that at the time for I didn't see it. Mr Oldgrove used to call on my people and me from time to time, and say it was growing. And he used to always laugh, and stop to talk to me, whenever he saw me trotting to school or back again. Then he died. Then my parents died. And I was alone, and a solicitor—not the one who was at the choosing of me, he had died years before—and this solicitor handed me a cheque, my fortune—by then it had grown to a hundred and twenty pounds. My office salary could keep me easily enough. I had no one in the world to think of except number one. So I set out to give number one the time of her life. I didn't think it was owing to me for anything I had done except to be lucky. So I made up my mind to blow the lot on a grand holiday. I bought a lot of clothes and I hired the motor car and the chauffeur and I didn't hire it until I'd gone a long way from my native home. See what a designing minx I was. And as soon as I saw you, see what a designing minx I am still, I said to myself, "If that man asks you to marry him— don't hesitate, say yes." But my conscience, you see there is such a thing as a minx conscience, said: "But only after I have told him what a cheat I am." Now you know, sir.

MAURICE Now I know I have my first kiss. (*She holds up her face, he kisses her, takes her face in hands and kisses her again.*)

MAURICE Do you think Tony would object to an old boy if I wrote also on the sand (*he writes*)

"TONY, WE HAVE THE GOOD THOUGHT FOR YOU STILL".

(*Taking* ALICE'S *right arm through his left hand and lifting her hand to his lips with his right hand. Exit both, right.*)
(*After a pause, enter on left* KITCHEN MAID *leading by the hand* CHAUFFEUR.)

KITCHEN MAID Oh, the air here by the sea tastes lovely after that stuffy old kitchen. Oh look! Look what somebody has written on the sand.

CHAUFFEUR I expect I know what it is, and who wrote it. It's something about a chap called Tony and my lady wrote it. Whenever we come to a bit of sea shore she always writes that (*looks down at sands*). Yes, that's her writing, but somebody else has copied it.

KITCHEN MAID How lovely, get me a stick and I'll write it myself (CHAUFFEUR *goes to left, breaks off small branch and brings it to the* KITCHEN MAID. KITCHEN MAID *with head on one side—considering writing—reads:*)

"TONY, WE HAVE THE GOOD THOUGHT FOR YOU STILL", your lady must be cracked.

CHAUFFEUR Not at all. She's a wise woman.

KITCHEN MAID What does it mean? What she's written.

CHAUFFEUR Ask me another.

KITCHEN MAID Well, she's rich and happy and grand, so here goes for luck (*writes on sand*). I'll tell all the girls in the hotel and we'll all have the good thought for Tony, whoever he is, and if he's dead let him rest his soul in peace and happiness. But perhaps you would sooner I didn't tell the rest—just to keep it to myself—to ourselves.

CHAUFFEUR I don't seem to care what you do about it.

KITCHEN MAID All right sniffy, here write it yourself, it can't do you any harm and might do you a bit of good, unless you're quite satisfied as you are.

CHAUFFEUR No, I would consider it too much of a presumption to write what my lady wrote—in a sense a kind of forgery.

KITCHEN MAID If that's all the forgery you ever do you'll do well. I'd write anything on any old strand in the wide world if I thought there was luck and virtue in it.

CHAUFFEUR Luck and virtue don't always go together.

KITCHEN MAID Now, Mr Petroleum, keep your wide eye on the wide ocean.

CHAUFFEUR All right, all right, I'll send you some post cards from some of the places I may be visiting with the car. I see a lot of places one way and another, and very interesting architecture—scenes in markets and what not, lakes and mountains, and I'm expecting to be on the Continent:

> On the Continong
> Tray bong, tray bong,

as the song says. Next season should be very instructive.

Monte Carlo, a shocking place for the gambling, and
Ostend, similar I understand, but different. Rome,
Venice, all canals, going around in boats, I believe. Ger-
many—lager beer in large china mugs, very nice too. I
like lager in the summer but for all the year round old
fashioned gold old four-ale takes a lot of beating. I like
it. But when I'm driving I touch nothing, lemonade and
a dash, no more. They can't bear the smell of liquor on
you. And, after lunch as soon as they climb in, I get a
whiff of every sort taken backwards. As it comes over to
me, Chartreuse Whiskey, Burgundy, Chablis, Sherry.
But I speed up pretty soon and when she gets going, the
breeze she makes carries the old scents, the perfumes of
the wash-'em-downs, away along the road behind us. I
daresay the hardworking country folk standing in their
little old fields enjoy the smell of other people's good
drinks what they'll never taste themselves. But I daresay
it may be a good thing for them, in the end, give 'em a
hope for better things, make 'em ambitious, if that's a
good thing. And as to smoking—no chauffeur that values
his place, smokes in his hours of duty. I think my people
have always thought almost worse of the smell of tobacco
than of liquor, and that's why, as we're not going out
again to-day, I'm going to light the pipe.

(*Takes out pipe and tobacco pouch, fills pipe and lights with
match. He sits on end of balustrade. He smokes, looking out to
sea.*)

There's something very imposing about the sea. I should
like to own a lot of sea, and I'd like to have a yacht to
go about on it. I've seen the very yacht that would suit,
painted all white with rosy coloured curtains on the
cabin windows. Fine large, long yacht with a bright brass
funnel, that'd take a lot of polishing I should think, but
I would have to do it . . .

(KITCHEN MAID *is slowly walking along sea to right.*)

I hate polishing brass work after a dirty run. Of course
in fine weather on dry roads it's nothing, it's child's play,

just a touch of the paste, let it settle itself and then rub it off—and there you are—they can see their faces in it. Make you laugh, some of them, you'd think they would sooner look at something better than their old phizzes. There's no accounting (KITCHEN MAID *moves off right*) for tastes . . . I'd sooner be looking at your nice little face, Miss Molly . . . hello, she's gone!

Curtain

SCENE 2: *Ten years later by a tropical ocean.*

(*Left and right palms; in front of them shrubs with large flowers. A distant point of land with trees.* MAURICE *and* ALICE *on a seat left.*)

ALICE We will soon have been completely round the world, won't we? We will be able to say we've been round the world. That used to be a wonderful boast with people one time. But there isn't anyone who could have had such a splendid and beautiful time as I have had, most happy of women, making a long circle with my Maurice.

MAURICE I'm too old for you, my dear. I'm not able to climb the highest mountains.

ALICE I have seen a plenty of men who could climb the highest mountains without loss of a breath, but I have with me one with whom I'd sooner climb a two-foot-high hillock, than own a mountain of gold, climbable or unclimbable; my man Maurice owns my heart. (MAURICE, *leaning towards her right hand which is on his shoulder, kisses it and recites*)

(*Pause*)

I've got a white hand on my shoulder
Such a beautiful white hand on my shoulder.

An old, broken-down sailor drifted into the bar of the hotel just now and gave us a song, he called it 'White Hand'.

ALICE Had he made it up himself?

MAURICE Oh, it was nothing, sentimental. He hadn't made it up, I heard it before—a week ago in one of those islands to the East'ard. He sang it all right but melancholy—I heard it before that again.

ALICE Don't bother about it.

MAURICE Well, it was a sad enough song.

ALICE Tell it to me and get it out of your mind or share it with me.

MAURICE (*who is now standing up*):

> Away Oh,
> Away Oh,

We got a ship—a happy ship and a happy crew

> Away Oh—
> Away Oh,

And a fine old man—and we got music too
A happy ship—and a happy crew

> And Away Oh,
> Away Oh,

> We're sailing away
> To where there's parrots
> Among the palms and girls
> In the shadow
> Shadow lands

> And Away Oh,
> Away Oh,

> But I've got a white hand on my shoulder
> Such a beautiful white hand on my shoulder
> Such a thin white hand on my shoulder
> Captain Death's got his hand on my shoulder

> Away Oh,
> Away Oh,
> Away Oh.

(*Pause*)

It's a miserable sort of song to sing out here. I think.

ALICE It is gloomy, but nothing could be gloomy here for long.

MAURICE No, not gloomy long, but long days can be too long.

ALICE This is a nice place to stay. I think we should stay here for some time.

MAURICE Yes, for some time.

ALICE Presently we'll get our things unpacked properly. I haven't remembered Tony yet, give me your stick.

(*She takes* MAURICE'S *stick and goes to water edge and writes on the sand.*)

MAURICE Tony must be remembered round the world now all the time. A great many people, far more than we ever knew anything about, must have written his epitaph. If we go round again we'll be tying a double true lovers' knot in his memory.

ALICE I'll go round the world with you as many times as ever you want to.

MAURICE We're fancy free, nothing to stop us except misfortune—other people's misfortune—or our own. We can keep moving like the finger on the wall but we don't write anything on the wall—only on the sand of the seashore.

(ALICE *comes towards* MAURICE *who looks right.*)

MAURICE I see a figure a long way off coming this way and I know who it is—it's my old lugubrious singing sailor—come we'll stand in the shadow of the trees and watch unseen while this old man of the sea comes to Tony's memorial.

(MAURICE *and* ALICE *stand to left.*)

MAURICE I don't suppose he has very good sight, or is much of a reader anyway. But I hope he won't pass by unseeing.

ALICE Oh, I hope not, I hope he will be interested. I hope he will follow my lead in honour of dear Tony. If he does it will be the first time I have actually seen anyone except yourself write my memory after me. You haven't seen anyone either, have you?

MAURICE Oh no, though I have several times seen the writing was fresh and new. Here he comes, he walks very stiffly, he's stiffer than I am and I am sure he's ten years younger than me. God give him good luck, I don't think he ever had much.

(*Enter* OLD SAILOR *right. He sees words on sand, looks down at them, takes from pocket glasses, puts them on, reads. He goes down on his knees, takes dash knife from his pocket, and with its point writes on the sand. Rises from knees and moves off behind trees left.*)

MAURICE (*looking left*) Here's someone else coming, it's a boy from the hotel, he's carrying a note or something for me on a tray.

(*Enter left brown native boy, carrying tray with cablegram on it—he wears a short white jacket and flowered cotton kilt.*)

MAURICE (*taking up cablegram*) I don't want this, I don't care about it. I wasn't to have any business messages at all, we neither of us were to be bothered. We left everything arranged for, didn't we? Yourself as to the home, and myself as to the office. Well, here goes.

(*He reads cablegram, he is moved, he looks towards* ALICE.)

Let us sit down just for a few minutes. My wife (*he pauses, then speaking slowly*), I have a sad story to tell. I am worth the money in my pocket—the clothes I stand up in. The new works have been burnt out. They were only half completed but nothing now remains. Every penny the firm had was in it. They were uninsured.

ALICE Come, my dear, let us go to the hotel, the room is shady. There is a fan working, don't talk about anything

for a little while, we are together now, we have each
other.

MAURICE (*rising*) Each other.

(*They move off left.*)

Curtain

ACT THREE

TIME: *Many years later.*

SCENE 1: *Same as Act Two, Scene 2.*

(*New seat left, bright chromium-plated, flowering bushes trimmed
down, but tall palms remaining. Enter* OLD SAILOR *more decrepit-
looking, with* VISITOR (*a man about 35 in grey linen suit, large
brimmed grass hat, guide book under arm*).)

VISITOR I suppose you know this Island well?

OLD SAILOR I know it, I suppose, as much as ever I will, I
have never moved from it since I was cast up on the
coast away there to the East (*points left*). I was a young
man then. The people on the Island thought a lot of me.
For three years I never did a stroke of work. The people
brought me anything I wanted, they thought I could
work miracles. The usual thing, you've read about it in
books, I have no doubt. They thought I could heal their
animals when they were sick, and themselves. I did what
I could. One thing I stopped them of, some of their most
awful cures, dreadful! shocking! I could tell you all about
them, freeze your blood, though that wouldn't be any
harm in this climate. Anyway, to hear me would only
bore you. When they were tired of feeding me for nothing,
they gave me a little canoe and I went fishing, and by
and by I got me a little patch, and I found I was able
to grow a few sweet potatoes and, one thing and another
I made out.

(*All this time the* OLD SAILOR *and* VISITOR *have been approaching the seat.*)

VISITOR Let's sit down, it's as cheap to sit as to stand.

(*They sit down,* VISITOR *on left—*VISITOR *offers tobacco pouch and cigarette papers.* OLD SAILOR *rolls cigarette as does* VISITOR, *who brings out match box and lights the* OLD SAILOR'S *cigarette— they smoke silently.*)

VISITOR You've had an adventurous life.

OLD SAILOR Humdrum enough—twelve years at sea, in sail all the time. I never stubbed a nail, never had anything worse to put up with but gales of wind until the old Phoebus Apollo, well, she wasn't an old ship, she was a lot younger than I was, about one quarter of my age and Phoebus Apollo wasn't her name, it was just what I like to call her. We were at anchor here in the bay, off-shore wind, what there was of it, when about the darkest hour of the night, the wind went slap round and blew straight into the bay and broke her up. On those rocks to the East, you could have seen them there at low tide. Me and the Old Man were all that got ashore alive and he died before morning. I think he got broke up inside pounding on the rocks, anyway he didn't seem to me to have any want to live. It was so dark, not a sign of a moon or a star, we couldn't see each other's faces. But he knew my voice. I couldn't know it was him by his voice, it was too far gone away, only by the feel of his sleeve with the braid on it. He heard no other voice but mine and he, I think, was pretty sure I was the only one left except himself. So just before dawn, he set out on his last voyage. Sir, I laid my ear flat on his breast and I never got a whimper out of it. Yes, I believe he was a fine man. He was going ashore for good after that voyage. They always say that. I'd never set eyes on him until I saw him standing in the office at the port we sailed from.

For years I was living nice and easy with my little garden patch and my fishing, and then another Alexander Selkirk come along and he traded with the inhabitants. He traded with me. Well, he was a man who was as little fond of hard work as I was, but he hated work and he fretted for hating it. I didn't fret. I think I fretted that night I was washed up as much as ever I wanted to. So it didn't fret me to catch fish and trade them with Alexander the Second. He'd opened a store by that time, and I took rum in payment for my trouble. Good genuine Sailor Man Rum it was too. First and last I must have consumed a row of barrels of it as'd reach from here to the beginning. After the passage of years Alexander got word of some sickness among the people. They weren't showing much interest in trade. So he got a doctor to come over to the Island and stay a while and make them so as they could trade again. Just before the doctor left, having cured the people so as they weren't listless any more—he gave me a sharp look and he told me to knock off the Demon Rum. He said if I didn't I was for the happy hunting grounds. I said, "What of it? Maybe I'll be the same there as here." "Maybe," he said, "but you won't have such an easy passage, you'll get complications. Shall I tell you some of them?" he said. "No," I said, "and if I want to, I can imagine better than you could tell me." I've got a vivid imagination, you require it on this Island if you're to hold your own against the extraordinary flowers and birds and insects and the colours of the illuminated seas that do abound. "Well," he said, "I've told you." "Yes," I said, "Doctor, in your capacity as a doctor you've told me." I took a last pannikin to him as his big canoe went over the tilt of the horizon. Last pannikin, I never took another.

VISITOR Did you not have any adventures with cannibals and such like?

OLD SAILOR When Alexander died, and he'd been making money, had it stacked up in a bank far away, his nephew came along with a couple of improved hard cases, and he handed over the store to them. They stayed with us a little while. They drank up all the rum that was left and then they just disappeared, melted out of the sight of men—some thought they took hands and floated out beyond the reef and sunk each other. The inhabitants said I was the natural heir to the store. I couldn't say anything about that, but I distributed everything on the

shelf fair and even among them. Then we all sat down
to wait. After a period of time a crowd of people came
from far away, well dressed, very clean. They came in a
big schooner with an auxiliary engine, first I ever saw,
very smart, and these people, they began measuring up
the flat land here by the beach, and they gave me a little
book and a pencil to make a note of the measurements
and they were making their own notes also. I considered
they were anxious to form an opinion of how much my
intelligence amounted to and how much experience I
had of the sins and sorrows of the great world from
which, they thought, they came. They went away and
presently they sailed into the bay again. They'd brought
carpenters and joiners with them and a lot of little white
tents for them to live in and they fell to and built a large
sized hotel. They sailed away then finally, they didn't
come back, no visitors came. There were no fixings in
the hotel. Just a beautiful shell. There was just one toy
they'd left behind them, one of these patent bottle
openers clamped to the counter. I'd never seen one till
I saw this one. They weren't invented when I was in the
world. But when the hotel builders went away it made
an amusement for us on the Island. We found three
bottles and a good double handful of corks, and any time
anyone felt like amusing himself he corked an empty
bottle, put the neck in the machine, jerked over the lever
and drew the cork. After a time the corks got completely
shredded out so we had to get some soft wood and make
our own corks. But they didn't come out of the bottles
so well. However we had our memories of the first corks
to fall back on. Memory is always a good garden to fall
back on. If you weren't so restless in your mind, sir, I
could tell you out some of my memories. I mean the ones
I manufactured for myself out of the ghostie air. These
boys and girls, old and young of this Island, have their
own special manufactured memories. Well they've all got
two sorts. The ones they talk of and the ones they keep
to themselves. So have I. You'll find yourself the same
way if you make a little stay here. But perhaps you're
moving on. Though I daresay they could make you
comfortable enough here. But on the other hand if you

take the next steamboat away to some other place you'll feel you've made a move and done something. The hotel up above us now is, I believe, very convenient and grand in every particular. I've never been through it, some time I might ask for the job of delivering some great personage's boots to him on a silver salver. But you mark my words, this hotel will never be to the old inhabitants of this place, the old ones that remember, but a poor misted shadow of the first one, which was rambled through up stairs and down stairs, and when the roof had fallen away and side planking moulded into dust, I tell you we that skipped through it were like moths in a skeleton. And when the people came and built this last hotel it would be hard for them to find the shape of the old foundations.

(VISITOR *is reading guide book.*)

I was always standing around while the building was going on and they got used to me. I was used to them, from the beginning. The architect, the directors of the company, plenty of them, all mighty flush of money I should say, and then the chef when he came; and the electrical engineer, who fixed up the lighting and all. I was used to them. The engineer thought he knew more than anyone, and he used to give the inhabitants little electric shocks, make 'em squeal. But there was one strong lad who thought he was so brave, he wouldn't give a twitter, and the engineer kept raising the strength and before he knew that he was up against an obstinate brave one, he pretty near shrivelled up that man of courage. He only just turned it off before it was too late.

VISITOR (*looking up*) No, it's not late, I don't think it's ever late in this place.

OLD SAILOR You're learning.

(VISITOR *reads guide book.*)

OLD SAILOR I used to talk a different way to each of these people just so as to suit the measure of their understanding, but it would be a mistake to make any attempt to alter oneself to talk to you, sir, for you are so simply, honestly, and straightforwardly true that falsehood would ring flat on you like a smasher's coin on a hard-wood floor. Later on, when the hotel got going, the visitors began coming and staying on, some of them, for a long time. The management found that the visitors got melancholy if they didn't have something they could understand to look at, and to be amused with. So they encouraged me to hang around the place and entertain the people—any old way. Tell them my life, my lives, shipwrecks by land and sea. The management thought I ought to give them some ancient legends of the old chieftains of the Islands. But when I tried to get the chief who was living then up in the hills to the back to talk, he wouldn't tell me anything unless I promised not to tell it off again to anyone. The management then told me to take a day off and make up some legends myself. But it was too great a strain, I wasn't able to make up anything. I wasn't scared that I'd lose my job because I knew the visitors wouldn't put with anyone but me. They were used to me. For a while, quite a while, two or three seasons I kept them interested in some paintings I got the knack of making. They were two in number, a distant Island green with palms like mop heads sticking up out of a blue sea. As well as blue and green I had some light red and a yellow, lemon yellow, and I gave them a picture of a canoe on the water with a sail, and a setting sun. They used to give me five dollars apiece for those paintings. I got the planking I painted on from the management. But after a lapse of time the visitors got to paying me ten dollars a head to give them the knack of it, and the most of them, those that had any power of concentration, got so as they could paint those two pictures themselves. So the painter-artist occupation died on me. However, like most of the people here, I could swim about a bit in the waves, and I used to go out with the bunch of swimming visitors. There were lots of the original inhabitants who could make rings round me as a swimmer, but the visitors felt safer if I was with them, than if they had half a hundred of the brown boys and girls dolphinating themselves among the tall green seas.

They believed that the shark always goes for the pale legs first. Fed up, they believed, long ago, with the brown and so the visitors thought if I kept farthest out Old Man Shark would swallow me, and while he was getting me down, they'd have time to go ashore. I swam around for years till I got a bit stiff for it. "Brave," you'll say. No, I wasn't particularly brave. You see, walking around the beaches for years under this sun with only a little kilt on me, my legs were only theoretically white.

The management of the hotel changed, from time to time, but I was always around getting the run of my teeth, and now and then, a stiver or so for pocket money. Not much dinner and very little dinarlee. You see, I had let them see how little contented me. I could do with very little of everything, and I hadn't got anyone who would particularly expect to have the shaking out of my long stocking. The management wouldn't have liked me to look too prosperous. I wouldn't have cut so much ice with the visitors if I'd appeared too grand. One time a visitor going away in the steamboat, as he was going up the side, let his swell white topi, with a green lining, flop into the water. I was there in my canoe, and I hooked it out of the sea for him, but he said "keep it". So for a few weeks I wore it around. But the management said, "No, I don't think so. The visitors aren't so keen about you in that. Makes you look like Government House. They like Government House all right sometimes. But they come here to get away from it." That was a long time ago. Things have all changed since them days.

(VISITOR *is unfolding map in guide book and studying it.*)

But so far I've been able to hold my own and I've been lucky, when one thing failed another came along. One customer sunk, another rising out of the sea. When I got tired of swimming around in the high breaking rollers I came inshore into the shallows, as you might say, where no shark with his wisdom teeth cut would think of coming. I discovered by a mere accident, that I had a husky old sailorman singing voice, and a few of the old inhabitants gave me praise for it, and I'll tell you, they are very particularly critical about singing. The young ones as well as the old ones don't mind criticising anything they don't think absolutely up to the mark, and in a way it's a compliment, because, if they didn't think something of you they'd just make a sort of purring noise and change the subject. They were made glad with my singing. I only had one old song; you've heard it I daresay, you've heard it often.

VISITOR Oh, yes, I heard it.

(*He folds up map and continues reading guide book.*)

Switzerland must be a very interesting country.

OLD SAILOR There's few who travelled these seas who haven't heard "White Hand" but most always they'd heard it sung by a tenor with a little round mouth always making too much of himself and not enough of the song. But when they heard my rum gum and old salt tack moan out that song with good respect, they were got right where they lived, and they stayed on, because they didn't use old "White Hand" up. After the first night they heard me they never would let me sing it more than once of a night. Like men in the shadows, with one candle, but plenty matches, they'd light and blow out light, light and blow out, making old "White Hand" and me last. You'll understand there was no question of passing round the hat after the song, nothing ever of that kind, always the artist. But the management appreciated the fact that I was keeping the visitors hanging on just to hear me sing "White Hand". You think you've heard it sung but not you, for you tell me you've never been here before, and unless you heard me and "White Hand" you never heard her. I am not conceited about it. No, I'm proud to be the lucky one caught with the right throat at the right period of my life to give out that song. And when I stopped singing it I stopped in full swing. You'll perhaps wonder why—it was a long time ago now when I stopped.

(VISITOR *turning to back of guide book, looking up something in the index.*)

OLD SAILOR Everything is changed. I'm changed a little myself. But before my joints got altogether stiff I got a new amusement for the visitors. The management thought a lot of it; they told me, actually told me, I was holding their slippery visitors from slipping away. I went up topside among the hills and I had one of the old inhabitants teach me a few steps of one of the old-time dances. It had to do with a harvest, much like you might have had away back home one time when they have thanksgivings and put corn in the churches, and pumpkins, and flowers of the corn, little blue ones and poppies; that's the flower they make the drug of, long sleep. I'll be thinking of my own long sleep sometime or other, I suppose. But the tourists; they thought it was a cannibal dance. The thanksgiving in the twirls of my legs they thought, were to signify the strength and elasticity I had taken to myself with the gobbling up of my enemy. Of course the tourists of those old days were an innocent type. I wouldn't say they were harmless. But they weren't very complicated in their minds, and they were generally satisfied with their own first view of anything—hit or miss. "Cannibal Dance," they said, and cannibal dance it was. What time is it?

(VISITOR *is reading, makes no answer.*)

Well, you're right, don't look at your watch; here, time isn't of any consequence. Everything is changed but there being no time they couldn't change time, not even the complexion of time. Another lucky touch I had for the visitors, and it was good for me personally, I got good hard money out of it, and I salted it away in the safe in the office and I drew on it. But unfortunately there was nothing much I could buy with it on account of me giving up the rum so long ago. So my capital lasted too long—like Dives in the Good Book it weighed me down. The way I made the money was cutting little toy canoes out of a couple of bits of bamboo and a leaf for a sail. And when the wind blew off shore, and out through the smooth water where the barrier was open, my little canoes would sail away and away oh. The visitors would buy these canoes for half-a-dollar each just to see them sail away. Strange, when I painted pictures of canoes I got a crown apiece. But when I made one, I couldn't get more than half-a-dollar. I tried to raise the price but they said they could make them themselves. They couldn't, not so's they'd sail away.

That trade lasted me a while but they tired of them in the end and I was glad; it got to be monotonous (*he looks off right*). Here's a woman, as fine a woman as ever lived, coming from the West.

VISITOR They seem very fine women to me.

OLD SAILOR Stand up Sir!

(*Enter right* ALICE, *now old and stooped; she is dressed in a thin grey linen—rather full skirt and jacket, wears a large brimmed grass hat. She carries a tray with cords over her shoulders—a few large shells are on the tray.* VISITOR *and* OLD SAILOR *stand up—* SAILOR *takes off his hat.* VISITOR *takes off his hat.* ALICE *bows, passes slowly across the stage by the water's edge and exits left.*)

OLD SAILOR Yes, I have reason to say as fine a woman as ever lived. When we got our first Governor here—he said as soon as he looked at me he felt discouraged and he wanted to retire me, and without pension—peremptorily like that. But this lady, she talked up for me, and I was retained, as before, without pay. The Governor said, "I'll call him the old souvenir", and he laughed and so the lady laughed and I laughed. She was always good and kind to me. Broke to the wide herself, she gave me the helping hand, let me work her garden a bit for her, raise the few vegetables for her and saw that the management gave me a little share of pocket money and my grub every day. And she had had her own troubles. She stood up to them like a good'un. When she first came here, with her husband, a fine man, as fine a man as ever I saw, though I saw him once only and for a short time. When she came here everything must have looked grand to her, fine Island, flowers the brightest in the world, fine hotel, and she and her husband with plenty of money to spend, to throw about them. And then in a moment— there comes a cable (came on the same steamer as themselves) packed aboard from the nearest cable station and that was far away. Hard luck, but anyway they had their last run in peace and quietness. And this cable her husband he opened it up and in a moment he took a seizure and died in an hour. He was broke. Everything at home gone up in flames. There wasn't the price of a drink left for the widow when the funeral was paid for. The management they acted fine and square I'll say. They never asked her to pay them anything ever. Presently they gave her a little grass-roofed house they had in the grounds with a little garden patch and all. When she had time to pull herself together she got into this trade of selling these shells. Visitors like yourself like to hold them to their ears—say they can hear the billows roar. It took her all her time to keep her courage. You see, every human being about seemed rich, the management and the visitors with money to spill, and the original inhabitants wealthy in their good nature. All rich except her and me. That's why she had a sort of pity for me. And another thing, I took her orders from the first. One night under the moon I was singing "White Hand" to the boys and girls. And after I was finished she came away from her cottage door and she said to me: "Don't ever sing that song again", and I quit it right then and there. I suppose it was a bit ridiculous me singing a song like that when my voice was beginning to get pretty well croaked.

All these years she's made out not so bad, enough to keep her alive and always in good heart. I never seen the cable that'd knock her out.

She's seen all the changes here same as I have. Governors—we've had them. She was here a long while before the first of them was wished on us, and he wasn't so bad. He was willing to learn. And we here, we Islanders, saw that he learnt a lot. We had him pretty well drilled. He sailed to his Boss away off, they had given him orders to show up somewhere else, but he died before he got there. I reckon he died of a broken heart. After that we had them in a string, one after the other, short term men, short term so's they couldn't get the cockles of their hearts tangled up too tight. As soon as they said "Earthly

Paradise" some little visiting bird, and not a bird of paradise, carried word away to the Boss, whoever he was. And the Governor packed his traps and lit out in a canoe, for the steamboat that had brought him his walking-away papers. The Captain's order was "Give him time to break the seal and read his letter, then blow your whistle high, and keep the steam squirting through it, till you see his canoe coming away from the beach." I know that's the facts, the Captain told me his own self. He is a noble Captain, he isn't of this world nor yet of the next. He's a kind of go-between, standing there on his bridge, with his hand on the engine-room telegraph, always whiffling in the soft airs between sky and seas. He has a heart in his breast he has, and he'd take the ring and pit himself against anything, his mate told me. He said, "You see him once butting into a hurricane, and you'll say what man like that does, man can do— with the help of God." I never knew but three steamboat captains and all since I washed in here. All good men first class. But this one, he's got a bit of a list, but he's going yet, is the King Pippin of them all.

Some of these Governors had hardly time to see their shadow in one full moon before the whistle blew for them. Then they bred a new kind of Governor, full of biz, doing things, making roads, cutting straight up into the country, all laid out with powdered coral, very fine to look at. By and by a burst of rain came and washed out the roadway, here and there, and everywhere. And there were the Governors who were all for suppressions. These stumps of trees here, that's the work of one of them and he's gone long ago, someone else had a better idea I suppose. Yes, those trees were of the flowering sort, large and full of scent, and the girls had the fashion of putting them in their hair so the Governor said, "It makes them too attractive", so he cut 'em down in their prime. Oh, yes, some of them had brains no doubt, misused brains, great on improving us. I'm improved, I'm sure, if you'd known me when I first came here you'd find it hard to recognise me now. I went to night school here, one or two rainy seasons, and you'd be surprised if you knew all I learnt. It's no burden to me and I'm thankful for that. The only thing I'm sure of is that I will die and I knew that from the first. Even you, sir, will die, I suppose you know that, unless you live until the world comes to an end under you, crumples up and sinks into the empty. Even then I don't suppose you'll consider it satisfactory living floating on the edge of empty.

But these suppression Governors, they didn't last much longer than the earthly paradise ones because they weren't able to show results. There was nothing left to suppress, not so they should notice. We got sly. This is the slyest Island on all the seas. I wouldn't tell you only I know you're not listening, you bloody little numbskull. These suppression Governors never did much good for themselves after they left here, I believe, because when the steamboat came for them they couldn't face defeat calm and quiet, and they used to fill themselves up with the home. And they mostly picked them out of the canoes in a bosun's chair, making Authority look like nothing at all. We've got no full Governor just at the moment. The last of the make-'em-goods suppressed himself out of this life by putting his foot through the bottom of a canoe. He said to the man who owned the canoe, "You shouldn't attempt to take passengers in that canoe, look, it's rotten", and he gave the bottom boards a bang with his foot, and he was right, the boards were rotten and he went through down to the bottom of the lagoon. They got him up and worked artificial restoration on him for a time but he never came back. A new Governor will be on the way out to us soon now (*looking left and standing up*). Here comes this lady with the shells (*he catches* VISITOR *by the shoulders with a tight clawlike grip*). You get up and buy two of her shells, one for each ear, give her two quid for the pair, no haggling, you've got it, haven't you?

VISITOR I've got it. (*Taking roll from pocket and standing up.*)

(VISITOR *and* OLD SAILOR *walk towards* ALICE: VISITOR *takes two shells and pays* ALICE: ALICE *hesitates, shakes her head.*)

ALICE It's too much.

(*But* SAILOR *insists on her taking the money, he closes her hand over it.* ALICE *moves along edge of sea and exits right.* SAILOR *makes* VISITOR *hold a shell to each ear.*)

Curtain

SCENE 2: *Same as Scene 1. A year later.*

(*Enter* VISITOR *right*—NEW GOVERNOR *left, he is wearing white topi, tussaud silk short jacket with three silver stars on left breast, pale blue shirt, turned down collar with black bow tie. Yellow cord riding breeches and high tropical laced boots. He has a revolver in holster and is leaning on a dark brown silver-mounted walking stick.*)

NEW GOVERNOR (*as they meet close to seat*) I give you good morning, sir, I am the Governor of this Island and I like to make myself known to all visitors. It is my invariable custom and I find it is appreciated. I have never yet received a serious rebuff; you, I understand, have made a previous visit here, I believe at a time when there was no Governor in residence and things were a tiny bit higgledy-piggledy. We have, I am glad to say, been able to put everything into order. Almost everything, of course there is always something in this part of the world among the outposts of civilisation where there is a little more to be done, a little more polish to be applied. You have hardly had time yet, no doubt, to compare the present with the past. Your previous visit was a year ago, I understand.

VISITOR I notice a very great improvement. There's an air of respect to be observed by the merest tyro in observation, everywhere.

GOVERNOR I am gratified that you were able to observe a change for the better. Though, of course, what you have observed must as yet be but a skimming of the surface. (*Impressively*) There is a deeper culture, a planned culture. This you will observe, I hope, later. Do you plan—intend to make a stay of some duration?

VISITOR I hope to be able to make a considerable stay if I

find myself comfortable. During the few hours I have been here I have experienced a strange, but very pleasant sensation, that of being in a chosen and appointed place. As though the Supreme Being and myself had collaborated in placing me here—my spiritual home.

GOVERNOR You want to watch out all the same. That feeling may come from the sense of order that is, and is to come. But we must recognise that man cannot live by order and order alone. There are other component parts such as hope—that is, the hope for more order.

VISITOR I feel that. By the way, there was a familiar figure to be seen when I was here before, an old man of the sea in worn clothes and a very poor hat.

GOVERNOR He died a few months ago. He sat down on the seat, he didn't move, and when I sent one of my native attendants down to see why he sat so long—I can see this seat with my binoculars from my study in Government House—he found that the old man was dead. He was quite a feature here, someone had given him the title of the Old Souvenir.

VISITOR Poor soul, he seemed to me very worried about something, I'm glad he's at peace. There was also a person here I noticed, a lady, no longer young, a peripatetic seller of sea . . . of shells. How is she?

GOVERNOR Dead, dead also. Only a fortnight ago. She had been ailing some time, but was cheerful, I understand.

VISITOR I'm glad of that.

GOVERNOR One evening she came down here just before the fall of night. She was observed to write something on the sand with a stick, no one was able, it appears, to discover what she wrote. I trust it was nothing scurrilous. There is a certain trouble here from time to time about slogans. But we will be able to get the matter well in hand I have no doubt. After the lady had left the strand I sent one of my attendants down to see for himself what was written. But the tide had risen over it, whatever it was. The lady couldn't be questioned because she was exceedingly ill; in fact, as soon as she regained her residence, a doctor had to be procured and, in spite of his every effort, she passed away before morning. Quite a large funeral— seeing the cavalcade was of such considerable dimensions

I thought it advisable myself to attend. I have had reason to believe that my action was appreciated.

VISITOR Her life had been a life of some severity, I was informed when I was here.

GOVERNOR I got no particulars. The people, including the hotel people, were vague.

VISITOR I don't like vagueness.

GOVERNOR Nor I.

VISITOR I used to be rather vague myself, always studying to improve my mind, listening to others, not listening to myself, letting myself be ridden over rough-shod. I wasn't a worm—but I was worm-like. Now I feel quite different, I feel at this moment a commanding something that envelops me and is part of myself. I have a desire to help others.

GOVERNOR That is most commendable of you and I am sure you will find many that you will be able to help. Even if they themselves do not realise it.

VISITOR In this matter of slogans I would suggest that certain slogans only be permitted.

GOVERNOR I am seeing to that, thanks for the suggestion all the same. I'm having a list of slogans prepared, any of which can be used.

VISITOR Right, and anything outside that list, any free-lance slogan, to be barred absolutely. That's the talk! I haven't as yet seen any writing on the walls.

GOVERNOR There aren't many walls. First take your wall, then write on him. That drives the people to the sandy beaches; we have plenty of them. In the old careless days they used to scrawl all over the Island shores personal remarks about the reigning Governor and his immediate friends in the community. It got so embarrassing that some of my predecessors used to employ a man and a horse to obliterate the writing with a brush drawn forward and backward by the horse. Evil persons who were not in true sympathy with authority used to detain the man, and the horse, by various dubious tricks. One was to tell the man that there was something most shocking written on a far beach. Something that should be removed before the people could see it. Then when he had hurried away out of sight, with his horse and harrow, they'd bring a large concourse of their friends down to our beach here to make merry over the work of the scandalous would-be wits. They drew caricatures on the sands, also of leading well-disposed citizens and of the Governor himself.

VISITOR That was too much.

GOVERNOR If you have any suggestion to make as to suitable slogans, it will give me the greatest pleasure to incorporate them. I have no apprehension in inviting *you* to make suggestions. But I was sadly disillusioned when I invited one or two of our visitors a week ago and found their only ideas were some purely ephemeral cry from the heart. I say cry from the heart, because their suggested slogans were only for the purpose of advertising some commodity in the manufacturing of which they had a personal interest.

VISITOR That is not right. You said just now, Governor, that walls were somewhat of a rarity here.

GOVERNOR Yes, very rare. The materials for building walls is rather a problem to come by. We have coral rocks but transporting them from the coast is very troublesome and labour here is diffident. But I like these problems, and no doubt I will find a way of procuring the right materials at the right moment.

VISITOR You, no doubt, have some sort of jail, probably surrounded with a wooden palisade. Poor stuff, doesn't make an impression like a wall. But you don't want a wall all round a jail. One good high wall standing up by itself, on a plain, is all that is required. If you build a wall to encircle your prisoners, after a few attempts to climb it, your prisoners, owing to low initiative caused by prison diet, give the thing up like an uncrackable conundrum and lie down in its shadow. But my idea is a single piece of wall, it can be a long or short piece, just as you think necessary. My single piece of wall, if it is properly constructed, high and difficult, attracts all the inhabitants who either attempt to climb it, or give advice and encouragement to others. The most alert and able, therefore the most criminal of your people, will be most active in the climbing. So there, at any time you want them, will be your criminals merely for the taking. I have

these ideas. I give them away as soon as they come to
me. See here, Governor, should you ever find yourself in
a corner of any kind, no matter how important, or how
trivial, just give me the word and I'll bend my mind on
to something. In this matter of permitted slogans—

GOVERNOR Would you like to see the list I have been prepar-
ing? Would you like to run your eye over it? (*Takes
typewritten paper from pocket and hands to* VISITOR) They're
alphabetical.

VISITOR (*looking down list*) Yes, yes, seems to meet every want.
You might add, "Art for Art's sake". I say, what's your
revolver for? Are you afraid of the natives?

GOVERNOR Not particularly.

VISITOR Is it loaded?

GOVERNOR Yes, there's one cartridge in it only.

VISITOR Isn't that a risk? You might miss with the first shot.

GOVERNOR No, I will not miss with the first shot.

VISITOR Well, you know your own business best. Now,
Governor, tell me something, here, sit down where the
Old Souvenir sat (*points to corner of seat.* VISITOR *walks up
and down, hands clasped behind his back*). Now, Governor,
tell me, where's your nearest inhabited land?

GOVERNOR About five hundred miles away.

VISITOR You've got no cable connection nearer than that?

GOVERNOR No, and not there.

VISITOR What's your link with the outside world?

GOVERNOR The steamer. The same as left you here just now.

VISITOR When do you expect it will call again? Not for a
month or so, I suppose.

GOVERNOR Since you ask, she'll be back here again tonight.

VISITOR The devil she will! That alters things. Oh, well. Quick
action is the best in the end sometimes. Why is she
coming back so soon and where's she been to?

GOVERNOR You are interested in her. Well, sir, the Captain
has sailed to the west, to an island, a deserted pineapple
island, and he aims to get a few bunches just as a private
venture.

VISITOR What time will he be back here?

GOVERNOR At the fall of night. He'll lay off until the moon
gets up; we've a full moon here tonight. He can't run in
through the break in the reef at night except under a full

moon. But as soon as the moon's up he'll steam right in and drop his anchor, right here in front of us. He aims to have a couple of days rest for himself and the crew.

VISITOR He does, does he?

GOVERNOR He deserves it. They all do. Getting a lot of pine-apples in the heat of the day is tiring work. He will be able to relax here.

VISITOR I sincerely hope he will be able to do so. You said just now, Governor, that I was a man of ideas, I am — Item A, Item B. You are a man trained in obedience and in training others to obedience. Well, I have no experience as a teacher or a trainer. Just now I got a genuine first-class idea. I'm going to remake this place, or rather start it right away from scratch. I'm going to make this place an independent State. You will retain your Governorship, with a slight difference. You will be called "Chief" just as the First Engineer on a steamboat is called "Chief", I will be the Evident — you know, Self-Evident.

GOVERNOR Dictator?

VISITOR No, no, "Dictator" suggests a time lag — a Dictator says do so and so and so, and then it gets done or sometimes it doesn't. I am the man who when he says a thing goes, it goes, I don't mean "goes away" so much as goes like a clock goes. Do you follow me? Do you take my point?

GOVERNOR Perfectly, it's self-evident.

VISITOR Well, the first thing we've got to set out is a Consti-tution. I'll rattle one out of my head right away. In the meantime there are some things for you to do. We've got to have something in the nature of an Armed Force, and something in the nature of a Flag. For the flag bring me here a collection of any materials suitable for a flag-making, from Government House, from the Hotel. And as to the Armed Force. How many men have you employed directly, or indirectly, about Government House?

GOVERNOR Eight houseboys, two carpenters, two painters, a couple of builders' labourers, a butler and five gardeners.

VISITOR How many is that?

GOVERNOR (*after counting*) Twenty, I make it.

VISITOR Good, are there enough arms for them?

GOVERNOR We've got a signal gun and two presentation swords, and we've got no ammunition for the gun.

VISITOR All the better, we don't want them to hurt anyone and we certainly don't want them by an accident hurting each other. Untrained men should never have firearms. They can carry spears with blunt ends. Got any spears?

GOVERNOR Not at the moment. But the carpenters can soon make some wooden ones. One-piece ones.

VISITOR And you might put a bouquet of flowers in the muzzle of each of the signal guns. Another thing we must have is a new Motor Road.

GOVERNOR There isn't a motor in the place, because up to this there hasn't been a single road suitable for motoring. There's a very ramshackle road, climbing into the interior, starting from the hinterland of the Hotel.

VISITOR I hate the word "hinterland"; it was very popular once; it always suggests, just what no doubt it is here, the ash heaps behind an hotel. You must have a Motor Road, we *must* have a Military Force, and we *must* have a Flag. You'll think "must" is to be the key word. But you'll find it's nothing of the sort. "Must" in plans should have a final letter added to it. The penultimate letter of the Alphabet. And so you get musty—that's rather funny, eh? I don't think being funny generally is such a bad thing in an Evident. But still sometimes it gives a wrong impression to people who don't understand fun. It's a queer thing but mostly everybody is impressed by solemnity. Even if they are solemn themselves. I shouldn't think all the same that our people were very solemn. I have, when I was here before, heard them laughing in the woods at night. About the Motor Road (*thinks with chin in hand*)—what time's low tide?

GOVERNOR Quarter past three.

VISITOR Very good, get your carpenters to prepare a quantity of rough stakes, then send any four unskilled men you have along the strand to the left here, and let them, on the smoothest part, stake out a double track motor road, for just as far as they can go. How far do you think that'll be, Chief?

GOVERNOR About seven miles, I should say. I've never been

all the way myself. It's a long way to walk, and I don't like walking in this climate. You know, Evident, your Evidence, that the tide will have turned and begun coming in a good way before the four men have finished marking out the road.

VISITOR What a mathematical brain you have (*claps his hands*). Put as many men as you can spare on the job and I say, this is good, let half start at each end, and then they'll meet in the middle, and if the tide begins coming in on them too fast, they must curve the road inwards in front of the tide. I should have liked to be able to say we had a dead straight Motor Road. But curved like Cupid's bow will be delightful. We have to constantly be adjusting ourselves in the face of the enemy. In this case "the Enemy" is the oldest one of all. By the way, how goes "the Enemy", (*he takes out watch which is in a fob pocket*) not so bad, we've only used up about half an hour so far. Ah, but there's still a lot to do. We've got to have a Swimming Pool. That's really one of the first things. Catches the idea of the youth. I don't know why it's necessary to catch Youth's Idea. I haven't time to go into it now. Where can we have our swimming pool?

GOVERNOR The people here have the entire Pacific to swim in, they wouldn't know what to do with a swimming pool.

VISITOR I'm sure you are right. But it doesn't make any difference. Get one of your painters to take a pot of aluminium, no I'm tired of aluminium, a pot of moonlight blue paint, and walk along the shore till he comes to a naturally formed pool among the rocks and then let him paint up the words "Swimming Pool".

GOVERNOR I don't think he'd know what moonlight blue was. Shall I send him down here to you with his paints and let you mix the shade you want?

VISITOR Oh, dear, no, thank you very much. I can't do everything. Let the painter choose any nice blue he likes. The great thing is to have him happy in his work. The foundations of our Society are to be built, as you will see, on happy craftsmen. Another thing we should have is a Picture Gallery. Have we got any pictures?

GOVERNOR I have a couple of the Old Souvenir's paintings,

and a mountain scene; it's after an oil painting. I picked it up myself, in a curiosity shop, just before I went aboard the ship to come here. I very nearly gave it to the Captain, as he took a fancy to it. But now I'm glad I didn't. It'll be a nucleus, and the Hotel has a number of engravings and a tinted portrait of one of the first directors. And there was a lady visitor who spent a season here many years ago, and painted a number of exotic watercolours of the Island and presented them to the hotel, in exchange for her bill receipted. I say "exotic" but don't misunderstand me, sir. This Island is exotic but these paintings were exotic in another way altogether. I wish the Old Souvenir was still with us, he'd organise a painting squad among the original inhabitants, some of them are very deft with their fingers and very competent draughtsmen, as we know by their caricatures on the strand. However, we're going to stop that part of their activity under the Limited Slogan Order.

VISITOR Oh yes, that must not be forgotten above everything else. The Limited Slogan Order. To return to our Picture Gallery. I suppose the hotel people would let us have their pictures on loan and give us the use of, perhaps, the large drawing-room. And how many pictures do you think you'll be able to get together?

GOVERNOR I couldn't say exactly, a few dozen anyway. The Hotel Management I am sure will give us every possible assistance they can—this not being the regular season, you yourself being the only visitor, they have time to be agreeable. When the rush is on they'll have no time to give to the music of the spheres which, as Pythagoras taught me, is a perfect harmony, and that is what we take it you aim at for our New State.

VISITOR You've said it.

GOVERNOR The Hotel Management in their days of rush recognise no chiming bells except the bells of the cash register.

VISITOR Wait a while, we'll tax that. In the meantime, what's the next thing we've got to have before our ship comes home, with the Captain in it? Everything must be working like clockwork. Everything, I say, before he arrives. We've got to do the best we can right away with the

materials we have to hand. Later on we'll be able to
work on the fine ancient system of trial and error. By
the way, that's an idea, I'll incorporate it in our Consti-
tution. The national motto shall be "By Trial and Error"
and there's more in it than meets the ear. Try your
criminal before he makes his first slip, his first Error,
and becomes a criminal, and draw lots, pick your victim,
put him in the dock, try him before a judge and jury,
convict him, or find him not guilty. Explain to him from
the first, of course, that it's only an imaginary trial. I
say "him" advisedly, because if we happened to draw a
young woman she'd argue—and that would bring our
courts into a farcical light, and the women would join
all together and laugh us out of court, out of our own
court. I may not be as brave as a lion but I know the
courage of a hen.

GOVERNOR I suppose I ought to be getting the various works
started.

VISITOR Yes, yes. And, I say, we will have to have a Race
Course.

GOVERNOR But there are no horses on the Island.

VISITOR Doesn't matter. First get your Race Course, then
somebody will bring the horses along. Horses won't race
without a race course and they won't race without book-
makers either. That's an idea—we might make ourselves
into a bookmaking firm. I'd cry the odds and you'd be
my clerk.

GOVERNOR Wouldn't that be derogatory to our position?

VISITOR No, not under the Incognito Rule—I'll have to put
that into the Constitution. The Evident and the Chief
will have the power of becoming invisible in law, at will.
And while we have decreed ourselves as invisible it will
be a criminal offence for any citizen to say, "I see you,
Evident", or "I see you, Chief".

I feel a little tired now. Before tackling the Consti-
tution, I think I'll have tiffin. Will you join me, Chief?

GOVERNOR I'd love to. I've never had tiffin with an Evident
before. But I'd like to get some of these matters, which
have to be put in order, started at any rate. I'll just get
a snack at Government House.

VISITOR Oh yes, and we must have a Library. Firstly, a Reference Library (we won't have *Who's Who*, I'm not in it), a ready-reckoner and the poets, and we will want an Atlas. Then in the Library proper, some fiction, crime tales. This, I know, is a practically crimeless Island, but the citizens won't realise that unless they've got some idea of the goings-on in other places. "You can't enjoy anything without contrast," as the Great Mogul said when he took iced rice with his curry. That's settled. You'll meet me here after I've had tiffin.

(*Exit*)

VISITOR (*returning*) I say, you don't think my title, "The Evident", will make people think of "the usual", like bacon and eggs for breakfast?
GOVERNOR It wouldn't have occurred to me for a moment.
VISITOR You're a good fellow, all right. "Evident" it is.

(*Exit*)

(GOVERNOR *fans himself with Topi.*)
(*Exit*)

Curtain

SCENE 3: VISITOR *discovered striding up and down in deep thought, hands clasped behind back. Enter left* GOVERNOR *followed by brown boy from Hotel who is carrying a great quantity of coloured curtains, chair covers and cushion covers.*

VISITOR What have we here?
GOVERNOR The Flag.
VISITOR Oh, I forgot the Flag. I've been so busy on the Constitution; well, first things first. Let's at it.

(GOVERNOR *signs to boy who drops the cloths in a heap partly over the seat and partly on the ground. He then stands by, turning his face in wonder from the* VISITOR *to the* GOVERNOR *and back again. The* VISITOR *and the* GOVERNOR *rummage among the heap. What the* VISITOR *doesn't approve of after holding up, he lets fall. What the GOVERNOR holds up, the* VISITOR *shakes his head at, and the* GOVERNOR *lets it fall, until the* GOVERNOR *finds two cushion covers, claret coloured and silver diamond. He hands them to the* VISITOR, *who is delighted with them, holds one up and admires it.*)

VISITOR It is our flag.

(*Arranges one of the covers over* GOVERNOR'S *left shoulder, keeps other in left hand.*)

Presently you'll have it run up to the top of the flag pole. And now for the Constitution (*he strides up and down*).

GOVERNOR (*to* BOY) Take these away (*pointing to a heap of cloths*) and return each to the place from which they came.

(*Exit* BOY)

VISITOR Be seated (GOVERNOR *sits down*).

VISITOR Complication is the thief of time. Therefore, by allowing a perfectly simple breeze of the brain to advise me, I have simplified the Constitution so that it will fit on half a sheet of notepaper. And then, I am speaking metaphorically, for our Constitution will not be a written one. It will be simply photographed on the tablets of our two memories. A kind of book-keeping by double entry. The Constitution is retrospective. Firstly, every citizen of this country has, always, been free. Secondly, the Government has consisted, always, of an Evident and his Chief, assisted by a Parliament, consisting of the Lefts and the Rights who are always equal and up to the present only the first part of the Constitution has functioned. The second part is now about to begin functioning.

GOVERNOR Excuse me, how are you going to keep the Lefts and the Rights equal?

VISITOR Beautiful simplicity again (*pointing to right over water*). See yonder in the lagoon, the Old Ceremonial Double War Canoe lying at anchor. That is our Parliament House. You and I will sit in the middle and the representatives of the two parties each in their own canoe, and you know how cranky these old war canoes are. If the number in one canoe exceeds the number of the other the whole concern will begin to tip over and I will then of course have my vote for what I think best, and should by any chance, owing to the different weight of individuals, there be any difficulty about trimming the two canoes, I will use you as a trimmer. So Parliament will float on an even keel.

GOVERNOR I see a difficulty in your scheme. The people here are splendid swimmers and wouldn't in the least object to upsetting Parliament.

VISITOR I've thought of that. None of the members will be allowed to attend Parliament except while wearing their best modern suits of clothes. This will make them careful. You and I will of course, wear our swim suits, in your case "with decorations". I see you have them. How have you been getting on with our plans?

GOVERNOR The carpenters are busy making stakes. We can't get along with the Motor Road, of course, until the tide has receded. The painter is painting his Swimming Pool Notice Board. In the meantime willing hands are marking out the Race Course. Others are assembling the pictures for the Picture Gallery. This is necessarily a rather slow piece of work, because my people having seen so few examples of Representational Art, are naturally very interested, and are constantly taking pictures out into the sunlight to view them better, and at their ease. If the attendant is alone in this viewing, he seems to be able to concentrate on the matter in hand, and to understand the picture, no doubt in his own way. But if two or three, with their pictures held out before them, happen to meet out of doors, immediately a discussion arises as to the merits or demerits of the various pictures. In some cases these arguments have engendered so much heat that it has been necessary to send out pickets to bring the picture bearers in. However, the exhibits are going up on the walls now, fairly smoothly. Though a certain amount of trouble is caused by partisans of certain pictures wanting them hung in the best places. The assembly of the Library is not giving so much bother, because unless the books have illustrations, my people

are absolutely impartial about them. Later on someone
will have to see that all the books are the right way up,
and arranged in some sort of order. The great thing is
to get the shelves furnished. It is a strange comment on
man in his more primitive form, that he should be most
anxious to understand what he sees. While he is often
entirely unambitious as to the understanding of what he
hears. Combining the eye of the eagle with the, compara-
tively, carefree ear of the parrot, who thinks human
speech was invented so that he could learn it off by heart.
This is an interesting thought. Do you not think so?

VISITOR I do, I do, indeed. How's the Armed Force getting
on? Have they had any drill yet?

GOVERNOR Oh yes, there is a lot of drilling going forward,
they are very enthusiastic about it. They take turns put-
ting each other through their lessons. They, of course,
have to select one of their number for the part of drill
sergeant in the more complicated items such as form
fours. They don't like drilling in their bare feet, they
consider that they are unable so to produce a martial
tread. Luckily I was able to find a cupboard full of old
boots in Government House. At this very moment they
are shaking the earth.

VISITOR The Parliamentary Canoe will have to be carefully
overhauled. But that needn't be done today. That's the
advantage of a retrospective Constitution. Parliament
has already functioned, in imagination's Echoing
Canoes. If I hadn't hit on this sort of Constitution we
would have been put to the pins of our collars to have
the whole concern in working order before the Captain
comes in tonight. As it is I know we won't be able to
rest on our oars until the day is far advanced. But before
the moon rises everything will be accomplished. I don't
suppose in the whole world so much will have been done
in so little time. Have you got your Slogan Notices made
out yet?

GOVERNOR They are now being made out by the receptionist
at the Hotel. She very kindly offered to help. She's very
intelligent. I daresay she's nearly finished them now. I'll
go up there and see how she's getting on.

VISITOR Yes, that would be well done. I'll be considering any further embellishments, which might tend to add to the importance and dignity of Our State. It's very hot down here, you might send a boy down from the Hotel with one of those large garden umbrellas.

(*Exit* GOVERNOR)
(VISITOR *sits on seat.*)
(*Enter boy with umbrella which he fixes over seat.*)

Curtain

SCENE 4: *The same; later evening. The stage is dimly lit.*

(*Enter left* GOVERNOR *dressed as before and* VISITOR *in full evening dress with flag round waist. Slogan Notice pasted on tree-trunk, right.*)

GOVERNOR See, I have got my Anti-unpermitted Slogan Notice up.

VISITOR I'm glad to see that. It is most important. Do you know as the hour grows nearer for the arrival of the steamer I have been getting just a little bit jiggity, and, as soon as I knew that it was actually lying out there waiting for the moon to come in to us, I was so worried about the Captain that I went and had a little talk with the lady receptionist at the Hotel. She completely reassured me.

GOVERNOR She is a most intelligent young lady, I have always found her so—and most helpful.

VISITOR Yes, indeed, I talked lightly about things in general for a few minutes, to put her at her ease, and then I asked her, plump, how would the Captain react to the New State and she told me that we need not give our-selves any trouble whatever on his account. She said, she knew for a fact, he had told her himself, that he was "absolutely fed up" (those were his words) with "ram-paging the wide oceans", and he'd welcome "with a heart and a half" the moment when he could retire from the sea and settle down somewhere on shore, and there was no place in the whole world he'd like better than this Island. Then without committing ourselves, I broached the subject of the crew and the ship. She said that I had no doubt heard that sailors were supposed to have wives in every port, and in the case of this special crew it might be said that they had wives in every port— but this one. That would be a reason for them being wishful, perhaps, to settle down here. Then I touched lightly on the subject of the ship, treating it rather as a joke. I asked if we could use it as the nucleus of a Navy, or perhaps as a Floating Summer Palace for you and me. She reassured me about that at once. She said they practically had the brokers in for months travelling with them, apparently to and fro all the time. She said the claim against the ship (she has a genuine business head that girl), could be satisfied by giving the brokers' men a quantity of unwanted fittings, a canoe, water, provisions, and full directions for getting home. She's taken a lot of worry off my spirits. (*Pause*) It's been a long day, a long day for both of us. I could have done nothing without you, Chief. What are ideas and plans without someone who will carry them out. (*Pause*) I wonder what the people up in the hills think about the New State?

GOVERNOR Oh, they've probably heard nothing about it yet, and even when they do, it will be next door to impossible to know what they are thinking about, or anything else. I don't think that they think as we understand the word. Their thought processes are of quite a different order to ours I do believe. But like the climate here, they are benign. Benignity is one of the most difficult things to deal with in a subject people. That is if you have to fill up any large space in your report for home. You see, they don't realise that they are a subject people at all.

VISITOR Well, they are not a subject people any more, and you don't have to send any more reports "home", as you call it. (*Slaps him on the shoulder.*)

GOVERNOR Of course not, I forgot that for a moment. I would throw up my hat in the air, but in this warm, and gentle climate, such exuberance would jar the sensibilities—all right in harsher, more northern latitudes, but not here.

VISITOR We've got everything through at such a pace today,

that we'll be glad to take a few days off. With ruck-sacks, we might go for a short walking tour into the interior, of course, only walking in the cool of the mornings and in the evenings, resting during the day. We might make ourselves up as natives of some distant Island, or at any rate we could wear false moustaches, like the Pasha and his Vizier, in the old story. We'd listen to everything we heard. You, I suppose, know the language?

GOVERNOR Only a word or two, I'm sorry to say.

VISITOR All right, then, we'll have to bring along an interpreter. He can carry our impedimenta. During our walk we will be able to make ourselves *au fait* with whoever are the most important people. The leaders of what we may call the Mountain Society. And then later, when we have our Floating Summer Palace in the lagoon we'll be able to give a reception. Of course the invitations will have to be sent out very carefully—the more I think of this walking tour the more important it becomes. You see we will have to understand perfectly the different stratums and cliques among the higher classes of the people. We don't want to step off the wrong foot. We'll have ice cream. There's sure to be a refrigerator on the steamer. That will be in our favour at once. Every guest, as they come on board, will be handed a cornet and the major domo will instruct the people how to lick them in the approved manner. After our rest among the hills we will come back to civilisation with such energy that the proroguing of Parliament will be child's place to us. I see the scene before me. The Great Double War Canoe now turned to the uses of peace, a sword beaten into a plough-share. Myself sitting up under the canopy in the forward part, and yourself, ever on the watch moving here and there. Seeing all the members into their places Left and Right. When the canoes have ceased rocking about, and are quite still, I will stand up. I think I will be wearing ceremonial robes of some kind. Something in the nature of regalia is always appreciated, and you must have a costume also. I may think these details out myself. But I rather think I will seek the advice of the young woman receptionist. I think she has taste, and at any rate a woman's nature lends itself better than a man's to the blending of shade. Man is ever rombustious and crude in these matters, delighting in sharp contrasts, like the Great Mogul. But I remember I used him before as a simile. That shows I'm really tired. Whenever I'm tired I begin repeating myself, and everything isn't finished yet. The meeting with the Captain is bound to be exciting. I first thought we'd meet him on the beach and welcome him to our New State. Then I thought that would be rather abrupt, knock him off his pins, his sea legs, as it were, so I got Miss Receptionist to agree to tell him about the change and then have him led towards the Picture Gallery, where we will be standing ready to receive him formally. I see you haven't changed, and I think you are right. My full dress appearance will symbolise authority at its blandest. First I thought of a black tie and a dinner jacket. But I discarded the idea at once. "Tails," I said to myself, "it must be." Uncomfortable, very, in the tropics but tumbling about in ducks, or a lounge suit, while symbolising Democracy at its highest, coupled with the Parliamentary Man and shining in the face of the eleven stars, is surely more than an anachronism, and far less than the Eternal Verities. "Captain," I shall say, "speaking for myself and for my intrepid, tireless and cultured fellow-worker on the Path of Freedom, I welcome you, wayworn from the deep and dangerous furrows of Neptune Realm, to our State which at one and the same time is the newest and oldest establishment of this planet, afloat and now ashore. The calm and urbane rigidity, no—placidity—of a firm land being substituted for a heaving deck. You behold us, no doubt, through rosy spectacles. After a while you will notice this island earth beneath you is trembling. Do not be alarmed. The trembling will be caused by the marching feet of myself and collaborator marching forward to greater expansion, remember that, as the poet says—

> Love itself
> Must rest

And where we rest we bivouac—on the Paths of Freedom."

(*Enter boy from Hotel, Left, carrying a note on a tray.*)

VISITOR A note for me (*holds it in his hand, turning it about*).
GOVERNOR Read it, sir.

> (VISITOR *opens note, reads hurriedly, he is distressed. Reads again, slowly.*)

VISITOR It is from the Receptionist.
GOVERNOR Yes, the Receptionist. What is it about? What does she say? Unless it's personal.
VISITOR No, it's impersonal. She says (*reading*) "You'll have to call your revolution off" ("Revolution"—I thank you Miss for that word) "until the end of the year. The pilot who brought the steamer in has just come up here in a hurry. He thought the management ought to know—the ship's full up of tourists. It's the earliest commencement of the season I've ever known."
GOVERNOR Anything else?
VISITOR "I have to jump to it now, yours in haste."
GOVERNOR Anything else?
VISITOR Only "Keep your chins up."
VISITOR (*after a pause*) I think I'll go in and change.

(*Exit* VISITOR)

> (GOVERNOR *sits down wearily in seat, takes off topi and wipes head—sits dejected, after a time rises, walks over and looks at slogan notice on the right, walks slowly across in shadow of tree left, when Enter right two Brown-Skinned Lovers. The moonlight is growing strong.*)

BROWN BOY (*handing girl his spear*) Write something good on the strand—something to bring us luck.
BROWN GIRL I can't see to write anything yet, wait a moment (*looks right*) until the moon comes up over the trees (*a pause*). What shall I write?
BROWN BOY Anything that will bring us good luck. I think the old things are best.
BROWN GIRL So do I. I'll write what we have always written (*she writes with spear point, saying the words*)

TONY—WE—HAVE—THE—GOOD—THOUGHT—FOR—YOU—
STILL.

GOVERNOR (*stalking across the stage*) What have you written?

BROWN GIRL Is that you, Governor? I've just written what we
always write.

(GOVERNOR *goes over and looks down.*)

GOVERNOR Is this taken from the list of Permitted Writings
put up on the tree there?

BROWN GIRL No, Governor.

GOVERNOR Did you read the notice?

BROWN GIRL Yes, Governor.

GOVERNOR Well, why do you think I put it up?

BROWN GIRL Oh, I thought you just put it up for putting up.
Anyway it's no harm what I've written. We say it brings
good luck. You try yourself. (*She puts spear in* GOVERNOR'S
hand.)

GOVERNOR Who was this Tony—some shepherd of the hills,
eh?

BROWN GIRL I don't know sir—he just brings us luck.

(GOVERNOR *drops his stick and takes up spear and writes,
saying:*)

TONY—WE—HAVE—THE—GOOD—THOUGHT—FOR—YOU—
STILL.

(*Enter left* VISITOR. *He has changed his tail coat and white tie
for his grey short coat and a black tie.*)

GOVERNOR (*looks at* VISITOR, *then down on sand at writing. The
moonlight is shining on his decorations Three Stars.*) What have
I done, I who was given these Three Stars (*he touches them
with his fingers*) each for seven years obedience and for
causing others to obey, I have disobeyed my own ukase.

But I have obeyed alone.
I have disobeyed alone.
I will die alone.

(*He pulls revolver from holster and raises muzzle to his chin.*)

VISITOR Don't let him—don't let him.

BROWN GIRL Oh no, Governor.

> (BROWN GIRL *throws arms around* GOVERNOR. BROWN BOY *seizes his right hand—and wrests revolver from him.* GOVERNOR'S *topi has fallen off—Girl and Boy release* GOVERNOR. *He stands with his face covered with his hands.*)

BROWN GIRL (*looking down on sand*) Don't be fretting yourself, Governor, look. (*She pulls his fingers away from his eyes.*) Look at the sea's edge! The tide is coming in now fast, look, look, the waters are covering up and washing away everything that we have written.

> (*As she speaks she and all the others, gazing down at the tide's edge, move slowly backwards towards the front of the stage.*)

CURTAIN

BIBLIOGRAPHY

BOOKS WRITTEN AND ILLUSTRATED BY
JACK B. YEATS

James Flaunty or the Terror of the Western Seas. London, Elkin Mathews, 1901.

A Broadsheet, edited by Jack B. Yeats. Illustrated by Pamela Coleman Smith, Jack B. Yeats, and others. London, Elkin Mathews, 1902, 1903.

The Scourge of the Gulph. London, Elkin Mathews, 1903.

The Treasure of the Garden. London, Elkin Mathews, 1903.

The Bosun and the Bob-tailed Comet. London, Elkin Mathews, 1904.

A Broadside, edited and illustrated by Jack B. Yeats. Dublin, Dun Emer and Cuala Presses, 1908–15.

A Little Fleet. London, Elkin Mathews, 1909.

Life in the West of Ireland. Dublin, Maunsel, 1912.

Modern Aspects of Irish Art. Dublin, Cumann Leigheacht and Phobail, 1922.

Sligo. London, Wishart, 1930.

Apparitions. London, Jonathan Cape, 1933.

Sailing Sailing Swiftly. London, Putnam, 1933.

The Amaranthers. London, Heinemann, 1936.

The Charmed Life. London, Routledge, 1938.

Ah Well. London, Routledge, 1942.

La La Noo. Dublin, Cuala Press, 1943.

And To You Also. London, Routledge, 1944.

The Careless Flower. London, Pilot Press, 1947.

In Sand. Dublin, Dolmen Press, 1964.